The Assessment of Multilingual Learners

Full details of all our publications can be found on http://www.multilingual-matters.com, or by writing to Multilingual Matters, St Nicholas House, 31-34 High Street, Bristol, BS1 2AW, UK.

The Assessment of Multilingual Learners

Supporting English Language Learners

2nd edition

Kate Mahoney

MULTILINGUAL MATTERS
Bristol • Jackson

DOI https://doi.org/10.21832/MAHONE4976
Library of Congress Cataloging in Publication Data
A catalog record for this book is available from the Library of Congress.
Names: Mahoney, Kate (Professor), author.
Title: The Assessment of Multilingual Learners: Supporting English
   Language Learners/Kate Mahoney.
Other titles: Assessment of Emergent Bilinguals
Description: Second Edition. | Bristol; Jackson: Multilingual Matters, [2024] |
   Includes bibliographical references and index. | Summary: "This book is a
   comprehensive introduction to the topic of assessing students who use
   two or more languages in their daily life. The book provides foundational
   information for assessing multilingual learners (ML) in schools, with an
   emphasis on school language and content. This 2nd edition has a
   greater focus on multilingual assessment"-- Provided by publisher.
   Identifiers: LCCN 2023057466 (print) | LCCN 2023057467 (ebook) |
ISBN 9781800414969 (pbk) | ISBN 9781800414976 (hbk) |
ISBN 9781800414983 (pdf) | ISBN 9781800414990 (epub)
Subjects: LCSH: English language--Study and teaching (Elementary)--Foreign
   speakers. | English language--Study and teaching (Secondary)--Foreign
   speakers. | Educational tests and measurements. | Education,
   Bilingual--Evaluation.
Classification: LCC PE1128.A2 M313 2024 (print) | LCC PE1128.A2 (ebook) |
   DDC 428.0071--dc23/eng/20240207
LC record available at https://lccn.loc.gov/2023057466
LC ebook record available at https://lccn.loc.gov/2023057467

British Library Cataloguing in Publication Data
A catalogue entry for this book is available from the British Library.

ISBN-13: 978-1-80041-497-6 (hbk)
ISBN-13: 978-1-80041-496-9 (pbk)

Multilingual Matters
UK: St Nicholas House, 31-34 High Street, Bristol, BS1 2AW, UK.
USA: Ingram, Jackson, TN, USA.

Website: https://www.multilingual-matters.com
Twitter: Multi_Ling_Mat
Facebook: https://www.facebook.com/multilingualmatters
Blog: https://www.channelviewpublications.wordpress.com

Copyright © 2024 Kate Mahoney.

All rights reserved. No part of this work may be reproduced in any form or by any means without permission in writing from the publisher.

The policy of Multilingual Matters/Channel View Publications is to use papers that are natural, renewable and recyclable products, made from wood grown in sustainable forests. In the manufacturing process of our books, and to further support our policy, preference is given to printers that have FSC and PEFC Chain of Custody certification. The FSC and/or PEFC logos will appear on those books where full certification has been granted to the printer concerned.

Typeset by Deanta Global Publishing Services, Chennai, India.

Contents

	Acknowledgments	vii
	Introduction	1
1	A Decision-Making Process Called PUMI	6
2	History: How Did We Get Here?	29
3	Validity	55
4	Methods	74
5	Content and Language	106
6	Psychometrics	133
7	Accommodations	150
8	Special Education *(co-authored with Laura M. Geraci)*	174
9	Accountability	197
	Advice for Instructors on Chapter Activities	207
	Glossary	221
	Index	226

Acknowledgments

I am grateful for my family (Jon Storm, Emma Kane-Mahoney Storm, Jack Mahoney Storm and Eva Jean-Mahoney Storm) – and also to my loving parents Pat and Bill Mahoney, and siblings Mary Andres, Jim Mahoney, Amy Mahoney and Daniel Mahoney. I am very grateful to the staff at Multilingual Matters for valuing this work and supporting me to be productive with the ideas in this book.

Permissions

Figures 5.3 and 5.4 are reproduced with kind permission of WIDA.
Figure 1.6 is reproduced by kind of permission of The Educational Testing Service. https://www.ets.org/
Table 1.3, Figure 5.2, Figures 7.1 and 7.2 and Table 9.2 are reproduced with kind permission of Taylor and Francis.
Figure 4.1 is reproduced with kind permission of Corwin Press.

Every reasonable effort has been made to locate, contact and acknowledge copyright owners. Any errors will be rectified in future editions.

Introduction

This book is intended to be a comprehensive introduction to the topic of assessing students in schools who use two or more languages in their daily life: the foundations of assessment for multilingual learners (MLs). The topic where assessment, measurement and multilingualism intersect is a complicated one. The content of this book breaks down the complex issue of assessment in a digestible way by providing in-depth chapters on the following areas: a decision-making process called PUMI (Purpose, Use, Method, Instrument), history, validity, methods, content and language, psychometrics, accommodations, special education and accountability. These major topics within assessment are all connected by a decision-making framework called PUMI, a framework that allows practitioners to better inform assessment decisions for bilingual children. Since 1999, I studied and began teaching courses on Bilingual Education and assessment. It was during this time that I developed the idea of PUMI (I didn't always call it this) to help teacher candidates understand and ask critical questions about assessment for bilingual children. Since teaching my first assessment course in 1999, I have conducted research on validity topics, taken advanced psychometric coursework, designed and taught assessment courses for Arizona State University and the State University of New York, as well as given workshops and interacted with teachers in professional circles across New York State on the topic of assessment; this second edition is the outcome of these cumulative experiences. I find this topic fascinating and relatively unexplored. I still have much more to learn – my hopes are that readers of this book find ways to further these ideas, conduct more research and change deficit policies and practice for future generations. The following sections provide more information about the organization of the book.

SNAPSHOTS

Most chapters contain 'snapshots' of real case scenarios mainly drawing from my experiences in the field. Pseudonyms are always used.

> **END OF CHAPTER ACTIVITIES**
>
> At the end of each chapter, there are activities that college instructors can use with their teacher-candidate students. At the end of the book, before the glossary, I also offer advice to instructors based on my own experience of implementing these activities in undergraduate and graduate assessment courses. The End of Chapter Activities are designed to be interactive in a face-to-face environment and to give students practice in digesting and processing some of the critical ideas in this book.

Themes in This Book

The following is a breakdown of each chapter and the main themes presented in each chapter.

Chapter 1: A Decision-Making Process called PUMI

(1) Teachers have to compromise along a continuum of assessment practices leading to deficit or leading to promise.
(2) Good assessment practices for MLs are grounded in four guiding principles or assumptions.
(3) A useful tool called PUMI can assist teachers in making informed and appropriate decisions about assessment.

Chapter 2: History: How Did We Get Here?

(1) The history of testing MLs includes many examples of inappropriate testing and misuse of results.
(2) Despite several decades of warning from the measurement community, test scores from tests given in English to students who don't know English are still being used for important education decisions.
(3) The current political climate favors accountability over validity.

Chapter 3: Validity

(1) Tests aren't bad; it's how we are using them that may be bad.
(2) Viewing ML test scores through the unified view of validity puts due importance on how we use ML test scores. This includes social consequences.
(3) Construct irrelevant variance (CIV) is a major validity threat for test scores of MLs.
(4) The social consequences of using test scores or 'side effects' are having wide-ranging impacts on the field of English as a new language (ENL) and multilingual education (ME).
(5) It should always be remembered that a test does not end with the student's score; it begins with test interpretation and use.

Chapter 4: Methods

(1) Selecting an appropriate method of assessment is directly related to aligning with the purpose of the assessment.
(2) Rubrics and checklists can be easily made from standards and criteria (purpose).
(3) Main categories of methods are one-to-one communication, written response, selected response and performance.
(4) Interviews, portfolios, storytelling and teacher observation are all very popular methods of assessment with MLs. Which one you should use depends on your purpose.

Chapter 5: Content and Language

(1) When assessing content, minimize or simplify the language so you can focus on content (you can never completely eliminate language, but there are ways to reduce it, without reducing content).
(2) Language is best assessed in context and over time. Language is not assessed well out of context (decontextualized) and at one point in time.

Chapter 6: Psychometrics

(1) Criterion-referenced tests (CRT) are more popular than norm-referenced tests (NRT); however, both have drawbacks.
(2) There are many types of scores but they are all generated from the same raw score.
(3) Teachers and parents have grown to not trust test scores due to multiple public test item or scoring errors made by testing companies.

Chapter 7: Accommodations

(1) We don't need accommodations if we create better assessments for MLs.
(2) Many accommodations are permitted with MLs, but few of them have research to suggest that they work.
(3) Linguistic simplification is a promising accommodation.

Chapter 8: Special Education

(1) There is significant federal and state policy governing the assessment of students who may have special learning needs.
(2) Many challenges regarding the education of MLs with special needs hinge on assessment.
(3) It's difficult to disentangle speech or language impairment (SLI) from learning disabilities (LD) from second language acquisition (SLA).
(4) The dominant practice of assessment in special education supports a fractional view of MLs.

Chapter 9: Accountability

(1) Accountability related to assessment has come to the forefront of education in the last 10 years.
(2) Accountability based on student assessment results has never been more intense and directly tied to assessment.
(3) Accountability without validity isn't meaningful (see also accountability/validity discussion in Chapter 2).

New to the Second Edition

The field of fair assessment for multilingual students has grown since the first edition of this book mostly due to the growing number of multilingual people in the world and a growing awareness of the inequities of practices in this field. Despite this, psychometric companies continue to produce monolingual tests and schools continue to administer and interpret them on behalf of multilingual students, despite glaring validity violations. Even when tests are translated into another language, this still supports a monolingual lens of assessment. This edition explores some of the creative ways that teachers can incorporate multiple languages into assessment.

Like the first edition, many of the examples in this edition apply assessment principles to emergent bilinguals in Spanish and English; however, some effort has been made in the second edition to address multilingual students beyond the Spanish/English context in the United States. The principles of PUMI have remained the same. A deeper discussion of translanguaging, how and when to assess it and more examples of it are included in this edition.

In this second edition, because the No Child Left Behind (NCLB) policy ended, the NCLB narrative has become historical, and in some places removed. However, discussions and explanations about NCLB remain in the book because many artifacts (and some scars) remain on the educational landscape of the United States, due to this federal policy. Detailed NCLB discussion such as annual measurable achievement objectives (AMAOs) and adequate yearly progress (AYP) have been removed. This second edition includes a greater emphasis on using assessment results in formative and summative ways, including ways to use/document formative and summative assessment methods. In general, more bilingual assessment examples have been added. In addition, there are more examples of peer and self-assessment (PASA) and more ideas about how to involve students more as agents of assessment.

Shortly after the first edition was published, Rick Stiggins (2017)[1] published *The Perfect Assessment System* in which he included a Students' Bill of Assessment Rights. I thought of including a similar list of rights for MLs in the final chapter of this book but instead decided to put them front and center (see below) to set a tone for this book about what we owe our students and how assessment practices that don't serve our students need to be put to rest. Below is my version of a Multilingual Student' Bill of Assessment Rights. In the end, our assessments are about students, communities and their practices; therefore, what follows is the Bill of Rights modified from Stiggins' work, to target the students and communities who are focal to this second edition.

Multilingual Learners' Bill of Assessment Rights
(idea borrowed from Stiggins, 2017)

(1) MLs have a right to see their community language practices in assessments.
(2) MLs have the right to count their community language practices as equal to standard and monolingual forms of languages, in assessment.
(3) MLs are entitled to be presented with the purpose and learning targets of each assessment and the way assessment results will be used, in a language and reading/speaking level that they can clearly understand.
(4) MLs are entitled to know the difference between good and poor performance on assessments, given in a language/level they clearly understand.
(5) MLs have a right to act as agents in their own assessment where they learn to self-assess and track their own progress toward mastery.
(6) MLs are entitled to assessment results that were gathered using high-quality assessments and yield valid results (with reduced bias and noise).
(7) MLs are entitled to communication of their assessment results and in a language/level that teachers, families and students can understand.
(8) MLs have a right not to be over-tested.

Terminology

This second edition replaces emergent bilingual (EB) with multilingual learner (ML) throughout the text. For this edition, I choose ML because it is promoted in New York, the state where I live, and it makes sense for the goals of this second edition. In some contexts other labels will be used.

Note

(1) My first introduction to assessment was a Rick Stiggins' workshop in California around 1995, at a CRESST conference (a research center for assessment and evaluation connected to the University of California, Los Angeles UCLA). Since that time, Rick Stiggins' logical approach to assessment ideas can be seen in many parts of this book, including Guiding Principle #2 in Chapter 1.

Reference

Stiggins, R. (2017) *The Perfect Assessment System*. Alexandria, VA: The Association for Supervision and Curriculum Development (ASCD).

1 A Decision-Making Process Called PUMI

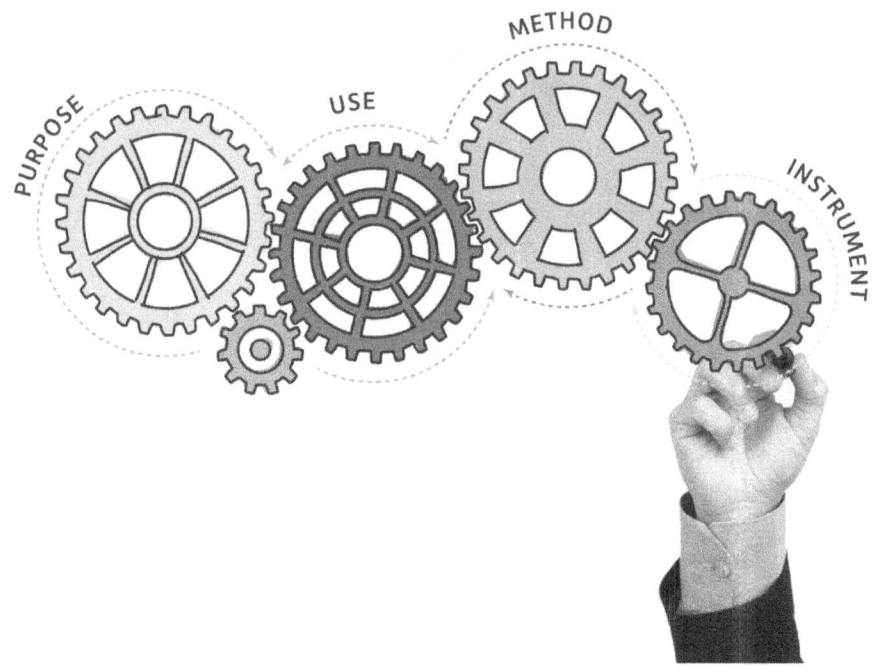

> **THEMES FROM CHAPTER 1**
> (1) Teachers have to compromise along a continuum of assessment practices leading to deficit or leading to promise.
> (2) Good assessment practices for multilingual learners (MLs) are grounded in four guiding principles, or assumptions.
> (3) A useful tool called PUMI (Purpose, Use, Method, Instrument) can assist teachers in making informed and appropriate decisions about assessment.

Key Vocabulary

- Assessment or testing.
- Assessment lens of promise.
- Assessment lens of deficit.

- Translanguaging.
- PUMI.

PUMI Connection: Purpose, Use, Method, Instrument

This chapter introduces the concept of PUMI which will be used in each chapter for the remainder of the book. PUMI is a decision-making process to help stakeholders make better decisions about assessment for MLs. It is recommended that when you are unsure about what questions to ask and what is important, start asking PUMI questions. What is the Purpose (P)? How will the results be Used (U)? What is the best Method (M)? What is the best instrument (I)? Finding the answers and understanding PUMI help slow down the process of assessment and lead us to using fewer and better assessments.

This foundational textbook has three primary objectives. First, it helps teachers and administrators understand the challenges with assessment and accountability for MLs that dominate the field today. Second, it prepares teachers, administrators and leadership teams to make decisions about how to use and select appropriate assessments for MLs. Third, this book prepares educators to advocate on behalf of MLs in regard to appropriate test-use policies and practices.

It's a Continuum: Promise to Deficit

Valid assessment for MLs is a complex scientific challenge, especially in a monolingual schooling context. The various approaches to assessing MLs in the field today draw on contrasting views of assessment and bilingualism. This section briefly reviews a continuum of views, followed by guiding principles that teachers and administrators can draw on as they make practical decisions about assessing MLs.

There are many ways to view the assessment of MLs, and these can be best understood as a continuum – a wide range of approaches with extremes on either end – ranging from deficit to promise. Promising approaches[1] to assessment highlight what the student knows and can do relative to multiple measures; on the other hand, deficit approaches highlight what the student doesn't know, usually relative to one measure. What is especially challenging is whether and how educators can look at MLs through a lens of promise within an accountability system focused on what children cannot do. Understanding this continuum will prepare the ground for better ML assessment policy, practice and advocacy.

The lens of promise is grounded in the ideas of dynamic bilingualism (García, 2009) and sociocultural assessment (Stefanakis, 1999), and is typically used in assessment courses and popular textbooks to guide educators in how to assess (and instruct) MLs within a meaningful and culturally relevant context. The lens of promise can also be seen in approaches like the WIDA (2019) 'Can do' philosophy and 'Can do' descriptors and rubrics. However, more often than not, and in contrast to a promising lens, deficit views of assessment dominate the policies and accountability system under which educators must perform. Deficit and promise are strikingly different, and educators are required to negotiate them in a public school setting in order to maintain good evaluations of their own teaching and do what is best for students. These two views are presented here as a continuum; that is, one end of the continuum differs extremely from the other end, but points near one another on the continuum may not be that noticeably different. These two views are not a dichotomy – mutually exclusive of one another, where educators must choose one view or the other. What is most common in schools today is a mix of both deficit and promising assessment approaches; state and district accountability systems are more often connected to looking for deficits or areas where children are lacking, whereas classroom assessment is more connected to the approach of promise. Usually, teachers negotiate both views. Figure 1.1 illustrates the idea of this continuum and Table 1.1 gives specific examples.

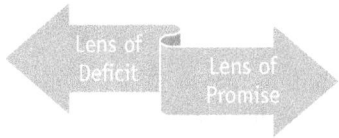

Figure 1.1 Assessment practices are on a continuum from deficit to promise

Assessment vs. Testing

Oftentimes in conversations that take place in schools, the words assessment and testing are mistakenly used synonymously. Assessment is a much broader concept than testing and can be thought of generally as the use of information from various sources to make decisions about a student's future instruction/schooling. Testing, on the other hand, is a measuring instrument that produces information we use in assessment. A test can be thought of generally to be like a measuring instrument such as a measuring cup or a scale or a tape measure, used to measure ideas to help make decisions in schools. The example given above is a very simplified view, just to point out the difference between assessment and testing. Measuring flour in a measuring cup is much easier than measuring language in a child emerging as multilingual. In addition to being easier, we simply do not have instruments to measure language with precision. Language assessment, in particular, functions differently from other content area assessments because language is complicated and not linear. Green (2014) says that language assessments are closer in nature to maps than to tape measures. Although tape measures may come in different sizes and shapes, they are all designed to measure length. On the other hand, maps represent and highlight different aspect of a multidimensional world according to the needs of the user (Green, 2014).

Support for MLs in Measurement Community

It is important to note that stand-alone tests themselves are not bad. However, with the increase in testing and the high-stakes decisions made from test scores, most educators have become very frustrated with the way test scores are used. The frustration is usually with the test-use, not the test, and especially for groups of students like MLs. Many times, policymakers, legislators, school boards, etc., use test scores for MLs in wrong – or invalid – ways. Examples of this from current practice include

Table 1.1 Comparing deficit vs. promising views of assessment

Leading to promise	Leading to deficit
Students are active participants or agents in the evaluation, which takes place in an authentic learning environment. • Example: Teacher shares rubric with students well ahead of assessment and students have the opportunity to ask questions and clarify what is expected.	Students are objects of evaluation – they do not know what is on the test; tests and responses to items are confidential. • Example: Teacher announces a 'pop quiz' and students don't know what to expect. • Example: State achievement tests are kept in locked cabinets until a state-sanctioned time and day.
Assessments look for what students can do – assessing *ability*. • Example: Teacher uses a portfolio to show writing ability/strengths/potential.	Assessments look for dis-ability or deficit in the child – assessing *dis-ability*. • Example: Teacher highlights items that are wrong on a multiple-choice test and results are compiled to create an academic intervention plan.
Each child represents an example of difference and complexity. • Students give an oral presentation of recent changes in their family with audio, visual, digital and artistic components.	The learning deficit is in the child/family. • A very low test score in math leads the teacher to say 'the child is at a disadvantage. He would do better if he had more support at home'.
Assessments are authentic and contextualized. • Unknown to the students, a teacher uses a checklist to observe and document use of English language during math problem-solving.	The assessment is decontextualized from authentic situations. • During an oral language standardized assessment, the administrator reads each item and none of the items are connected or real. For example, 'How many hands do you have?' and scores the response.
Several measures are used to make a decision (similar to the idea of triangulation in research). • A teacher uses the results of a reading retell, book discussion and standardized reading assessment to make decisions about what level of reading the student should advance to.	A single measure determines a decision – frequently a high-stakes decision like reclassification or graduation. • A student has to score 65 or better on a state test to graduate from high school.
Instructional decisions are made on an individual basis. • A student with high reading levels in the home language is selected to be the leader of a bilingual dictionary activity.	If a child does not meet an expected norm, remediation is required. • All students below the 50th percentile on an English-only math achievement test are automatically assigned to a pull-out remedial math course.
The assessment occurs over many points in time and with conferences and feedback from teacher and peers. • Writing in the new and home language is assessed every five weeks to look for changes. Results are sent home to parents with a personal note from the teacher.	The assessment occurs at one point in time. • Testing day is April 10 from 9am to 11am.

using achievement test scores to judge language ability (wrong construct), using only one test score to reclassify a ML (never use one score to make a big decision) or using test scores from a test that MLs cannot read very well (not a fair or accurate measure). It is important to point out that the educational measurement community does not support these types of test-use practices, and they do, in fact, support promising practices for MLs. Despite the measurement community's supportive position toward fairness for MLs, the production of large-scale tests designed *for* multilingual children is still a novel idea.

The term 'measurement community' refers to measurement scientists who have studied educational measurement, covering topics such as fairness and validity, for several decades. The three organizations that dominate the science and use of test scores in the United States are the American Educational Research Association (AERA), the American Psychological Association (APA) and the National Council on Measurement in Education (NCME). The study of (educational) measurement is basically the practice of assigning numbers to traits such as achievement, language, interest, aptitude and intelligence. Assigning numbers to traits such as language(s) is more challenging than other constructs, from a mathematical perspective because language is multidimensional and can change dramatically based on context and affective variables (think affective filter). Oftentimes, measurement scientists (also called psychometricians) design research studies to try to validate whether those numbers really represent the trait. As a result, they make recommendations about how to use test scores; however, it is up to policymakers to write good policies about how to use test scores. This is usually where 'a disconnect' occurs, leading to deficit assessment practices. This disconnect is also visible when psychometricians (or test technicians) do not have the authority to assure that tests are used appropriately and test politicians (policymakers impacting testing policy) propose and make policy not aligned with the blueprint of a test, in particular the published uses of a test. An analogy for this is if you purchase a table saw and disregard the owner's manual – it will likely not function properly or not at all – more so, someone could get hurt. To further illustrate this disconnect, Rick Stiggins (2017) opens Chapter 1 of his book *The Perfect Assessment System* with a quote from E.F. Lindquist about the role of the measurement scientist:

> If measurement is to continue to play an increasingly important role in education, those who measure must be more than technicians. Unless their efforts are directed by a sound educational philosophy, unless they accept and welcome a greater share of responsibility for the selection and clarification of educational objectives, unless they show much more concern with what they measure as well as with how they measure it, much of their work will prove futile and ineffective. (Stiggins, 2017: 1)

This disconnect also plays out when test publishers bypass professional educators altogether and sell their products directly to untrained legislators, turning testing into an increasingly political and financial enterprise; since 2010, the United States has spent hundreds of millions of dollars on developing new multistate standardized tests whose scores are of little direct instructional value (Stiggins, 2017). Just imagine, the hundreds of millions of dollars spent on creating tests for a monolingual audience could have been spent on creating tests to include the language practices of multilingual children, or perhaps purchasing multilingual libraries in schools/communities or addressing other sociolinguistic challenges that MLs face in monolingual mindset schools. Chapter 9 (Accountability) in this book expands on who in the educational community is accountable to students for better use of assessments.

Ten years ago, the measurement community published the new *Standards for Educational and Psychological Testing* (AERA, APA, NCME, 2014) where standards for fair test-use were made explicit for the first time in a separate chapter on 'Fairness in Testing'. Fairness, especially with subgroups like 'individuals with disabilities' and examinees classified as 'limited English proficient' received increased attention from the measurement community (AERA, APA, NCME, 2014). In this important document, fairness in testing is considered a central idea, as those responsible for test development are held to the standard of designing all steps of the testing process to be accessible to the widest possible range of individuals, removing barriers, such as English proficiency, that may create unfair comparisons or interpretations of test scores (AERA, APA, NCME, 2014). Details about standards for fair testing are presented, especially on topics such as validity, test design and accommodations. Unlike previous versions of these standards, the importance of testing MLs (and other groups who have been marginalized from fair test development and interpretation) in a fair way has become a central idea. What is needed to move forward in the field of assessing multilinguals are tests designed *for* multilingual students where monolingual and bilingual children can be assumed/included in the design of the test, not an afterthought of accommodation after the instrument is published. Perhaps this will be the focus of future editions of this book, but for now – the position paper written by the NCME (2020) described below draws attention to critical issues when designing an English monolingual test to be used with multilingual children, who are not yet proficient in English. While the eight factors listed below are a step in the right direction, much work is needed to operationalize these eight factors at the design level. Although these eight factors may be newly articulated to the measurement community, the ideas below are already familiar ideas to teachers of multilingual children.

This increased attention is from a national-level high-profile organization (NCME) who published a position paper (2020) specifically addressing the testing of MLs, asking that special attention be given to the following eight factors when designing and evaluating a test for MLs. The NCME believes that careful consideration of these eight factors will lead to valid and fair inferences about what MLs are learning as they progress through their educational experiences (NCME, 2020).

(1) Language is culturally grounded and culture is partly expressed through language. Because the language used on a test is often embedded in sociocultural contexts, care must be taken to ensure that this language will be accessible to MLs.
(2) The language in which a test is given should, whenever possible, coincide with the language in which a ML student is receiving instruction.
(3) The degree of familiarity a ML student has with a test administration mode – who may have limited experience taking a test on a digital interface.
(4) A critical issue when testing MLs is whether they have sufficient proficiency with the language in which a test is being given. The test results for a ML student should always be contextualized with this information.
(5) Test developers should be aware that the productive and receptive language skills of MLs develop differently, and that this may interfere with their ability to engage with a test.
(6) Productive and receptive language skills develop differently; test developers can improve fairness by enabling response methods that allow students to

demonstrate their abilities on the target construct or domain, regardless of the balance of productive and receptive language skills.
(7) Testing challenges may be most pronounced for MLs with special needs or specific learning disabilities; such unique learning needs must be accommodated as appropriate and consistent with the Individuals with Disabilities Education Act (IDEA).
(8) Policies and practices for testing MLs should be informed by research. In particular, there is continuing need for rigorous experimental research on the use of language supports to promote valid test score inferences in a way that does not fundamentally alter the meaning of the test construct.

Home Languages are Typically Undervalued or Ignored

Home languages can be used in a variety of ways in education to secure a child's important position in education. Although federal, state and most district accountability systems focus primarily on the assessment of English in the United States, this book emphasizes the importance of recognizing multilingualism through assessments. A fundamental assumption of research and practice in the education of MLs is that the students' home language(s) is a resource to include and nurture, not a problem to overcome (Ruiz, 1984). Promising assessment practices focus on how students really use language(s) in authentic ways, and in ways that reinforce individual and group cultural identity. The personal linguistic map idea shown in Figures 1.2 and 1.3 asks students to draw the important and complex ways that students use language with their family, community and educational practices. This allows teachers to assess students' linguistic assets to be used in culturally relevant instruction and assessment.

This is one example of how to highlight and gather information (assess) and document what languages and cultures can be used as assets that lead to many meaningful uses of the home language throughout the year. For more lesson plans, videos and ideas, see https://www.cuny-nysieb.org/meet-the-first-grade-team/. This book encourages the reader to use PUMI to better understand all assessments. For example,

Figure 1.2 Students at the center of making 'personal linguistic maps' in first grade at Dos Puentes school in NYC (https://www.cuny-nysieb.org/meet-the-first-grade-team/). This linguistic map shows how Isaac uses Hebrew, English and Spanish in his life and arrows are drawn to examples of people/contexts where he uses each language.

Figure 1.3 'Family linguistic maps' displayed as part of a multilingual ecology in first grade at Dos Puentes school in NYC (https://www.cuny-nysieb.org/meet-the-first-grade-team/)

one might use the following PUMI statements about the linguistic map assessment: The Purpose (P) is to assess language-use for child with family and community. The information is Used (U) to design instruction using language as an asset. The Method (M) of assessment is written response and the Instrument (I) used is a flexible linguistic map outline (to include as many languages as the child connects to). Linguistic maps are an example of how to assess home languages used by the student.

In addition, the use of home languages in content area assessments is widely underutilized. Content area assessment whose purpose is to measure content (not language) can be given (or received) in any language(s), because content is separate from language. If the purpose is to measure content knowledge in history or social studies, then the assessment can be conducted in English, Spanish or a combination of two or more languages that are meaningful to the student, with the goal of better showing what the child knows (see Figures 1.4 and 1.5 for examples of student responses using translanguaging in a content area assessment). Figures 1.4 and 1.5 show English curriculum-based assessments where the student responds in what languages they want. For Figure 1.4, the goal is to assess social studies content in the United States (facts about the War of 1812). The first prompt is given in English and the student response is in Spanish. The second prompt in Figure 1.4 shows the student using key English words from the prompt to start a response, then finishes the response in Spanish; this is a simple example of translanguaging in assessment responses.

In assessment, teachers want to promote the fluency of content knowledge by using home languages in prompts or responses. The two examples given in Figures 1.4 and 1.5 show a relatively easy way to allow more opportunity for students to demonstrate their knowledge because the English-only prompts are unchanged, and the responses are open-ended and therefore open to multiple languages (there is no fixed or binding rule that responses must be in the language of the prompt). This is in direct opposition to requiring students to respond in English only, which in this case (Figures 1.4 and 1.5) may have resulted in no or a fractional response resulting in a low or zero score. This type of language restrictive environment triggers many negative consequences related to self-efficacy, culture and language. Teachers unable to read student responses in multiple languages should not preclude them from using home languages in assessment. Linguistic resources, such as other/older multilingual students, teachers, staff and translation applications are readily available to help monolingual teachers translate between languages and may include image options to scan student work. However, it should be noted that students need practice and assurance that using their home language is 'OK' or allowed because

Figure 1.4 Example 1 of translanguaging in assessment response

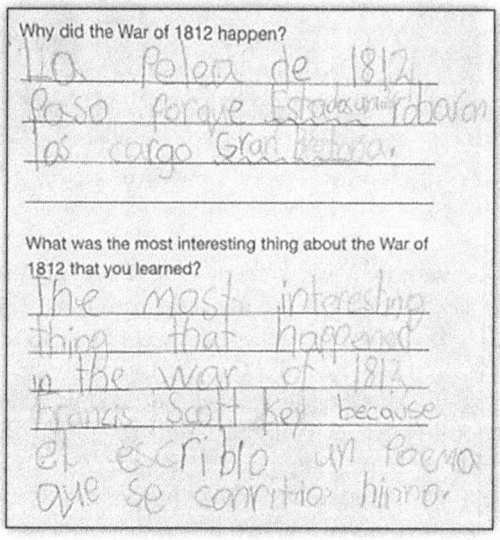

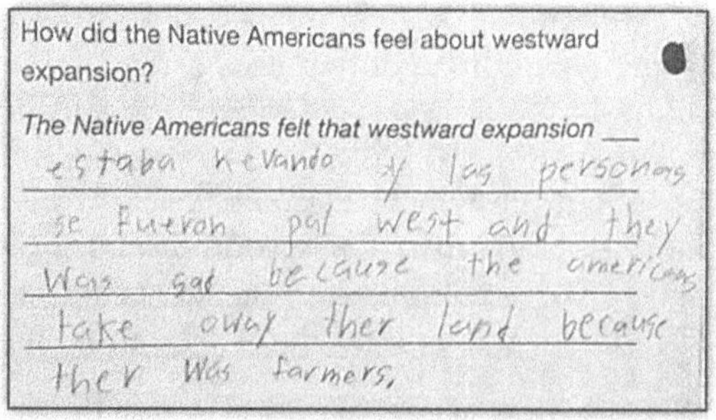

Figure 1.5 Example 2 of translanguaging in assessment response

even in classrooms considered 'inclusive', there may be strong messages in the curriculum, instruction and school environment that home languages do not belong in school. To counter this, the teacher can model or show models to students of how to use their linguistic repertoire in assessment. If the assessments in Figures 1.4 and 1.5 were given in English only or Spanish only (monolingual approach to assessment), the teacher would have a fractional view of what the student knows in social studies. Using translanguaging in assessment departs from the traditional monolingual approach to assessment.

Translanguaging in assessment can be viewed through assessment input and output. The input is all of the assessment material presented to the student (prompts, questions, multiple-choice options) and the output refers to the answers generated, or produced, by the student. Decisions about input and output should be made based on the linguistic profile of the students, the language of instruction and the student's strength to optimize showing what the student really knows. A restrictive and punitive approach to assessment for MLs is when the language of the test, instruction and rubric is English-only where responses in any other language are marked incorrect. This clearly puts bilingual and multilingual students at a disadvantage.

To extend this idea of translanguaging to standardized testing, Lopez *et al.* (2019) explored with designing computer-based items where the locus of control about which languages to use (input or output) is with the students. Students decide whether to use Spanish, English or a mix of Spanish and English (translanguaging) to see an item (language tabs), read an item (using read aloud recordings), write a response (such as the examples given earlier in this chapter), say a response (using a recording) and review synonyms. In their study, the directions to a test item may state: 'Answer the question below; you can write or say the answer in English or Spanish or a combination of both. To read the question in Spanish, click the Español tab'. This experiment was carried out using a computer-based platform (Lopez *et al.*, 2019). This type of translanguaging approach allowed bilingual students (Spanish and English) to use their entire linguistic repertoire to answer the math questions. This idea has the potential to be extended to multilinguals by adding more language tabs to the platform (such as Bengali, Arabic, Chinese) (Lopez *et al.*, 2017). One item from an assessment is shown in Figure 1.6.

Home Language Assessment

Typically, there are very few or no published/commercial assessments available in schools for home or multiple languages, which in this age of accountability leads to a de-emphasis of languages other than English. (if it's not tested, it's not taught). Another aspect of this issue is accountability. The increase in accountability to measure and show gains in English that came during the No Child Left Behind (NCLB) era (2001–2015) caused schools – and some bilingual schools – to abandon instructional time for developing the home language because school leadership was not held accountable for showing growth in home languages. And in some cases, schools abandoned bilingual programs altogether. Kate Menken and Cristian Solorza (2014) studied the decline of bilingual education in New York City schools in the NCLB era. Through qualitative research, they studied 10 city schools that have eliminated

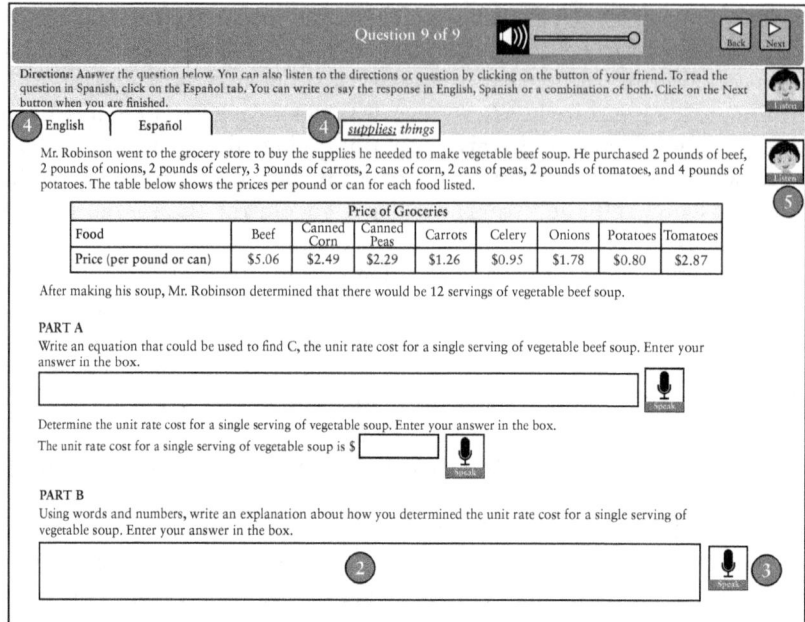

Figure 1.6 Sample bilingual assessment resources, as shown in Lopez *et al.*'s (2019: 7) ETS Research Report Series, ETS-RR-17-07

their bilingual programs and replaced them with English-only programs. The authors found that testing and accountability (high accountability of English, little to none of Spanish) were used as justification and created a disincentive to serve MLs through bilingual education. Since the end of the NCLB era (2015), dual language bilingual education programs are on the rise both in New York City and nationally.

Also, many teachers refrain from additional tests beyond those mandated; they feel that their students are already burdened with too many tests. This concern is warranted because many times MLs are tested up to double the amount of non-MLs. If you take each test for MLs and add together the amount of instructional time lost due to testing and teacher absence due to scoring and training for testing, the 'cost of testing' for MLs becomes evident. Unfortunately, not to assess the home language is to leave out important information that could be used to inform instruction and build on students' strengths.

Common in schools today is the overwhelming dominance of relatively inflexible assessment practices with MLs. Most assessment and accountability systems focus exclusively on English (or the dominant language of schools), reflecting the assumption that English is the only relevant language when instructing and assessing. Common assessment practice with MLs tends to measure each language separately, or not assess the home language at all. For example, in the United States, MLs are regularly tested in English using a mandated standardized test, and if the student is in a bilingual program, on a separate day with a separate instrument, perhaps they are also tested using a Spanish language proficiency test. Typically, the two results are combined to represent the child's bilingualism. In reality, this is considered to be a very narrow view that critically underestimates what the child can actually do as a multilingual person. Separate language tests or full translation of a test in the home language still support the idea of monolingual assessment.

SNAPSHOT: WHICH LENS?

Assessment practices may lead to promise: Efrain attends an English-only school in Arizona. Efrain's teacher invites him to create a writing portfolio to demonstrate how his writing ability in English has improved over the first two marking periods. The primary theme of the portfolio is 'change', and the teacher and Efrain conference together to decide that the four writing samples in English that he will showcase in his portfolio will each describe a recent change in his family (these changes include: a new dog, his grandfather and cousin from Mexico are living in their house for four months, his brother moved out and got an apartment two blocks away) with attention to how these changes influence his everyday life. Reflecting the teacher's understanding that reading and writing are interconnected, as are all of the languages in Efrain's linguistic repertoire, the teacher includes evidence in Efrain's portfolio of reading comprehension in Spanish. Efrain reads several award-winning children's stories about being Mexican in the US Southwest, focusing on the changes that children go through in the United States. Efrain reads the books in Spanish and records a summary of the books in Spanish. The recordings and reflections are included in a section of the portfolio about home language. Also included in Efrain's portfolio is a page on which Efrain reflects on the quality of his work over time, as well as a page on which the teacher evaluates Efrain's writing in stages (using a rubric aligned with state English language proficiency [ELP] standards) and provides feedback. Efrain uses the portfolio to demonstrate his writing ability to his teacher and parents. This exemplifies promising assessment practices because the portfolio is designed to show Efrain's writing ability, and he is expected to be an agent of the assessment process by including a self-assessment of his own work and also by selecting the topics based on recent changes in his own life. This is also an example of how promising assessment is culturally relevant. Culturally relevant instruction/assessment is when teachers respond to the differences in students while focusing on the strengths of students. It often mediates the mismatch between home and school that many schools experience. Results from the portfolio are compared to Efrain's interactive journal writing samples and the standardized English (writing portion) test score to chart his progress and determine programmatic changes (if any).[2]

Assessment practices may lead to deficit: Efrain's teacher announces that according to state policy, April 10 will be the day he takes the Content and Language Instruction Performance (CLIP) – a state-mandated ELP test. Starting in January, Efrain is reminded on a daily basis how important this test is and his teacher provides 10 minutes of CLIP practice every day to prepare for the big test in April. The test contains multiple-choice items and prompts in English to generate writing samples upon which Efrain will be evaluated. The standardized prompts change from section to section and are unrelated. For example, first Efrain is asked to write about a day at the beach (this prompt is difficult for Efrain because he lives in the Sonoran Desert); next, he is asked to write about nature versus nurture; lastly, he is asked to write about the types of things he can learn from peers while playing a sport. Efrain and his teacher are the objects of the assessment – the assessment is being performed *upon them* – and the items and prompts are designed by outside evaluators (a psychometric company) unfamiliar with Efrain's language, culture and geography. The creation of the actual test items and most of the scoring are done outside the state, and the test scores are analyzed to show what parts of Efrain's writing need improvement. The focus is on what Efrain cannot do in writing (searching for deficits). The results arrive at the school in June and Efrain's new teacher reads the results in August. An academic intervention plan to remediate the identified deficits is designed for the next school year; and Efrain is tested the following April to see if the deficiencies have been remediated. Based on the test score generated on the ELP test, Efrain will either remain officially designated as an English learner and continue to receive English as a second language (ESL) services, or be mainstreamed (not receive ESL services).

Discussion questions

- What assessment practices lead to promise or deficit for MLs?
- How can you negotiate both views (promise, deficit) to create a 'compromise' plan that benefits students?
- How can you advocate for better assessment practices for MLs?

Four Guiding Assessment Principles in This Book

The following four guiding principles – both theoretical and practical – guide the work throughout this book:

- **Guiding Principle 1: Assessment practice for MLs is viewed through a lens of promise.** This guiding principle largely draws from the assessment ideas of Evangeline Stefanakis (1999, 2003, 2011) and the author's own practical experience. This book assumes that bilingualism is an asset and that assessment methods should highlight this asset (not point to perceived deficits). Assessment is an interactive process that should be integrated into daily routines that occur within a culturally relevant pedagogy (Ladson-Billings, 1994, 2021). Instruction and assessment should be student centered, involving students and peers in the act of assessment (administering and scoring) and organizing what they know. Assessment should also be multifaceted, involve multiple culturally relevant perspectives and provide authentic and meaningful feedback to improve student learning, teachers' instructional practice and educational options in the classroom.

- **Guiding Principle 2: Only high-quality assessments are acceptable.** This guiding principle draws from the work of Rick Stiggins and Jan Chappuis (2011, 2016) and Rick Stiggins (2017). High-quality assessment adheres to the following five standards: (1) clear objectives, (2) focused purpose, (3) proper method, (4) sound sampling and (5) accurate assessment free of bias and distortion. To violate any of these standards places students' academic well-being in jeopardy. In addition, an assessment system helps to maintain each student's sense of academic self-efficacy and willingness to continue learning, and it does this by helping all students:
  - Become key players in the self-assessment process as they learn and rely on that involvement to promote their own success.
  - Stay aware of where they are within whatever learning progression they are ascending and of what comes next for them.
  - Use continuous evidence of changes in their own levels of mastery to monitor and feel in control of their growth over time.

  It is important to expand assessment's role from identifying achievement problems to helping to solve those problems. Results from formative and summative assessments can inform instructional decisions focused on individual student success and it can be used for classroom, school, and district levels. With evidence like this arising from classrooms, schools, and districts, standardized tests as we have known them are no longer necessary. We don't need all students to respond to exactly the same items at the same time to address student learning needs (Stiggins, 2017).

- **Guiding Principle 3: Validity is a unified concept.** Proof that assessment results are valid for MLs should be presented before assessments are used to make important decisions. The idea of validity should include the adequacy and appropriateness of inferences and actions, including social consequences, based on test scores or other modes of assessment. This guiding principle draws from the work of Samuel Messick (1989).

- **Guiding Principle 4: Translanguaging during assessment is important for MLs.** For multilingual students, translanguaging as a pedagogical practice can serve to validate their home language and cultural practices; plus, in assessment, simply put, students can show more of what they know with the use of translanguaging in assessment. In assessment, if the purpose of the assessment is to assess content (math or science for example), then translanguaging in assessment will more validly show what students know. Ofelia García (2009) uses the term 'translanguaging' to describe the language practices of bilingual people (active) as opposed to the language of bilingual people (static). This focus on dynamic language practices (languaging – translanguaging) is now one of the better-known holistic conceptualizations of language used by researchers and practitioners. Guiding Principle 4 draws from the work of Ofelia García (2009) and my practical work with the City University of New York–New York State Initiative for Emergent Bilinguals (CUNY NYSIEB) team.[3]

Guiding Principle 4 is demonstrated in Figures 1.4 and 1.5. The purpose of these assessments was to measure social studies content. The use of translanguaging in assessment helps students show more fully what they really know because they can use their full linguistic repertoire, which creates more opportunity for accessing content and for assessing a holistic picture of what they know as opposed to a fractional picture when students are limited to one language (Celic & Seltzer, 2013; García, 2009). Using translanguaging in assessment is good pedagogical practice for English as a new language (ENL), bilingual and mainstream teachers – everyone. This is easier to do when teachers have control over classroom-based assessments; however, it becomes more difficult to implement as an assessment practice when local, state or national governments control assessment, when the idea of integrating translanguaging in assessment becomes much more difficult.

Together, these four guiding principles create a foundation to increase the quality of assessment for MLs. Teachers and administrators can draw on these guiding principles as they make decisions about assessment. The remainder of this chapter introduces a practical and easy-to-remember decision-making process called PUMI that will help teachers adhere to the four guiding principles reviewed above.

PUMI (Purpose, Use, Method, Instrument): A Framework for Decision-Making

This section introduces the 'PUMI' framework, which teachers and administrators can use to make decisions about assessment for MLs. PUMI is an acronym for purpose, use, method and instrument. The PUMI framework is essentially a series of critical questions that educators need to ask in order to select the most appropriate method of assessment and improve the condition of assessment for MLs. Figure 1.7 represents the four major steps in the PUMI framework used throughout this book.

Purpose: First, educators need to ask themselves and each other, 'What is the **P: purpose** of this assessment?' or, more pointedly, 'Why are we doing this?'. For MLs, we often assess for the following purposes: to measure oral language, to measure achievement against a set of standards or to measure ELP development in content-based instruction. The purpose of an assessment is usually in relation to a set of standards. Learning targets (another name for purpose) must always

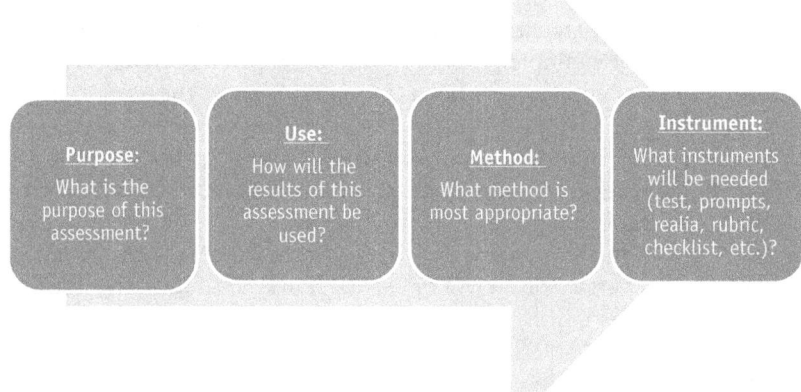

Figure 1.7 A decision-making process called PUMI (Purpose, Use, Method, Instrument)

be translated into student-friendly terms and into a language the student understands. When answering the first question in PUMI, the answer usually begins with **'to measure…' or 'to assess…'**. What is it we are trying to assess or measure? Every assessment is designed to have a purpose and to measure something, regardless of whether it is developed as a large-scale assessment, mandated by a state as part of its accountability system or is a classroom assessment designed by a single teacher or a team of teachers.

Just as builders need detailed plans (blueprints) to construct a building, test makers need a blueprint to build a test and give instruction about how to use the results appropriately. To determine the purpose, articulate exactly what you are trying to measure. If you are using a commercial or state-mandated test, the purpose of the test has already been determined by the test authors. For a commercial test, the purpose is always revealed at the beginning of the technical manual (sometimes called the 'blueprint'), but most teachers would be surprised to read what the test authors say the purpose is – always check. Further, it's important to identify the conceptual or theoretical framework upon which the test was built. If possible, read in the technical manual (some refer to as the blueprint) how the test constructors define language (if it is a measure of language) and on what conceptual or theoretical framework the test is built. Beware of language tests that are vague about articulating a language theory or tests built on the judgment of a committee of experts. If you still don't know the purpose of an assessment, ask your administrator to clarify. Be cautious about moving forward with the assessment without understanding the purpose. If the purpose is difficult to identify, start your sentence with, the purpose is 'to assess' _____ or the purpose is 'to measure' _____.

Use: Next, teachers and administrators need to ask critical questions about **U: use**. Use of data is the most important question to address. How exactly will the results of the assessment (data) be used after the assessment is completed? The stakes are high for many assessments in schools. There are roughly two ways to use assessment results: **formative** or **summative**. Formative ways of using assessment results include supporting student learning while you are still forming your professional judgment of what students know. Summative ways are when assessment results are used to summarize what students know. The results of assessments are commonly used to determine what program a ML student will go into or exit from, whether a child will be classified as a ML in schools and therefore receive targeted language services, classification into special education or whether a teacher is effective or not, to name a few. The results of assessments are also used for daily classroom-level decisions, such as how much scaffolding is needed, how to group students, mastery of content, pace of the lesson or unit and so on. Many people confuse purpose and use, so you can think of it this way: The purpose is identified before the assessment is designed, and the use occurs after the test results are collected. Basically, imagine yourself holding a piece of paper with assessment results. What will you do with them? This is use.

Method (M): It is important to ask PUMI questions in the P*U*M*I order. Following the order, after careful consideration of P: Purpose and U: Use, it is time to select the appropriate **M: Method** and instrument. It should make sense that selecting the method and instrument without understanding the purpose and use of an assessment can lead to inappropriate assessment practices. When it is time to consider method, imagine the most authentic situation in which the student is 'doing' the content or language objectives and pick your assessment method as close as possible to the real task. This authenticity should also be present in the instruction, which leads to promising culturally relevant instruction and assessment. If you are assessing speaking, then – for the assessment method – ask MLs to speak in a natural setting, about something they are comfortable speaking about (speaking with rubric); if you are assessing problem-solving, then pick a method where you watch them solve a problem and ask them questions about how they solved it (observation with rubric); if you are assessing writing in an academic setting, then obtain a sample of writing during a social studies or science lesson (written response). This author categorizes all assessment methods into the following four categories: selected response, written response, performance and one-to-one communication. Chapters 4 and 5 provide a deeper focus on methods of assessment.

Instrument (I): Outside of education, you can think of a bathroom scale as an instrument to measure weight, a measuring tape as an instrument to measure length, etc.; instrumentation can be thought of as the tools needed to carry out the assessment. Interpreted broadly within education, the instrument consists of the things necessary to carry out the assessment, such as an outline, a graphic organizer, writing prompts, a rubric,[4] a checklist, a standardized test score sheet, props and realia. After you choose the method, it is easy to select the instrument, by thinking about what things are needed to support the purpose, use and method. Instrumentation depends on purpose, use and method and is the final step in the PUMI decision process.

SNAPSHOT: A TEACHER'S JUDGMENT COUNTS

Mrs Ortiz is a sixth-grade teacher who assesses MLs in a variety of ways throughout the first two weeks of school to find out important factors she knows affect schooling and language acquisition. She assesses important areas such as schooling history (school intake forms or interview family member), attitudes about English and the home language (questionnaire), ELP during a content area lesson (observation of student speaking in content lesson), translanguaging patterns (All About Me poster with emphasis on language use at home) and ELP (state-mandated assessments). However, it has always bothered her that nobody assesses the reading and writing skills of her students in the home language. She understands that the child's home language makes up the whole child (and that viewing the student through English-only assessments may represent only a fraction of the child); she knows that understanding literacy levels in the home language is also a valuable instructional tool to leverage content, learn more English and learn more home language. In addition, her state is now mandating that schools identify students with interrupted/inconsistent formal education (SIFE). With all this in mind, Mrs Ortiz was introduced to the General Home Language Reading Assessment Rubric at a workshop and decided to use PUMI to make decisions about whether this assessment would meet the needs in her classroom. Mrs Ortiz made a quick PUMI table similar to Table 1.2 and, based on the PUMI analysis, she decided to proceed with using the General Home Language Reading Assessment Rubric.[5]

Table 1.2 Mrs Ortiz uses PUMI to make decisions

Purpose (P)	Use (U)	Method (M)	Instrument (I)
To assess reading ability in the home language	To design appropriate instruction using reading in the home and new language	Category: One-to-one communication; reading with rubric	The General Home Language Reading Assessment Rubric
	To design intense alternate program (such as SIFE or newcomer program) if home reading skills are absent		

Discussion questions

- How does this snapshot relate to the four guiding principles presented earlier in this chapter?
- How does Mrs Ortiz use PUMI to help guide her assessment decisions?

Translanguaging and Assessment

Translanguaging is increasingly seen as an important design principle in instruction and assessment. The following section shows how some researchers are studying the topic of translanguaging and assessment.

For example, Ascenzi-Moreno (2018) conducted case studies of three teachers in the US who used an adapted miscue analysis when assessing reading. This adapted version introduced two additional components to the typical miscue analysis to allow exploration of the impact of language (or home languages) on the reading assessment results. In this study, she closely documented how using formative reading assessments through a translanguaging lens can best document the full range of MLs' abilities. (See Chapter 5 for more on Ascenzi-Moreno's study.) The next authors study how dominant assessment practices threaten the unique cultural and linguistic diversity of Australian students. Steele *et al.* (2022) explored translanguaging and assessment of Australian Aboriginal students who may speak Standard Australian English (SAE), Australian Aboriginal English, Creoles and traditional languages such as Kija and Martu. These authors adopted the term transmodal (assessment) or transmodality to describe not only the language of the assessment, but also the modality. They argue that (in Australia) the dominant assessment modes of reading/writing/literacy reflect current sociopolitical values, colonizer values and the superiority of SAE. These misaligned assessment practices threaten the unique linguistic diversity of Australia and do not allow access to the inner workings of the human mind, languages and culture of their students. Therefore, transmodal assessment includes the entire linguistic repertoire and/or semiotic systems. Transmodal assessment allows individuals to express their knowledge and understanding using, for example, drama, music, narration, gestures and hand signals in written or oral form and in both standard and non-standard dialects. These can be layered, intertwined and infused (Steele *et al.*, 2022).

But many monolingual teachers who believe in this more holistic assessment still struggle to enact translanguaging pedagogies in their assessment practices. Fine (2022)

Table 1.3 Ways monolingual teachers adapt to formative assessments in Science where students used translanguaging

Code	Sub-code	Definition	Example
Talk moves	Pausing	Pausing the flow of conversation to consider students' science ideas that included translanguaging	'What does that mean?'.
	Consulting with students	Talk that suggests teachers check-in with specific students to ask about their multilingual work	'I'll have to ask that student'.
	Lack of linguistic knowledge	Talk where collaborative members refer to their own lack of multilingual knowledge	'Well. I don't know anything. And I'm listening to Spanish everyday'.
	Modeling	Modeling how to interpret students' science ideas that included translanguaging	'In the Spanish language don't they put the adjective after the object?'.
	Using multiple linguistic resources	Drawing from prior knowledge about a language that students used in their written/spoken work	'Because pure oxygen is better. Right? Because 'mejor' is 'better'.
	Agency	Exhibiting agency in interpreting student ideas that include translanguaging	'So, I'm assuming he's interpreting as if like fire is something that's actively being moved. Like fire is something that's acting on its own. That's how I'm taking it. Like I'm just listening to the conversation, but more like he's thinking, like conceptually in science wise, he thinks fire can come and go when it wants to. Yeah, that's how I am taking it'.
Activity structures	Student science ideas sorting activity	Teacher activity to sort student work by science ideas (including work that includes translanguaging)	'What did you note about students' science ideas? What buckets did you sort student work into?'
	Student translanguaging ideas routine	Explicit routine during the reflect and modify meetings where teachers discuss student work that includes translanguaging	'So I have a kid using English to label their model. But Spanish to answer the written part'.
	Visual elements	Focusing on the visual elements of student work, such as recorded videos, scientific posters, drawings and models	'This is the group that recorded one in English and Spanish. And the one they did in English, they covered up their eyes with the little sunglasses. And then the one they did in Spanish, they didn't cover themselves'.
Tools	Internet-based translation tool	Using internet-based translation tools	'What if you type the whole thing in – that whole phrase into Google Translate. I wonder what it says'.
	Internet-based bilingual dictionary	Using internet-based multilingual dictionaries	'Try Word Reference'.
	Transcription	Expressing interest in transcriptions of students' oral multilingual ideas	'It is really hard for me to understand what students say in their videos. I think if I had a transcription of their multilingual ideas, I would be better able to interpret them'.

Source: From Fine, 2022.

studied monolingual teachers' interpretive power when teachers do not share multiple linguistic resources with their students. This study took place in a suburban school in a Rocky Mountain state in the United States. The focal teachers were deeply committed to equitable pedagogies but lacked concrete ways to interpret the results of formative science assessments. The results focused on ways the *teachers* adapted to the translanguaged formative science assessment. Table 1.3 (from Fine, 2022) shows how monolingual teachers adapted to the formative science assessment using translanguaging. In short, the focal teachers adjusted their interpretive power by talking through the interpretation, structuring activities differently and using internet-based tools.

Schissel *et al.* (2018) also worked with teachers in their translanguaging research. They found language teachers in Oaxaca, Mexico, to be more open to expanding ML practices in instructional pedagogy but found tensions supporting translanguaging within institutional practices because of the societal monolingual (Spanish) proficiency norms. This research study validated the practices of communities in Oaxaca who spoke languages such as Zapotec, Mixtec, Chatino, Triqui and Mixe.

The following study focused on how young children translanguage in formative literacy assessments in the US. Bauer *et al.* (2020) studied six kindergarten students in a Midwest US Spanish/English bilingual program to see how they translanguage during informal literacy assessments. During assessment, all students were able to use translanguaging to effectively narrate a story. The authors showed that the students brokered and leveraged their multilingual tools when they engaged with Spanish literary texts and concluded that if assessments are multidimensional, they will capture translanguaging practices (Bauer *et al.*, 2020). The authors emphasize how binary terminology such as English dominant or Spanish dominant fails to capture the rich and complex diversity of dialect and language exposure, knowledge and use. The mismatch of the monolingual accountability system becomes a problem for MLs in general. For an example of the rich and complex language profiles of these young children, see the descriptions of the languages of the students who participated in this study (Table 1.4). The language profiles in Table 1.4 ends the chapter by

Table 1.4 The complexities of participant languages in Bauer and colleagues (2020)

	Description of students' languages
Angel	Parents are immigrants from Mexico, who insist Spanish be the language of the home. He has older siblings and they converse in Spanish and sometimes in English.
Ayame	Mother is African American and father is from Mexico. Ayame speaks in English with her mother. Her father speaks to her in Spanish and she answers in English (this changed over the course of the year). She is the older of two girls.
Gabrielle	Lives with her mother. Her mother is white and her father is African American. Her mother speaks only English. Mother reported that Gabrielle is not an AAVE speaker. Gabrielle is one of three children, the middle child.
Joslyn	Lives with her parents, who are both from Mexico. She is the youngest of four children and the only girl. Spanish is expected in the home.
Reins	Lives with her mother and father. She is one of two children. Her brother is 10 years older than her. Her parents expect Spanish in the home.
Tamara	Lives with her mother. Her mother is African American. She is an only child. Both mother and child speak AAVE.

Source: Bauer *et al.* (2020).
Note: AAVE: African American vernacular English.

reminding us how assessment, especially language assessment, should work towards capturing rich linguistic profile of multilingual students.

> **END-OF-CHAPTER ACTIVITIES (Instructors: See advice at the end of the book)**
>
> By completing Activities 1 and 2, the reader will be able to:
>
> (1) Discuss assessment practices that lead to promise and those that lead to deficit for MLs.
> (2) Order the steps to PUMI and briefly explain each step. Use PUMI to better understand a mandated English proficiency test in your area.
>
> **Activity 1**
> Discuss assessment practices that lead to promise and those that lead to deficit for MLs.
> Either as a whole group or a small group, students will place the instructor-made sticky notes in a blank T-table (formatted similar to the following table), read the clue to the class and briefly discuss why it fits there.
>
> | Leads to deficit | Leads to promise |
> |---|---|
> | | |
> | | |
> | | |
> | | |
>
> **Activity 2**
> Order the steps to PUMI and briefly explain each step. Use PUMI to guide the decision-making process about assessment for MLs.
> Find another student to be your partner. The instructor will pass out four index cards per pair. Each card will display the letter P, U, M or I. With each student taking a turn, explain what each letter means (not just the word – but a definition in your own words). Many people confuse Purpose with Use. Hint: When talking about Purpose, start with 'to measure…' or 'to assess…'; with Use, think about, once you have the results in your hand, now what will you do with them (what decisions will be made, for example)? Explore a different order of PUMI and explain why you like/dislike it. Be prepared to share your definitions of PUMI and one example to the whole class. If you live in the United States and you are 1 of the approximately 40 states that use the World-Class Instructional Design and Assessment (WIDA)[5] test called ACCESS for MLs, complete a PUMI table for the ELP test called ACCESS (currently used by 40 of 50 United States). Otherwise, use a mandated ELP test in your area. For example, New York is not a WIDA state, so with your partner, create a PUMI table for the New York State Identification Test for English Language Learners (NYSITELL) or the New York State English as a Second Language Achievement Test (NYSESLAT) and other assessments used in the identification process.[6]

Notes

(1) The lens of promise can also be called 'strengths-based' or 'asset-based' assessment. All these labels indicate that we are focusing on what students can do instead of emphasizing what students cannot do.
(2) In reality, many of these practices using home language are not allowed in Arizona. Despite decades of research results showing that using home language increases learning, Arizona is the only state remaining to outlaw Bilingual Education.
(3) CUNY-New York State Initiative on Emergent Bilinguals (NYSIEB) was a collaborative project of the Research Institute for the Study of Language in Urban Society (RISLUS) and the PhD program in Urban Education funded by the New York State Education Department.
(4) Remember: A rubric is not an assessment method; it is a scoring device (or tool) to help make assessment results more reliable and therefore more valid. Broadly thinking, it can be thought of as a tool or instrument to carry out an assessment.
(5) This General Home Language Reading Assessment Rubric can be found in García, O., Herrera, L., Hesson, S. and Kleyn, T. A CUNY-NYSIEB Framework for the Education of Emergent Bilinguals with Low Home Literacy: 4–12 Grades. (https://www.cuny-nysieb.org/wp-content/uploads/2016/05/CUNY-NYSIEB-Framework-for-EB-with-Low-Home-Literacy-Spring-2013-Final-Version-05-08-13.pdf). The rubric can be found in Appendix A.
(6) WIDA is no longer using this acronym-definition because it no longer represents their mission. Just WIDA now.

References

AERA, APA, NCME (2014) *Standards for Educational and Psychological Testing*. Washington, DC: AERA.

Ascenzi-Moreno, L. (2018) Translanguaging and responsive assessment adaptations: Emergent bilingual readers through the lens of possibility. *Language Arts* 95 (6), 355–369.

Bauer, E., Colomer, S. and Wiemelt, J. (2020) Biliteracy of African American and Latinx kindergarten students in a dual language program: Translanguaging practices across informal assessments. *Urban Education* 55 (3), 331–361.

Celic, C. and Seltzer, K. (2013) *Translanguaging: A CUNY-NYSIEB Guide for Educators*. New York: CUNY-NYSIEB, The Graduate Center.

Fine, C. (2022) Translanguaging interpretive power in formative assessment co-design: A catalyst for science teacher agentive shifts. *Journal of Language, Identity, & Education* 21 (3), 191–211.

García, O. (2009) *Bilingual Education in the 21st Century: A Global Perspective*. New York: John Wiley.

Green, A. (2014) *Exploring Language Assessment and Testing: Language in Action*. London: Routledge.

Ladson-Billings, G. (1994) *Dreamkeepers: Successful Teachers of African American Children*. San Francisco, CA: Jossey-Bass.

Ladson-Billings, G. (2021) *Culturally Relevant Pedagogy: Asking a Different Question* (Culturally Sustaining Pedagogies Series). New York: Teachers College Press.

Lopez, A., Turkan, S. and Guzman-Orth, D. (2017) Conceptualizing the use of translanguaging in initial content assessments for newly arrived emergent bilingual students. Research Report ETS RR-17-07, December 2017.

Lopez, A., Guzman, D. and Turkan, S. (2019) Exploring the use of translanguaging to measure the mathematics knowledge of emergent bilingual students. *Translation and Translanguaging in Multilingual Contexts* 52, 143–164.

Menken, K. and Solorza, C. (2014) No Child Left Bilingual: Accountability and the elimination of bilingual education programs in New York City schools. *Educational Policy* 28 (1), 96–125.

Messick, S. (1989) Meaning and values in test validation: The science and ethics of assessment. *Educational Researcher* 18 (2), 5–11.

NCME (2020) National Council on Measurement in Education (NCME) position statement on testing English Learners. https://higherlogicdownload.s3.amazonaws.com/NCME/4b7590fc-3903-444d-b89d-c45b7fa3da3f/UploadedImages/English_learners_Statement_sept_2020.pdf

Ruiz, R. (1984) Orientations in language planning. *NABE Journal* 8, 15–34.

Schissel, J., De Korne, H. and López-Gopar, M. (2021) Grappling with translanguaging for teaching and assessment in culturally and linguistically diverse contexts: Teacher perspectives from Oaxaca, Mexico. *International Journal of Bilingual Education and Bilingualism* 24 (3), 340–356.

Steele, C., Dovchin, S. and Oliver, R. (2022) 'Stop measuring Black kids with a White stick': Translanguaging for classroom assessment. *RELC Journal* 53 (2), 400–415.

Stefanakis, E. (1999) *Whose Judgment Counts? Assessing Bilingual Children, K-3*. Portsmouth, NH: Heinemann.

Stefanakis, E. (2003) *Multiple Intelligences and Portfolios: A Window into the Learners Mind*. Portsmouth, NH: Heinemann.

Stefanakis, E. (2011) *Differentiated Assessment: Finding Every Learners Potential*. Wiley-Jossey Bass Series. San Francisco, CA: Jossey-Bass.

Stiggins, R. (2017) *The Perfect Assessment System*. Alexandria, VA: The Association for Supervision and Curriculum Development (ASCD).

Stiggins, R. and Chappuis, J. (2011) *An Introduction to Student-Involved Assessment for Learning* (6th edn). New York: Pearson.

Stiggins, R. and Chappuis, J. (2016) *An Introduction to Student-Involved Assessment for Learning* (7th edn). New York: Pearson.

WIDA (2019) The WIDA Can do philosophy. See https://wida.wisc.edu/sites/default/files/resource/WIDA-CanDo-Philosophy.pdf (accessed 18 February 2024).

2 History: How Did We Get Here?

THEMES FROM CHAPTER 2

(1) The history of testing multilingual learners (MLs) includes many examples of inappropriate testing and misuse of results.
(2) Despite several decades of warning from the measurement community, test scores from tests given in English to students who don't know English are still being used for important education decisions.
(3) The current political climate favors accountability over validity.

Key Vocabulary
- Class analysis argument.
- Cultural argument.
- Eugenics.
- Genetic argument.
- No Child Left Behind (NCLB).
- Test fairness.
- Test misuse.

PUMI Connection: Use

This chapter focuses primarily on the U (Use) of test scores for MLs. By providing a history and presenting the damaging mistakes that have been made in the past, it is hoped we can prevent the misuse of test scores in the future, and better understand where we are today.

This chapter may seem rather gloomy but its aim is to help explain the present. The author wanted to include a variety of historical perspectives regarding testing, which may be of particular interest to readers who wish to know how present practices took root. First is a review of the history of test misuse among non-English-speaking and other groups of people, followed by some theoretical frameworks that contradict the old but strong genetic argument of school success/failure. These frameworks may also help educators understand and explain alternative/additional reasons why today, some students succeed and others don't. The second section of the chapter provides a major-event history table documenting important and influential policies in the history of ML assessment over time. The final section emphasizes the changes in assessment introduced in 2001 by the NCLB, and an overview of the current Every Student Succeeds Act (ESSA) that began in 2015. These federal US policies greatly impact the assessment, in particular, the testing of MLs on an individual level.

A History of Misuse

Historically, the mission of education has been to sort students into various levels of social and economic systems, and assessment has played the lead role in ensuring this sorting. A history of discrimination exists in US education and abroad whereby non-English-speaking children have been denied equal educational opportunity based on the use of standardized tests. Standardized tests in English, when presented to non-English-speaking students, raise several obvious validity concerns (a detailed discussion of validity is forthcoming in Chapter 3). The issue of fairness in testing has attracted scrutiny since the 1960s, yet federal and state mandates requiring the testing of students in a language they do not know have increased since 2000. Two types of standardized tests introduced major obstacles to ML populations in the early 1900s, especially immigrant groups: literacy testing and intelligence testing. Literacy testing was used to block access to civic participation (such as voting) of people such as immigrants and African Americans in the south of the United States. Although more often, these tests and the consequences of the white supremacist sentiments of the time were put in place often with the intention of harming the lives of language-minoritized bilinguals (Schissel, 2019).

Understanding test fairness was less of a concern before the 1960s. Many examples exist, pre-1960, of the misuse of intelligence tests to gatekeep[1] or advance some racial groups over others. During this era, for example, some educators, psychologists and others used intelligence test scores to describe American Indian and Mexican children as having many negative qualities such as 'dullness'. For example, Lewis Terman,[2] who was most famous for his Stanford–Binet Intelligence test first used in schools in 1916 (and a version of it is still used today, 100 years later), was also a well-known eugenicist.[3] At the same time that he became a champion for 'gifted' children, he also promoted a very dark social agenda for 'other' groups of children. Terman and other eugenicists claimed that the smartest or more fit people, such as the wealthy with European ancestry, were reproducing too slowly and in danger of being overwhelmed by more 'feeble-minded' races (non-wealthy and non-European). Terman also promoted the idea that America was being jeopardized from within, by the rapid proliferation of people lacking intelligence and moral fiber and warned that the unchecked arrival of immigrants from southern and eastern Europe would drag down the national stock (Leslie, 2000).

As Leslie (2000) reports, early eugenicists such as Terman managed to advocate and pass several laws aligned with their social agenda. Thirty-three states, including California, passed laws that required the sterilization of about 60,000 men and women at mental institutions. Early eugenicists also affected immigration policy; in 1924, Congress set quotas that drastically cut immigration from eastern and southern Europe (Leslie, 2000).

In 1916, while Terman promoted his Stanford–Binet Intelligence test in schools, he also published a book called *The Measurement of Intelligence*. In this book, Terman discussed his findings after administering the Stanford–Binet test to Spanish speakers and unschooled African Americans. This only supported his preference for white European racial groups over others. In his words:

> [a] high-grade or border-line deficiency... is very common among Spanish Indian and Mexican families of the Southwest and also among negroes. Their dullness seems to be racial or at least inherent in the family stocks from which they come... children of this group should be separated into separate classes... They cannot master abstractions but they can often be made into efficient workers... from a eugenic point of view, they constitute a grave problem because of their unusually prolific breeding.

Although this quote is extreme and old (it dates back to 1916), many still question the roots of intelligence tests used today – especially as entrance criteria for gifted programs and other similar programs. It is a well-known fact that such programs exhibit an under-representation of minorities, with almost no ML representation. Because MLs come from non-dominant cultural and linguistic groups, they are most vulnerable to test misuse based on race or language. Figure 2.1 is a cartoon, dated 1922, showing the powerful assessor and the child as an object of the assessment. This cartoon is a nice visual for some of the powerful dynamics of assessment in schools and especially the mission of schools to sort children into different levels of the social and economic system. As depicted in the cartoon, the assessment is based on intelligence testing and psychological theories (see psychology books shown directly below the magnifying glass). This is new and an improvement on the 'old method' where students were sorted based on race and class. Since this cartoon dates back to 1922, the new and the old method are old to us now. However less explicit now, schools still serve as the main sorters of economic and social classes. This underlying mission of schools has changed in the current century, but assessment methods have not.

Figure 2.1 School as sorters. (Source: Paul Davis Chapman from Stefanakis, E. [1999] *Whose Judgment Counts? Assessing Bilingual Children, K-3*. Portsmouth, NH: Heinemann)

Measurement misuse in order to advance one racial group over another can be traced back even further to the use of craniometry in the 19th century. This now-laughable practice measured cranial features in order to classify intelligence and race superiority as well as temperament and morality. Those who practiced craniometry believed that measurements of skull size and shape could determine traits such as intelligence and capacity for moral behavior. The British used such measurements to justify racist policies against Africans, Indians and the Irish. The Nazis and Belgians used similar craniometry methods to claim their superiority. In *The Mismeasure of Man*, Stephen J. Gould (1981) implies that craniometry in the 19th century gave way to intelligence testing in the 20th century.

In 1969, researchers Chandler and Plakos designed a research study to investigate how intelligence (IQ) tests were being used with Spanish-dominant Mexican American children. They selected 47 Spanish-dominant students to be a part of the study, all of whom were enrolled in educable mentally retarded (EMR) classes after being assessed on the English-only IQ test. Chandler and Plakos retested all 47 students with the Spanish language version. In most cases, the Spanish-dominant children were found not to be EMR; the decision to classify them as EMR was therefore based on an invalid use of the English IQ test scores. The study concluded that many children of Mexican descent were inappropriately placed in EMR classes.

During the 1960s and 1970s, test fairness became a concern for many. Testing standards used since this time in the United States showed an increase in addressing test fairness. In particular, changes to the testing standards (*Standards for Educational and Psychological Testing*) illustrated the growing concern by the measurement community over testing fairness for non-English-speaking children. The 1966 version of the Standards focused on what is required for test manuals. The 1974 version, however, for the first time included standards for the use of tests. A decade later, the 1985 Standards included a section on standards for 'particular' applications, with a section specifically designated for the testing of linguistic minorities. The 1999 version dedicated one-third of the book to fairness in testing, with a focus on testing individuals of diverse linguistic backgrounds, and the most recent version (2014) includes a more articulated chapter on fairness with more examples than before of MLs (American Educational Research Association [AERA], American Psychological Association [APA], National Council on Measurement in Education [NCME], 1966, 1974, 1985, 1999, 2014). Despite several decades of warning from the measurement community, test scores from tests given in English to students who are not yet proficient in English are still being used today for important decisions.

The issue of fairness in the assessment of MLs gained more nationwide attention as legislation such as NCLB mandated the inclusion of all children in large-scale assessments as a way to provide equal learning opportunity. August and Hakuta (1998) warned of the great need to develop guidelines for determining when MLs are ready to take the same assessments as their English-proficient peers, and when versions of an assessment other than the standard English version should be administered. They also emphasized the need to develop psychometrically sound and practical assessments, and assessment procedures that incorporate MLs into district- and state-assessment systems.

As reviewed in Chapter 1, standards from the measurement community have warned researchers and practitioners about the potential validity threats for MLs taking tests in English. For non-English speakers and those who speak some dialects of English, every test given in English becomes, in part, a language or literacy test (AERA, APA, NCME, 1985: 73). The 1999 version of the same standards warns that test norms based on native speakers of English either should not be used with individuals whose first language is not English, or such individuals' test results should be interpreted as reflecting, in part, their current level of English proficiency rather than ability, potential, aptitude or personality characteristics or symptomatology (AERA, APA, NCME, 1999: 91). Also in 1999, the National Research Council (NRC, 1999), which formed the Committee on Appropriate Test Use, echoes the same message: The test score for MLs is likely to be affected by construct irrelevant variance (CIV; a full discussion of CIV is forthcoming in Chapter 3) and, therefore, is likely to underestimate his or her knowledge of the subject being tested.

Many educators are aware of the history of test misuse for MLs and have tried to move away from the deficit perspectives of non-English-speaking children in schools, but the practices dominating schools and policies today perpetuate these old ideas. Test misuse and assessment play a role in whether students succeed or fail in school. Since the 1960s, several frameworks for interpreting success and failure in schools have been explored to counter the dominant genetic argument so popular in the 1800s and 1900s. To help understand a broader context of school success/failure, frameworks from Guadalupe Valdés and John Ogbu are explored below to help educators interpret and explain the factors and different perspectives on the success/failure of MLs in schools.

Theories that Explain Success and Failure

Throughout history, myriad and complex theories have attempted to explain why some children succeed in school and others do not. The question is generally approached through two broad conceptual frameworks – the deficit argument and the difference argument. The *deficit argument* holds that the 'impoverished' child is failing in school because he or she is not ready for school. The communities, homes and cultures from which the child comes are lacking, and this leads to a disadvantage at school. The *difference argument* targets the school as being unready, rather than the child, and claims that the deficit argument is based on ethnocentric research plus White middle-class norms and values.

Guadalupe Valdés (1996) suggested that explanations of school failure can be categorized in terms of the genetic argument, the cultural argument and the class analysis argument. The genetic argument (discussed earlier in this chapter) has been out of favor for a number of years; it views some groups as genetically more able than others, and because of these inherent differences, children of different racial and ethnic groups perform differently in schools.

The cultural argument proposes that children who perform poorly in schools are either culturally deprived (devalues the child's culture) or culturally different (values the child's culture) and therefore mismatched with schools and school personnel. In general, cultural deprivation takes the position that non-mainstream parents do not have the 'right' attitude toward the value of education, do not prepare their children well for school or are not sufficiently involved in their children's education. Valdés (1996) states that there is a fine line between the culturally deficit and culturally different explanations. The cultural difference argument supports the idea that the experiences of all children are rich, even if they are not the values respected by the educational institution.

The class analysis argument ascribes school failure to the role of education in maintaining class differences (that is, maintaining the power of some over others). For this argument, it is no accident that children of the middle classes are primarily sorted into the 'right' streams or tracks in school and given access to particular kinds of knowledge. The role of the schools, using testing as a sorting tool, is to legitimize inequality under the pretense of serving all students and encouraging them to reach their full potential. The system succeeds because, although the cards are clearly stacked against some students, these students come to believe that they are in fact given an opportunity to succeed. They leave school firmly convinced they could have done better – perhaps achieved as much as their middle-class peers – if only they had tried harder or worked more. They are then ready to accept low-paying, working-class jobs, and the working class is thus reproduced (Valdés, 1996).

In a classic study that documented the class analysis argument, Jean Anyon (1980) studied a sample of schools from the working class, the middle class and the affluent professional class. In the working-class schools, schoolwork consisted of following the steps of a procedure. The procedure was usually mechanical, involving rote behavior and very little choice or decision-making. In the middle-class schools, work consisted of getting the right answer. If one accumulated enough right answers, one received a good grade. Directions often called for some figuring, some choice and some decision-making. In the affluent professional schools, work was a creative activity, carried out independently. The students were continually asked to express and apply ideas and concepts (Anyon, 1980). This differentiated schooling, as highlighted in Anyon's research, inevitably leads to a replication of the social class structure and helps to explain the class analysis argument for school success or failure.

Another theoretical framework through which to view student success and failure is John Ogbu's (1978, 1998) cultural-ecological theory. John Ogbu was an educational anthropologist who sought to explain current practices in school through history. Ogbu is well known for his explanation of how minority students are classified based not upon numbers but upon their different histories. Differences in student performances, explained through a two-part theory, are the result of the treatment of minority groups within both school and society at large, as well as minorities' perceptions of that treatment and their responses in school.

The first part of Ogbu's theory, which concerns what he terms 'the system', explains the way minorities are treated or mistreated in education in terms of educational policies, pedagogy, returns for their investments or school credentials. The second part of the theory concerns 'community forces' – the way minorities respond to schooling as a consequence of their treatment. These minority responses are also affected by how and why a group became a minority.

Autonomous minorities are people who belong to groups that are small in number. They may be different from the dominant group in race, ethnicity, religion or language. Examples of autonomous minority groups in the United States are Amish, Jews and Mormons. Although these groups may suffer discrimination, they are not totally dominated and oppressed; thus, their school achievement is no different from the dominant group (Ogbu, 1978, 1998). Voluntary (immigrant) minorities are those who have more or less willingly moved to the United States because they expect better opportunities (better jobs, more political or religious freedoms) than they had in their homelands or places of origin. Involuntary (non-immigrant) minorities have been conquered, colonized or enslaved. Unlike immigrant minorities, non-immigrants have been permanently incorporated into US society against their will. Involuntary minorities in the United States are original owners or residents of the land who were conquered – American Indians, Alaskan Natives and early Mexican Americans in the southwest. This also includes Native Hawaiians and Puerto Ricans who were colonized, and Black Americans who were brought to the United States as slaves.

Although Ogbu's theories date back to the 20th century, they are relevant today. For example, the guiding principles of the City University of New York (CUNY) Initiative on Immigration and Education (IIE) (Kleyn *et al.*, 2023) reflect Ogbu's 20th-century ideas about the importance of articulating the different histories and how that impacts educational experiences/outcomes. One of the guiding principles from this NYC-based organization is 'We are not all Immigrants' and it posits that the fabric of the United States includes not only immigrants but also the Native

Americans whose land was stolen in the creation of the United States, as well as the descendants of enslaved people who were brought to this land against their will. Saying statements like 'we are a nation of immigrants' or 'the US was built by immigrants' further invisibilizes the Native People and the lived realities of slavery and the Black experience in the United States (Kleyn *et al.*, 2023). This present-day example of a guiding principle aligns with Ogbu's (1978, 1998) cultural ecological theory. Decolonial theory has become a popular way to explain school success and failure as well as other societal inequities. Decolonial theory calls to take away colonization where colonization is thought of as one group taking control of lands, resources, languages and cultures over others.

María Cioè-Peña (2022) has a decolonizing way of explaining why some kids succeed and others don't. A famous quote from NYC poet Audre Lorde is 'the master's tools will never dismantle the master's house' (1984); Dr Cioè-Peña used this quote but replaces the word house with school to describe what she sees as the reason some students succeed and others don't. Cioè-Peña (2022) writes that the racialization (the processes by which a group of people is defined by race) and the pathologization (the act of unfairly or wrongly considering someone as a problem in schools) that happen in schools through language continue to systemically promote colonial ideals and power structures. These take the form of linguistically rooted assessments and evaluations that are used to determine program placement and significantly impact student outcomes and equity. One way to interpret this is that monolingual tests are the tools of those in power (white, middle-class, English speakers) and are used to keep themselves in power; this type of thinking promotes a settler or colonial mentality. Until we decolonize applied linguistics and eliminate linguistically bound, standard-driven evaluations, especially for disability and ML categories, we will continue to replicate the racist and ableist ideologies in policy and practice (Cioè-Peña, 2022). This perspective aligns with the class analyst argument described above.

Schools as sorters appears as a theme across the centuries and assessment has played a major role in the sorting. Rick Stiggins (2017) refers to the mission of schools to sort students into social and economic levels as the 'old mission', and the mission of schools since the turn of the 21st century where schools provide all students with the lifelong learner proficiencies that will allow them to keep up with the rapid pace of change as the 'new mission' of schools. The 'old mission' was accomplished by setting a fixed amount of time to learn (one year per grade level) and allowing the amount learned during that time to vary across students. Some students complete their first-grade year having learned a great deal, while others learn less. Those who learn well in first grade carry that advantage into second grade and generally continue to grow at the same pace. Those who didn't learn as much in first grade tend to lag behind in second grade. This range of achievement widens year after year as students ascend through the grade levels. The end result is a dependable 'rank in class' at the end of high school. Students who see the evidence of their struggles in the form of their assessment results become frustrated at their chronic failure and give in to hopelessness; about a quarter of them, on average, drop out.

The traditional role of assessment was to provide the evidence of student achievement that underpins the 'old mission'. Stiggins (2017) further explains that there is an underlying motivational belief at work in the 'old mission'. Society and its educators have believed that by limiting opportunities for ultimate success, they can create a competitive environment that will drive students to strive for more learning. This belief holds that those who have achieved a high level will strive to remain on top and those ranked lower than they want to will work harder to improve their grades and accept their position in the pecking order. This belief also extends to those who suffer from chronic failure and achieve very low rankings, that they must just not care or don't want to work hard. And when they drop out, the educational resources available can be redirected to those who are willing and able to learn.

Standardized achievement tests that emerged last century and remain in place today were, and are, designed to fit into this 'old mission' institutional sorting routine (Stiggins, 2017: 19–20). Since 2000, we have expanded the social and economic mission of schools and because of this we need to abandon some of our old assessment practices that continue to function, such as schools as sorters.

Clearly, the 'achievement gap' problem is a complicated one, connected to history, society and power. The next section focuses on one very influential US policy called NCLB that changed the landscape of assessment for MLs indefinitely.

Accountability With(out) Validity? NCLB

Educators and families are due more accountability and more validity for MLs. The following section will take the reader through arguments of accountability and validity. Do we have to sacrifice one for the other?

What is NCLB?

The No Child Left Behind Act started in 2002 and ended in 2015; however, its impact will remain for many years to come. Educational reform efforts in the United States in the early 21st century can be largely defined by two characteristics: (1) schools labeled as excellent are those that have good test scores in math and reading, and (2) the use of standards and test-based accountability is the way to achieve such excellence. The intent of NCLB was to provide every child in the United States with a good education so that 'no child is left behind'. However, the law's definition of a good education – a high score on standardized tests in English and mathematics – is one with which most educators would disagree. To support this definition, NCLB required that all children in third through eighth grades, even MLs, be given state assessments each year in reading and mathematics.

If a child failed the test, he or she was judged to have not received a good education. If a school or district didn't make adequate yearly progress (AYP), it was labeled 'in need of improvement' and subject to some kind of major change, such as allowing students to move to another school, moving the principal and half the staff out of the school, closing the school and/or other major consequences. Students who performed poorly on math and reading were considered at risk of school failure, regardless of how they performed in other subjects. The logic of NCLB made sense, unfortunately the test and punish methods did not.

The passage of NCLB completely changed the accountability landscape for MLs. The era before NCLB (pre-2002) can be classified in general as *less accountability/more validity* because teachers had more flexibility to choose valid measures of what exactly MLs knew. Advocates for MLs supported state-level policies that delayed the requirement that MLs take content-area standardized tests in English until they obtained sufficient levels of language proficiency; the definition of 'sufficient language proficiency' varied from state to state. These state-level policies were put in place largely in response to years of research showing that as language proficiency increases, so does academic achievement. One way to interpret this is: we have the best chance to show what content a ML student knows if we wait to assess until their English proficiency is higher. Schools were seldom asked to be accountable for MLs before MLs could comprehend the language of the tests. In fact, it was common for MLs to have at least three years (or more) of exemption before they were required to take the standardized tests in English for any purpose (accountability or otherwise). This backfired, though, because delayed accountability for MLs often led to inferior programs and instruction during these formative language-learning years. Advocates for MLs were unhappy with the lack of accountability, arguing that schools and policies continued to ignore the needs of MLs.

The pendulum swung fast and far after NCLB was passed. Accountability for MLs went from nearly non-existent to attaching ultra-high stakes to the performance of MLs on standardized tests in English. Despite the language of NCLB that called for 'valid and reliable' assessments, the law also required that MLs be tested in English before they knew English – a highly contradictory stance.

The era after NCLB (post-2002) can therefore be described, in general, as a *more accountability/less validity* era during which the struggle to find assessment methods to validly measure what MLs knew continued, after the accountability was determined. The following examples demonstrate this struggle. In August 2006, under the Bush administration, the federal government created a new (English language learners/limited English proficient [ELL/LEP]) partnership in Washington, DC, to discuss assessment requirements for MLs. One of the main goals of this meeting was to provide states with the technical assistance they needed to develop valid and reliable assessments for MLs. Three years later, a public forum was commissioned by Barack Obama's administration and was held by the US Department of Education on December 2, 2009, in Denver, Colorado. Three prominent researchers were invited (Jamal Abedi, Charlene Rivera and Robert Linquanti), who called for a number of dramatic changes in the way MLs were tested. In the same year (2009), a working group advisory board for MLs was formed through the Center for Applied Linguistics (CAL) to prepare a set of recommendations for the federal reauthorization of the Elementary and Secondary Education Act (ESEA). The board's recommendations focused on improving education outcomes for MLs. Meetings focusing on Race to the Top (RTTT) competitive grants and a new set of tests for the Common Core Learning Standards (CCLS) followed in January 2010.

The sequence of events described above led to heated debates in the field of education, as educators were split about whether to support, through advocacy, much-needed accountability at what many say was at the expense of validity. Most educators would rather choose neither (less accountability/more validity nor more accountability/less validity) because they strive for a better balance between accountability and validity. Some say that the former ignored the needs of MLs and the latter delivered more harm than benefits to them. One negative result of NCLB was the creation of a two-tiered educational system, in which those who can't pass the test revert to a repetitive, test-preparation curriculum, while those who pass the test receive a high-level, higher-order thinking curriculum aligned with college preparation and professional careers. One side of the debate argues that NCLB actually caused the same inequities that most people believe the law was designed to eradicate, all with a huge dollar sign attached to it.

Scholars in the field documented the harmful effects of NCLB as (1) dismantling bilingual education programs as a result of low English language arts (ELA) and English language proficiency (ELP) test scores (e.g. see Menken & Solorza, 2014); (2) narrowing the curriculum to focus on content areas (English and math) that count for AYP – the narrowing due to NCLB is in addition to an already narrowed curriculum related to limited choices in upper-level courses (Kanno & Kangas, 2014); (3) declining graduation rates (as school ratings rose, graduation rates went down); (4) increasing the number of MLs classified as having special education needs; (5) creating more situations where bilingualism is a 'problem' and schools and teachers are discouraged from working with students who may have difficulty passing the test; and (6) undermining the goals of dual language bilingual education (DLBE) programs (Henderson & Palmer, 2020). They say that high-stakes accountability, though, seems to magnify the challenges of implementing DLBE by drawing resources away from the kinds of material and time investments necessary for success, to distract and confuse teachers as they attempt to make sense of the various demands (Henderson & Palmer, 2020: 114). Wayne Wright (2002) interviewed teachers to explore the effects of high-stakes testing from their perspective and reported effects such as narrowing of curriculum, linguistic bias, sociocultural and class bias plus feelings of inadequacy in many teachers and students.

The idea of a student feeling inadequate is shown in Figure 2.2 with a student drawing, reflecting how he feels about being tested in English. Often, student effects are observed in schools, but rarely are students asked how they feel about standardized testing. The illustration in Figure 2.2 was created by an ML student in Arizona when his teacher asked him to draw a picture to show how he feels about taking the state's high-stakes test.[4] As seen in the picture, his response was 'I felt like not knowing nothing'. The drawing also depicts the student slumped at his desk. Clearly, in addition to a low score, taking the test led him to feelings of inadequacy. A student's emotional response to assessment results will determine what that student decides to do about those results: keep working or give up. These emotional dynamics of assessment should be considered when determining whether or not an assessment is high quality. When a student tries to learn and fails, the experience can trigger uncertainty about one's ability. The resulting loss of 'smart status' and fear of future failure can freeze cognition; if this becomes chronic, it can give rise to hopelessness and pessimism in the classroom (Stiggins, 2017).

Figure 2.2 Drawing by ML elementary student in response to a high-stakes test: 'I felt like not knowing nothing'

How Adequate Yearly Progress was Used under NCLB?

A key covenant of the No Child Left Behind Act (2002–2015) was to ensure AYP for all students. Schools and districts had to demonstrate AYP to their state departments of education and, in turn, state departments had to demonstrate to the Federal Department of Education – that all students were showing adequate progress. Schools could not submit test scores as an average achievement score of the whole school because this might 'hide' the low performance for a specific group of children, like MLs. Such an increase in state- and federal-level accountability was unprecedented and many believed that the emphasis on accountability for MLs was much needed in US schools. At the time of NCLB, the federal government outlined the process that individual states must follow to develop systems that measure the progress of all students, but the way to best measure AYP for MLs was left unspecified (as is often the case with federal direction for MLs). The general process for 'all students' included setting challenging academic standards, developing annual state-level assessments that address state learning standards, setting an initial starting point, specifying successive targets for AYP and providing increased support to schools that consistently fail to meet AYP.

When NCLB was first passed in 2002, it required each state to set its own AYP targets the same for all students, regardless of the educational challenges that some students face. Each state in the United States has its own system of accountability, which is separate and sometimes strikingly different from the federal school accountability system. It was possible for a school to be 'passing' according to the state system but 'failing' under the federal system. The MLs students at a school form a subgroup of students who are examined; if the school does not show AYP for this subgroup, the entire school 'fails' (in theory leaving no child behind, even MLs). However, shortly after the Bush administration passed the NCLB law, it quickly became apparent that AYP for MLs contained fundamental flaws. Schools with large numbers of MLs were behind because the subgroup of MLs always had lower proficiency in English (hence their ELL/LEP label) and tended to score low on tests in English partly due to their status as MLs (not knowing enough English to participate meaningfully). Because of this Catch-22 situation (Wright, 2002), the Bush administration announced more flexibility in the law for the ML subgroup, allowing former MLs to be included in the ML subgroup for up to two years. Also, newly arrived MLs were allowed a 12-month exemption from ELA assessments. However, anyone familiar with second language acquisition (SLA) knows that newly arrived MLs cannot reach the required level of proficiency needed to garner valid results in a single year – another fundamental flaw that undermines the accountability of schools for MLs.

The law overlooked MLs in many ways; therefore, amendments were introduced to try to 'fix' things. Another amendment soon expanded the subgroup of MLs to include fluent English proficient (FEP) students. In the years immediately following passage and amendments, the US Government Accountability Office (GAO) conducted a study that focused on the 2003–2004 school year. The GAO asked several questions: To what extent were MLs meeting academic progress goals? What were states doing to ensure the validity of their ELP tests? How was the Department of Education supporting state-level efforts to meet the 'valid and reliable' requirement? In the study, which was published in 2006, the GAO found that 25 states did not provide adequate evidence to ensure the validity or reliability of academic test results for MLs. Moreover, a 2005 Department of Education-funded technical review of the available documentation for 17 ELP tests found insufficient documentation of the validity of the assessment results (GAO, 2006).

One example of the use of AYP is a set of statistics published on the New York State Education Department website: 'The Good News: Approximately 64% of schools make AYP for MLs in ELA and 98% in math. The Bad News: The failure rate for MLs in ELA is by far the highest of any group – almost twice the rate of Students with Disabilities (SWD)'. This result is not surprising for teachers who understand that it takes four to nine years to learn academic language, otherwise known as language used for academic purposes, which is a partial prerequisite for scoring high on the ELA exam. For policymakers unfamiliar with the length of time it takes to learn a language, however, it might sound alarming. Keep in mind that the same students who cannot pass the ELA test may be progressing very well in their second

Table 2.1 Pros and cons of AYP for MLs

Pros	Cons
Increase accountability for MLs.	Assumptions underlying AYP are too simple (don't account for the complexity of second language acquisition [SLA]).
Focusing on progress is a positive thing.	MLs likely can't read the test very well that is used to measure AYP; therefore, test scores don't really show what they know.
	MLs were an afterthought to the AYP concept (as shown by two amendments published shortly after the law passed).

language development according to more authentic measures of language. Because AYP was so problematic, it is no longer a federal requirement. With the passage of the ESSA (Public Law 114-95) in 2015, AYP is no longer a federal requirement; however, individual states may choose to continue to require AYP. Table 2.1 outlines the pros and cons of applying AYP to MLs.

Doubts about NCLB

The logic of NCLB targeted two 'gaps' in achievement. One gap is the differences in test scores and the quality of schooling among subgroups within the United States (e.g. White vs. Black or MLs vs. native English speakers). What has become increasingly clear across many decades is that the introduction of new standards, tests and policies has not diminished the gap between MLs and non-MLs. The other gap is the difference in test scores between the United States and other countries. Comparing the United States to China, Yong Zhao (2009) authored a book titled *Catching Up or Leading the Way* in which he questions whether test-driven accountability will empower the United States to 'lead the way' in quality schooling and innovation or whether it will put the United States in a position where it must try to 'catch up' with other nations that have tried test-based accountability for years and have begun to abandon it. As an example, Zhao demonstrated how China began to abandon its use of test-based accountability and test-based curriculum because of negative consequences such as a lack of innovation and the narrowing of skill sets and curriculum. He argued that since NCLB, US schools are not emphasizing the skills students truly need – such as the new globalization and technology goals – and that such neglect undermines traditional US thought and strength. He also noted that countries such as China were changing their education systems to emulate the pre-NCLB US educational system. Many researchers, including David Berliner and Stephen Krashen, point to the long history of research on achievement gaps and how gaps in test scores primarily reveal one thing: the most influential factor in achievement – poverty. When compared to other countries with similar degrees of poverty, the United States actually fares quite well on a global level. Berliner (2009), a well-respected researcher, argued that six out-of-school factors (OSFs) cannot be ignored in any discussion or policy aimed at closing the achievement gap. The six OSFs include (1) low birthweight and non-genetic prenatal influences on children; (2) inadequate medical, dental and vision care, often a result of inadequate or no medical insurance; (3) food insecurity; (4) environmental pollutants; (5) family relations and family stress; and (6) neighborhood characteristics (Berliner, 2009: 1). Berliner argued that these six OSFs are related to a host of poverty-induced physical, sociological and psychological problems that children often bring to school, ranging from neurological damage and attention disorders to excessive absenteeism and oppositional behavior. Schools in high poverty neighborhoods face significantly greater challenges than those serving wealthier families, and efforts to improve educational outcomes in these schools – such as driving change through test-based accountability – are unlikely to succeed unless they are accompanied by policies that address OSFs. According to Berliner (2009), if the writers of NCLB had taken into account the complexities of poverty and passed co-requisite policies to target them and how they affect schooling, a reduction in achievement gaps might have become a reality. But this did not happen.

Diane Ravitch (2010), an educational historian, explained that during the NCLB years, the Standards Movement was 'hijacked' by the Testing Movement. She noted that the law bypassed curriculum and standards altogether; it demanded that schools generate higher test scores in basic skills, but it required no curriculum at all nor did it raise standards. Moreover, NCLB ignored important topics such as history, civics, literature, science, the arts and geography. Ravitch realized that the new reforms had nothing to do with the substance of learning, and that accountability makes little sense if it undermines the larger goals of education. This realization led many unhappy parents to remove their children from the tests altogether.

Led by New York State, there was a national 'opt-out' movement led by parents to withdraw their children from high-stakes testing programs because they saw no educational value in these tests. What motivated these parents was fear that the emphasis on high-stakes testing was emotionally damaging their children (Stiggins, 2017). Parents in the United States rallied across the country in a movement called the National Opt-Out Movement. Parents opted out of state-mandated testing by keeping their children at home or requesting a separate location in school so that children could 'refuse' to take the test. Pennsylvania experienced a five-fold increase in parents 'opting out' between 2012 and 2015. Some school districts in New York experienced over 50% of students opting out of the state-mandated math test. News like this was broadcast across social media and was popular on public radio stations (see, for example, 'Why some Parents are Sitting Kids out of Tests', March 5, 2015).[5]

Support for NCLB

Despite all the negatives discussed thus far, NCLB delivered one large and significant positive effect for MLs: a new focus on accountability. If MLs don't perform well, it's everyone's problem. Because of NCLB, principals, superintendents and state departments of education were talking about the quality of education for MLs, as well as possible solutions. Learning how to appropriately educate MLs was seen as the responsibility of the whole school, including English as a new language (ENL) and non-ENL teachers. In New York, for example, as of 2014 those who are a candidate to become teachers, in all certification areas, have to pass a test called Educating All Students (EAS) to receive state certification. The EAS test has nine indicators on it that directly target an understanding of how MLs learn best. Before NCLB, these conversations rarely happened in the mainstream education environment, and mainstream teachers could become certified without knowing anything about the needs of MLs. NCLB also ushered in higher-quality, large-scale assessments for MLs. According to expert Jamal Abedi (2008), the guidelines set forth by NCLB in 2002 also improved the overall quality of large-scale ELP tests compared to those used before NCLB.

A History of Assessment Events

Table 2.2 presents a range of historic events that impacted assessment in the United States. Table 2.3 shows another perspective on how NCLB, a particularly

Table 2.2 Important historical events affecting assessment and accountability in the United States

Year	Event	Importance
1954	Brown v. Board of Education	The outcome of this landmark case was that 'no state shall deny any person within its jurisdiction the equal protection of the laws'. This ruling opened the door to future litigation limiting discriminatory practices against students based on language, race, ethnicity, disability, culture, etc.
1964	Elementary and Secondary Education Act (ESEA) enacted	Government funds are granted to meet the needs of 'educationally deprived children'.
1968	Title VII Bilingual Education Act, an amendment to the ESEA	For the first time, federal funding provides support to programs specifically designed for MLs, including bilingual education.
1970	Diana v. State Board of Education	Diana, a Spanish-speaking student, was diagnosed with mental retardation (MR) due to her low score on an IQ test given to her in English. When given the test again from a bilingual psychologist, Diana no longer qualified for special education. This resulted in a consent decree that mandated that IQ tests could not be the sole criteria or primary basis for diagnosis.
1972	Guadalupe Organization v. Tempe Elementary School District	The plaintiffs request was to require bilingual/bicultural services to non-English-speaking Mexican American and Yaqui Indian students. Similar to Diana, this consent decree specified that IQ tests could not be the sole criteria or primary basis for diagnosis.
1974	Lau v. Nichols	Supreme court case; establishes that language programs are necessary to provide equal educational opportunities.
1981	Castañeda v. Pickard	An appeals court establishes a three-part test to determine whether schools are taking appropriate action under the 1974 Equal Educational Opportunity Act: (1) programs must be based on sound theory, (2) programs must be supported by adequate funding and (3) programs must show effectiveness after a certain amount of time.
1984	A Nation at Risk	Fear-driven report that blames the poor education system for the country's ills. This report led the United States down the path toward greater federal control.
1991	First National Standards	In 1991, the mathematics education community spearheaded the first standards of its kind. National Standards were written by the National Council of Teaching Mathematics (NCTM).
1994	George W. Bush becomes governor of Texas	The 'Texas Miracle' begins. Bush holds office as governor from 1994 to 1999. The Texas Miracle impresses Congress and convinces legislators that such a model of accountability can work. Researchers McNeil and Valenzuela (2001) report that the Texas Miracle harmed the education of poor and minority students.
1997	First national ELP standards	ESL standards for pre-K–12 students is the first set of national ELP standards.
1997	Individuals with Disabilities Education Act (IDEA) Revisions of 1997	This particular version of the law, among other things, mandated that parent consent procedures must be in the native language, and evaluation materials be free from bias of race and culture and must be provided in the child's native language.
1998	Proposition 227 passes in California	This proposition severely limits the use of home languages in California public schools. The US 'English Only' movement is official.
1999	National Research Council forms Committee on Appropriate Test Use	Committee statement: The test score for ML students is likely to be affected by construct irrelevant variance (CIV) and therefore is likely to underestimate his or her knowledge of the subject being tested.

Table 2.2 (Continued)

Year	Event	Importance
2000	George W. Bush becomes President of the United States	The Texas Miracle concept is adopted as a draft of No Child Left Behind (NCLB).
2000	Proposition 203 passes in Arizona	Like California, Arizona voters severely restrict the use of home languages in public schools. The 'English Only' movement grows stronger.
2001	NCLB becomes law	NCLB is signed into law. The Elementary and Secondary Education Act (ESEA) is reauthorized as NCLB.
2002	Question 2 passes in Massachusetts	Like California and Arizona, voters in Massachusetts restrict the use of home languages in public schools.
2002	Title III of NCLB	This requires states to (1) develop and implement ELP standards; (2) implement a single, reliable and valid ELP assessment aligned with ELP standards that annually measures listening, speaking, reading, writing and comprehension; and (3) establish annual measurable achievement objectives (AMAOs) and report progress annually. See Table 2.2 for a more detailed examination of the changes that NCLB brought to assessment of MLs.
2002	NCLB Enhanced Assessment Grant	Provides state support to develop an ELP instrument. Four different consortia of states develop ELP tests in an attempt to address the new requirements of NCLB. All new tests focus on the concept of academic language or using language for academic purposes.
2002	World Class Instructional Design and Assessment (WIDA) is born	WIDA Enhanced Assessment Grant is awarded to Wisconsin Department of Public Instruction, WIDA's first home. Eventually, more than 45 states join the WIDA consortium.
2002	Title VII eliminated	The Title VII (Bilingual Education Act) created in 1968 is eliminated and replaced by Title III (Language Instruction for Limited English Proficient and Immigrant Students).
2004	Rod Paige announces changes to NCLB	Secretary of Education Rod Paige announces two significant changes to NCLB pertaining to MLs: (1) LEP students may be exempt from English language arts exams for one year; and (2) for AYP purposes, fluent English proficient (FEP) students can stay in the LEP subgroup for two years. The fact that this was announced two years later, demonstrates that MLs were not a priority (more of an afterthought) when NCLB was written.
2004	Pennsylvania challenges ML test validity in state court	*Reading School District v. PA Department of Education:* Challenge denied. It was determined by state court that it was not practical for the Department of Education to administer tests in the child's primary language.
2005	State standards required	NCLB requires that all states develop standards in science by 2005 (English and math in 2002).
2007	National experts gather	Federal government calls a meeting of national experts (five years after NCLB passes into law) to define what is valid and reliable assessment for MLs. The question remains unanswered. Another example of MLs as an afterthought.
2008	California challenges ML test validity in state court	*Coachella Valley v. California:* Nine school districts asked the state to provide tests in Spanish or simplified English. The request was denied and upheld by the state.
2009	National experts gather (again)	Federal government calls a meeting of national experts (seven years after NCLB passes into law) to define what is a valid and reliable assessment for MLs. The question remains unanswered.

(Continued)

Table 2.2 (Continued)

Year	Event	Importance
2009	Obama administration's American Recovery and Reinvestment Act (ARRA) of 2009	Economic stimulus package signed into law by Barack Obama – $831 billion from 2009 to 2019. The US Department of Education calls upon schools to use assessment data to respond to students' academic strengths and needs.
2010	Common Core State Standards (CCSS) released in ELA and math	Design of standards is coordinated by the National Governors Association (NGA) and the Council of Chief State School Officers (CCSSO). Forty-eight states join in an unprecedented level of national participation in a single set of standards (in ELA and math).
March 2010	US Department of Education announces grant to develop CCSS assessments	Grant reflects concerns about CCSS, including the incorporation of fair and reasonable accommodations for MLs and students with disabilities (SWD). Nearly 10 years after the NCLB law required 'valid and reliable' assessments for MLs, the Department of Education still cannot define what that means.
2010	Two assessment consortiums launched (Smarter Balance and Partnership for Assessment of Readiness for College and Careers [PARCC])	Smarter Balance (Assessment Consortium, awarded $175 million) and PARCC (awarded $185 million) are launched with funding from the US Department of Education to create assessments aligned with the CCSS and to be fully operational by the 2014/2015 school year. PARCC has 26 states as members and Smarter Balance has 31 states as members. ML advocates complained that there are no tests in Spanish or other languages. Initially, 46 states participated in consortiums. By 2017, participation had dropped to 20 states. In 2022, only two states participated. Since 2010, hundreds of millions of dollars have been spent on developing these standardized consortia (no longer used) tests.
2011	ESEA Flexibility program introduced	More flexibility for NCLB: President Barack Obama invited each state education agency to request flexibility on behalf of itself, its local educational agencies and schools. Nearly all states had plans approved.
2014/2015	Forty-two states commit to use common test	Consortia member states commit to and implement the common assessments as their NCLB assessments. Race to the Top (RTTT) funds pay for the design, development and piloting of the assessment system, plus other costs.
2015	NCLB replaced by ESSA	The NCLB Act was replaced by the ESSA. Signed by Obama, the intent of the law was to reduce federal involvement in public schools and send much of that authority back to states and local districts. This reauthorized the ESEA of 1965.
2016	Proposition 58 passes in California	Proposition 227, restricting bilingual education in California, is repealed. In addition, during this decade, dual language bilingual education (DLBE) in the United States is experiencing a 'dual language revolution'. It is estimated that 2000–3000 new DLBE programs were opened between 2005 and 2020 (Henderson & Palmer, 2020).
2016	ELPA21 (English Language Proficiency for the 21st Century) is born	Offering ELP standards and tests (like WIDA), ELPA21 is offered and housed at the National Center on Research on Evaluation, Standards and Student Testing (CRESST) at the University of California in Los Angeles (UCLA). Now states can choose WIDA, ELPA21 or create their own ELP standards/assessments for MLs. Federal criteria must be met.
2017	Consortia membership declines	Consortia membership (PARC and Smarter Balance) drops from 46 to 20 as states favor state-developed standards and tests.
2020	Most states are served by WIDA	Thirty-five states joined WIDA, seven states joined ELPA21 and the rest created their own ELP standards for MLs that correspond to college and career readiness standards and assessments to measure these standards.
2021	CCSS repealed or revised in 24 states	Over half of the original states who adopted Common Core State Standards no longer use the original standards. These standards were mostly rejected by conservatives who viewed the CCSS as 'national standards' and a violation of state rights.

Table 2.3 Results of NCLB and ESSA: Major changes that affect MLs

Before NCLB	After NCLB	After ESSA	Implications of change (positive and negative)
MLs have a three-year waiver.	MLs must take content-area tests; no exemptions.	Annual testing of ELA and math in Grades 3–8 and high school.	(+) Increased accountability for MLs. Schools are worried about the appearance of low test scores and are thus motivated to improve schooling for MLs.
	MLs must take ELP tests after one year.	States still required to track the progress of separate subgroups of students including MLs.	(−) Decrease in validity. MLs are taking tests when they are (by definition) not proficient in English. There is no valid use for these scores. The negative effects of using these scores outweigh the benefits.
ELP standards are not required.	States are required to develop and implement ELP standards.	The requirements for ELP standards and assessments and the expectation for MLs to make progress in learning and ultimately attaining English proficiency remain the same.	(+) Consistency: When students move from district to district, they receive a similar curriculum.
		Like NCLB, there will be some allowances for testing in home languages.	(−) Districts lose autonomy. Standards may not be written well, but districts are stuck with them.
Districts may choose a language proficiency test from a list of tests.	States are required to implement a single, 'reliable and valid' ELP assessment aligned to ELP standards that annually measure listening, speaking, reading, writing and comprehension.	ESSA removed requirements that teacher evaluations be tied to student test scores.	(+) Consistency across districts. Before this change, a child may have been classified ML in one district and not ML in another because he or she took a different language proficiency test. (+) Psychometric qualities of ELP assessments improved (Abedi, 2008).
			(−) Districts can no longer choose. The one test chosen by the state department might be too easy or too hard.
		Like the flexibility plan, states are given greater flexibility for goal setting and how they will intervene in low-performing schools. States can now consider factors other than test scores in their accountability system, which opens up space for consideration of students' level of proficiency and other.	
Annual measurable achievement objectives (AMAOs) do not exist. States are not required to report annual ML progress.	States are required to establish AMAOs and report progress annually.	MLs still have to take ELA and math tests with no exceptions; however, there is some flexibility with how the scores are used for accountability. We hope 'the greater flexibility afforded to states to design their own accountability systems opened up the possibility for more realistic expectations for MLs students, more attention to their linguistic needs and the potential for greater support for bilingual education programs'.	(+) Increased accountability for MLs. Schools with low-quality ENL and bilingual programs need to show evidence of progress.
			(−) Beginner MLs grow more quickly, and more advanced MLs grow more slowly. AMAOs are not aligned with second language acquisition (SLA). Demanding that students 'move along' with language acquisition is not enough.

influential policy, changed the face of education, in particular, for MLs. In December 2015, the NCLB Act was replaced by the ESSA. President Obama signed the ESSA into law in December 2015. The new law ended heavy federal involvement in public schools and sent much of that authority back to states and local districts. The final section of this chapter provides an overview of the ESSA.

The Every Student Succeeds (ESSA) Act of 2015

We are ready to move beyond a time with an obsessive belief that standardized achievement tests are so powerful they can improve schools and teacher quality. When the ESSA was signed into law (ESSA, 2015), NCLB ended. Accountability through the results of standardized tests and all the inherent problems (for MLs) remains the main tenet of ESSA, as it was in NCLB. The ESSA is still bad news in the sense that it still obsessively focuses on accountability testing as the answer to school improvement instead of crediting the importance of things like formative assessments and how they can improve schools. Without explicitly saying it, the shift away from federally mandated assessments to inviting states to explore alternative innovative uses of assessment is because the heavy-handed federal mandates in the prior decade did not work. But the federal belief that the best way to use test results is to hold schools accountable for raising annual scores is inherent in ESSA. The positive and negative effects of this type of accountability as reviewed earlier in this chapter, for the most part, still apply to the ESSA.

The main ideas behind NCLB remained with the introduction of the ESSA in 2015. States still utilize yearly ELP standards/assessments to track student progress and hold schools accountable for ML student achievement. With ESSA, states gained more power to determine how to improve their schools with lower test scores, including improving schooling for MLs. In ESSA, states are given more flexibility for goal setting and for determining how to intervene and 'improve' low-performing schools. States are required, however, to track the progress of separate subgroups of students, including MLs, rather than lump students together in a single super subgroup. Specifically, ESSA realigned with NCLB on the topic of tracking progress for subgroups of MLs. The accountability subgroup introduced by NCLB remains in ESSA instead of collapsing the data for the ML subgroup with a super subgroup of all 'at-risk' students. The concern about aggregating (or collapsing) the subgroup of MLs into a super subgroup (Baker & Wright, 2021) is that the unique linguistic/cultural needs of MLs may be washed out.

ESSA recognizes some of the failures of NCLB, including its unrealistic achievement expectations and overreliance on high-stakes standardized tests as the sole measure of student achievement (Baker & Wright, 2021). With ESSA, all MLs are still required to take math and ELA exams regardless of their length of time in the country. However, ESSA allows states the flexibility (two options) to use/interpret these data for accountability purposes. The first option is for test scores for ML students to count toward a school's rating only after they have been in the United States for one year; the second option is for test scores to be reported to the public but they won't count toward a school's rating. However, by the second year in the United States, states must incorporate MLs scores for both reading/ELA and math, using some measure of growth; and the third year in the United States, ML scores are incorporated just like those of non-MLs. After the passing of the ESSA, the law had a slow roll-out due to Trump's election, his appointment of DeVos as Secretary of Education, and disruption from the Covid-19 pandemic. We hope 'the greater flexibility afforded to states to design their own accountability systems open up the possibility for more realistic expectations for ELL students, more attention to their linguistic needs and the potential for greater support for bilingual education programs' (Baker & Wright, 2021: 196).

Overall, the 2015 renewal of NCLB called the ESSA has done little to change the deep-rooted test and consequence educational culture created with NCLB. Overall, ESSA allows states to decide when to provide assessments in languages other than English and is characterized as being designed to provide more support for MLs. Despite this, NCLB and ESSA are best known as continuing a long history of assimilationist and anti-bilingual education/English-only educational policies that largely reflect an assimilationist language ideology (Henderson & Palmer, 2020: 13). For bilingual programs, despite the NCLB and ESSA policies having mainly created obstacles to a pluralist language ideology and goals supporting them, these ideologies and goals are growing. The biggest challenge for teachers in support of bilingual programming is the goal of developing two languages within a system where accountability is only on one language (Henderson & Palmer, 2020: 94).

For example, a network of Dual Language schools in the Midwest United States documented that as state standardized tests became increasingly high stakes, the discourse shifted away from equity – to the deficiencies of African American students. In particular, Black students were labeled as languageless and targeted as problems – problems that may have led to the failure of this group of Dual Language programs (Dorner *et al.*, 2021). All in all, educational policies such as NCLB and ESSA carry with them subtractive assimilationist ideology. This is also sometimes reflected in the name of the policy. For example, Title III 'English Language Acquisition, Language Enhancement, and Academic Achievement Act' replaced Title VII the 'Bilingual Education Act', thus deleting the word 'bilingual' from the law, reflecting the underlying subtractive and assimilationist language ideology evoked by both NCLB and ESSA federal policies in the US.

END-OF-CHAPTER ACTIVITIES (Instructors: See advice at the end of the book)

By completing Activities 1-4, the reader will be able to:

(1) Order 10 important historical events that influenced the history of assessment for MLs.
(2) Categorize popular reasons for school success/failure through different arguments and relate them to personal experiences and assessment.
(3) Compare and contrast the benefits and risks of validity and accountability scenarios for assessing MLs.
(4) Make two comments in an academic discussion about school practices today and how they relate to the history of assessment for MLs.

Activity 1
Order 10 important historical events that influenced the history of assessment for MLs..

Pairs of students will practice the order of historical events and the implications of these events. The instructor will bring paper and sticky notes to class for each pair of students to create a timeline. The instructor will post a list of historical events (from Table 2.2) out of order and ask students to order them with a partner on their 'timeline' and explain why the event was important. The sticky notes are used so that students can reorder events and change the order of events while discussing/learning. An alternative way to introduce this activity using more movement is to create a 'human timeline'. Pass out 10 index cards with the name of an important historical event and have the whole class input on how to order the students holding the cards. This allows for a group discussion of the historical events.

Activity 2
Categorize popular reasons for school success/failure through different arguments and relate it to assessment.

In a group activity, be prepared to state two reasons why some students succeed in school and others don't. After the group activity, give assessment examples in each part of a word web and share with a partner.

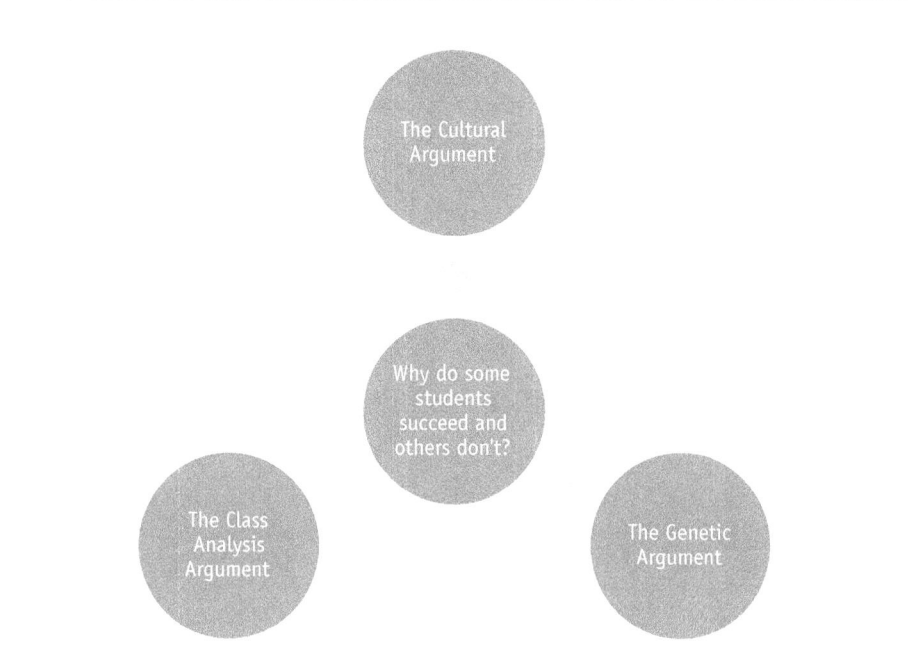

Activity 3
Compare and contrast the benefits and risks of validity and accountability scenarios for assessing MLs.

In groups of three or four students for small-group discussion, answer the following questions and be prepared to share with the whole class: (1) name and describe the two validity accountability scenarios discussed in this chapter: (2) list two specific examples per scenario.

Activity 4
Make two comments in an academic discussion about school practices today and how they relate to the history of assessment for MLs.

After reading this chapter, come to class prepared for an academic discussion worth points on the syllabus (this also models authentic assessment). Each student should be prepared to comment twice in the academic discussion and will be scored on the following rubric. This assessment method is called discussion with a rubric.

Quality of Comments. Student contributes at least two timely and appropriate comments, thoughtful and reflective, responds respectfully to other students' remarks and provokes questions and comments from the group (suggested *four points*).

Resource/Document Reference. Clear reference to chapter being discussed/has done the reading with some thoroughness, comment contains detail or critical insight (suggested *four points*).

Active Listening. Posture, demeanour and behaviour clearly demonstrate respect and attentiveness to others (suggested *two points*).

Notes

(1) The word gatekeeper literally means a person whose job is to stand at a gate and control who goes through it. In assessment, tests are often referred to as 'gatekeepers' because many times they control who advances (college entrance, high school graduation, voting rights, etc.) in society.
(2) Lewis Terman is also noted as a pioneer in educational psychology for his research with 'gifted' children by Stanford University. In addition, he served as president of the American Psychological Association.
(3) A eugenicist is a person specializing in eugenics. Eugenics is a social philosophy advocating the improvement of human genetic traits through positive genetics – the promotion of reproduction among people with desirable traits, and negative eugenics – reducing the reproduction of people with undesirable traits.
(4) The drawing is part of an unpublished study to explore the feelings of MLs taking achievement tests in English in a restricted language policy state (Arizona). Mahoney, K., Mahoney, A. and Rossi, R. (unpublished).
(5) https://www.npr.org/sections/ed/2015/03/05/390239788/why-some-parents-are-sitting-kids-out-of-tests.

References

Abedi, J. (2008) Measuring students' level of English proficiency: Educational significance and assessment requirements. *Educational Assessment* 13, 193–214.

Abedi, J. and Sanchez, C. (2021) Historical milestones in the assessment of English learners. In B.E. Clauser and M. Bunch (eds) *The History of Educational Measurement* (pp. 87–110). New York: Routledge.

AERA, APA, NCME (1966) *Standards for Educational and Psychological Tests and Manuals*. Washington, DC: Author.

AERA, APA, NCME (1974) *Standards for Educational and Psychological Tests*. Washington, DC: Author.

AERA, APA, NCME (1985) *Standards for Educational and Psychological Testing*. Washington, DC: Author.

AERA, APA, NCME (1999) *Standards for Educational and Psychological Testing*. Washington, DC: Author.

AERA, APA, NCME (2014) *Standards for Educational and Psychological Testing*. Washington, DC: AERA.

Anyon, J. (1980) Social class and the hidden curriculum of work. *Journal of Education* 162, 67–92.

August, D. and Hakuta, K. (eds) (1998) *Educating Language Minority Children*. Washington, DC: National Academy Press.

Baker, C. and Wright, W. (2021) *Foundations of Bilingual Education and Bilingualism* (7th edn). Bristol: Multilingual Matters.

Berliner, D.C. (2009) *Poverty and Potential: Out-of-School Factors and School Success*. Boulder, CO/Tempe, AZ: Education and the Public Interest Center & Education Policy Research Unit. See http://nepc.colorado.edu/publication/poverty-and-potential.

Cioè-Peña, M. (2022) The master's tools will never dismantle the master's school: Interrogating settler colonial logic in language education. *Annual Review of Applied Linguistics* 42, 25–33.

Dorner, L.M., Moon, J-M., Bonney, E.N. and Otis, A. (2021) Dueling discourses in dual language schools: Multilingual 'Success for all' versus the academic 'decline' of Black students. In N. Flores, A. Tseng and N. Subtirelu (eds) *Bilingualism for All? Raciolinguistic Perspectives on Dual Language Education in the United States* (pp. 88–110). Bristol: Multilingual Matters.

Every Student Succeeds Act (2015) Public Law No. 114-354.

GAO (Government Accountability Office) (2006, July) *No Child Left Behind Act. Assistance from Education Could Help States Better Measure Progress of Students with Limited English Proficiency*. GAO-06-815 no Child Left Behind. chrome-extension://efaidnbmnnnibpcajpcglclefindmkaj/https://www.gao.gov/assets/gao-06-815.pdf.

Gould, S. (1996) *The Mismeasure of Man* (revised edition). New York: W.W. Norton & Company.

Henderson, K.I. and Palmer, D. (2020) *Dual Language Bilingual Education: Teacher Cases and Perspectives on Large-Scale Implementation*. Bristol: Multilingual Matters

Kanno, Y. and Kangas, S. (2014) 'I'm not going to be, like, for the AP': English language learners' limited access to advanced college-preparatory courses in high school. *American Educational Research Journal* 51 (5), 848–878.

Kleyn, T., Figueroa, A. and Stern, N. (2023) City University of New York (CUNY) Initiative on Immigration and Education (IIE). See https://www.cuny-iie.org/grounding-principles (accessed 18 February 2024).

Leslie, M. (2000) The vexing legacy of Lewis Terman. *Stanford Alumni Magazine* July/August.

Lorde, A. (1984) The master's tools will never dismantle the master's house. In A. Lorde *Sister Outsider: Essays and Speeches*. Berkeley, CA: Crossing Press.

Menken, K. and Solorza, C. (2014) No Child Left Bilingual: Accountability and the elimination of bilingual education programs in New York City schools. *Educational Policy* 28 (1), 96–125.

McNeil, L. and Valenzuela, A. (2001) The harmful impact of the TAAS system of testing in Texas: Beneath the accountability rhetoric. In M. Kornhaber and G. Orfield (eds) *Raising Standards or Raising Barriers? Inequality and High Stakes Testing in Public Education* (pp. 127–150). New York: Century Foundation.

National Research Council (NRC) (1999) *High Stakes: Testing for Tracking, Promotion, and Graduation*. Washington, DC: National Academy Press.

Ogbu, J. (1978) *Minority Education and Caste: The American System in Cross-Cultural Perspective*. New York: Academic Press.

Ogbu, J. (1998) Voluntary and involuntary minorities: A cultural-ecological theory of school performance with some implications for education. *Anthropology & Education Quarterly* 29 (2), 155–188.

Ravitch, D. (2010) *The Death and Life of the Great American School System: How Testing and Choice are Undermining Education*. New York: Basic Books.

Schissel, J. (2019) *Social Consequences of Testing for Language-minoritized Bilinguals in the United States*. Bristol: Multilingual Matters.

Stiggins, R. (2017) *The Perfect Assessment System*. Alexandria, VA: The Association for Supervision and Curriculum Development (ASCD).

Terman, L.M. (1916) *The Measurement of Intelligence*. Boston: Houghton Mifflin. https://doi.org/10.1037/10014-000.

Valdés, G. (1996) *Con respeto*. New York: Teachers College, Columbia University.

Wright, W. (2002) The effects of high stakes testing in an inner-city elementary school: The curriculum, the teachers, and the English Language Learners. *Current Issues in Education* 5, 1–40.

Zhao, Y. (2009) *Catching Up or Leading the Way: American Education in the Age of Globalization*. Alexandria, VA: ASCD.

Recommended reading

Abedi, J. and Sanchez, C. (2020) Historical milestones in the assessment of English learners. In B. Clauser and M. Bunch (eds) *The History of Educational Measurement* (pp. 87–110). New York: Routledge.

This chapter provides a 24-page history of the assessment of English learners (ELs) in the United States with an emphasis on testing accommodations. The first author is the leading expert on accommodations for ELs.

Baserra, M., Trumbull, E. and Solano-Flores, G. (eds) (2010) *Cultural Validity in Assessment: Addressing Linguistic and Cultural Diversity* (Language, Culture and Teaching Series). New York: Routledge.

The authors address the disproportionately negative impact on students who do not come from mainstream middle-class backgrounds. The book is unique in that it accounts for cultural validity by articulating through validity terms the cultural and linguistic variations that jeopardize assessment results. Criteria for culturally valid assessment are included.

Schissel, J. (2019) *Social Consequences of Testing for Language-minoritized Bilinguals in the United States* (Bilingual Education and Bilingualism Series). Bristol: Multilingual Matters.

This book constructs a social narrative to examine the social consequences of testing faced by language-minoritized bilinguals in the United States. This historical analysis adds an important perspective for educators and researchers concerned with inequities in the testing of language-minoritized bilinguals.

Glass, G. (2008) *Fertilizers, Pills, and Magnetic Strips*. Charlotte, NC: Information Age Publishing (IAP).

Glass argues and shows with data that the central education policy debates at the start of the 21st century (vouchers, charter schools, tax credits, high-stakes testing and bilingual education) are really about two underlying issues: (1) how can the costs of public education be cut? and (2) how can the education of the white middle class be privatized at public expense? He uses demographic data across 30 years to support these points.

Henderson, K.I. and Palmer, D. (2020) *Dual Language Bilingual Education: Teacher Cases and Perspectives on Large-Scale Implementation*. Multilingual Matters.

This book provides a first chapter articulating the abbreviated history of dual language bilingual education. The authors also provide teacher case studies documenting teacher efforts to provide learning opportunities within sometimes very challenging policy contexts.

McNeil, L., Coppola, E., Radigan, J. and Heilig, J. (2008) Avoidable losses: High-stakes accountability and the dropout crisis. *Education Policy Analysis Archives* 16 (3). See http://epaa.asu.edu/ojs/article/view/28.

These researchers used large-scale data to show that the current high-stakes, test-based accountability system puts our most vulnerable youth – the poor, MLs, African American and Latino children – at risk of being pushed out of their schools so the schools can reach acceptable status according to NCLB.

Ravitch, D. (2013) *Reign of Error: The Hoax of the Privatization Movement and the Danger to America's Public Schools*. New York: Alfred A. Knopf.

In this book, Diane Ravitch argues that graduation rates are the highest and dropout rates the lowest they have ever been. She argues that NCLB and RTTT set unreasonable goals and punish schools and teachers in an unfair way. She also documents how Wall Street, individual billionaires and major foundations are eyeing public education as an emerging market for investors, which will lead to its downfall.

Stiggins, R. (2017) *The Perfect Assessment System*. Alexandria, VA: ASCD.

According to James Popham in the foreword (Stiggins, 2017), this book invokes a theme that has governed most of Rick Stiggins' career. Stiggins wants us to make sure that our assessment practices are linked to student's motivation in a manner that engenders student self-esteem rather than damages it. More than any other writer, Stiggins has reminded us that if our educational tests lead too many students to conclude that they are not smart or capable enough and school success is out of their reach, then the entire use of testing is dysfunctional. This book focuses on using classroom assessments for student learning rather than as tests of student learning.

Terman, L.M. (1916) *The Measurement of Intelligence: An Explanation of and a Complete Guide for the use of the Stanford Revision and Extension of the Binet-Simon Intelligence Scale*. Boston: Houghton, Mifflin.

This historical book, published over 100 years ago, allows you to see first hand the thoughts and ideas behind Lewis Terman and this popular intelligence test.

3 Validity

> **THEMES FROM CHAPTER 3**
>
> (1) Tests aren't bad; it's how we are using them that's bad.
> (2) Viewing multilingual learner (ML) test scores through the unified view of validity puts overdue importance on how we use ML test scores. This includes paying more attention to the social consequences of test-use.
> (3) Construct irrelevant variance (CIV) is a major validity threat for test scores of MLs.
> (4) Social consequences of using test scores or 'side effects' are having wide-ranging impacts on the field of assessment for multilingual children.
> (5) It should always be remembered that a test does not end with the student's score; it begins with test interpretation and use.

Key Vocabulary

- Unified view of validity.
- Construct.
- CIV otherwise known as bias.
- Test interpretation.
- Test score use.

PUMI Connection: Use

This chapter primarily focuses on the U (Use) by explaining a theory of validity called the 'unified view of validity'. The unified view of validity shifts the thinking on validity from validating tests (outdated thinking) to validating how we use test scores (current thinking). This is an important shift because it places more emphasis on test score-use, which will lead to more appropriate and fair decisions about testing for MLs.

This chapter is the most theoretical of all the chapters in this book. After this chapter, the remainder of the book focuses on the practical issues of assessing MLs. The author uses the concerns over assessing MLs (achievement and language) in the United States as the context to better understand the important topic of validity. This chapter raises concrete concerns about the validity, ethics and ideologies of using test scores. It is important for the reader to process some of this theory/framework to draw more meaning from the practice-oriented chapters immediately following this chapter.

In the past, we asked: Is this test valid or not? Now we ask: Is a particular test score-*use* valid for MLs? This change represents a fundamental shift in thinking about validity, from validating the instrument (presumably for all students) to validating how we use test scores for a particular purpose. Although different types of validity still exist, it is now considered inappropriate not to consider this unified view. Most people refer to the *unified view of validity* as *validity* now.

Validity threats can lead to unrelated factors raising or lowering test scores in ways they should not. For MLs, whose language and culture typically do not match the school and test culture, unrelated factors such as language and culture can decrease test scores in systematic ways. When this happens, whether the results increase or decrease systematically the results are said to be biased. Bias can creep into assessment results from many directions, for example, cultural and linguistic assumptions in the test items, poorly constructed items or scoring, inappropriate reading levels or the language of the test. It would be nice if it was possible to determine the percentage of bias in each test score (that will vary by student) before assessments are administered and definitely before the results are used, but we have no way of easily detecting this. We must rely on teachers' keen sense of validity and fairness in assessments and the wherewithal to speak up. If any of these unrelated factors are impacting assessment results, the fairness of the assessment is called into question. For tests, please know that measurement experts are trained in sophisticated ways of detecting biases in the pilot phase of designing a test; however, that is if the pilot sample of students is similar to your own. This may reduce bias but it does not eliminate it. When in doubt, raise a red flag – many times, educators have the best ability to spot biases as they are closest to the students, and to the tests.

Construct-Related Validity Threats

If schools/teachers are collecting inaccurate evidence of student achievement and making instructional decisions based on these data, interventions based on these benchmark data will not serve students well. Because of this, it is important to be aware of, and learn ways to reduce CIV, a major threat to the validity of using ML test scores. CIV is a systematic measurement error that reduces the ability to accurately interpret scores or ratings (Haladyna & Downing, 2004). Simply put, tests in English are likely measuring something other than what it seems for MLs, at least partly, and in a systematic way that may go undetected.

To break CIV down – *construct*[1] is the concept we are attempting to measure. With MLs, we often measure the construct of language proficiency and/or academic achievement, with high stakes attached to test-use. The term 'construct' reminds us that these ideas are constructed by experts in the field and are informed by a theoretical or conceptual framework chosen to guide the test construction. We are also reminded that we call many of these 'psychological constructs'. Like other constructs that psychologists have tried to measure (such as intelligence, critical thinking or social development), there has been a great deal of disagreement about the existence and nature of language ability, and views have shifted over time (Green, 2014). *Irrelevant* means not relevant to the construct. *Variance* is a way of explaining what accounts for the test score in a statistical way. No psychological construct is perfectly definable or perfectly measurable; language proficiency and achievement are no exceptions to this rule.

CIV is a major validity threat for MLs because irrelevant constructs often contaminate test scores. In other words, if the CIV is high, then the test may be measuring something different than it was designed to measure. Measurement scientists mostly call these construct irrelevant variables, but some call them nuisance variables, extraneous variables, noise or contaminants. For example, if a ML student takes a math test in English that is full of word problems, the assessment becomes more of a measure of language than of math. The CIV in this case is language because the assessment was designed to measure math. The term CIV can also be replaced with the term bias.

Another validity threat related to the construct is when the test does not cover the entire construct (the term for this in the measurement field is 'construct underrepresentation'), like language for example. For instance, many tests narrowly measure speaking, listening, reading and writing and many times not very well, but they claim the test measures 'language proficiency'. This is an example of the test claiming to measure language, but in reality only a very small fraction of language is measured. As the name implies, this type of validity concern is known as construct underrepresentation.

Most experts that study language become frustrated with the way schools define and assess language in such narrow and calculated ways, and with so many high stakes attached (advancement of grade, graduation from high school, entry to special education [SPED] or gifted programs, etc.). Elana Shohamy points out that our conceptions of language should include multimodal representation such as visuals, graphics, images, dance and even silence. These forms of 'languaging' are far more representative of real language use for ML children. She also says that when language is treated as discrete categories with fixed boundaries, political entities use such boundaries to maintain an 'us versus them' attitude and give preference to some language varieties over others in order to harness political power (Shohamy, 2006). Those having political power give preference, and privilege, to certain forms of language, like Standard English over non-Standard English. This privilege is then justified through test results. These types of validity threats lead to one group claiming superiority over another (see Chapter 2 for a historical documentation of this).

Language-Related Validity Threats

Although they function closely together, language proficiency and academic achievement are two distinct constructs and should be measured separately. Language proficiency signifies knowing a language, whereas academic achievement signifies knowing a particular domain of content made available through formal schooling. On the one hand, the emphasis of academic achievement is on content, which consists of the concepts and generalizations within a subject matter. Language proficiency, on the other hand, is the medium through which students access these domains of content. Academic achievement is the result of cognitive learning, whereas language proficiency is a result of language acquisition and/or language learning. Because language proficiency is a medium for academic achievement, the task of measuring each construct and separating how one influences the other has proved to be an important scientific challenge.

There is no denying a strong relationship between language and achievement. The relationship between language factors and student performance in content-based areas has been well established in the literature (see, for e.g. Abedi, 2003). When two constructs, such as achievement and proficiency, function so closely together, how much of the test score is due to true achievement and how much is due to CIV? Educators understand that language factors threaten the validity of achievement test scores because they are trained in how to instruct and assess MLs, taking language factors into consideration, through concepts such as scaffolding and comprehensible input. However, non-educators may not see the harm in testing MLs in English on academic achievement tests. When those who advocate for testing MLs in English are asked why they think this is a good idea, two responses are typical. First, for many, it's the law. State and federal laws in general leave no option but for schools to comply with mandatory testing. State policymakers rationalize that scores need to be collected right away, sometimes even before a student can speak English, to provide solid 'baseline data'. Second, it is argued that even though the test may not be a good measure of content, at least it can measure language. In fact, some state policies use content-area test scores to inform the identification process for MLs. School districts rationalize this because children must know English reasonably well to understand the questions of a test – lower scores reflect limited knowledge of English and higher scores reflect greater knowledge of English. Many researchers point out that an achievement test, not specified by second language acquisition theories to measure language, is inappropriate and that children may score low on a standardized achievement test for reasons wholly separate from language.

Because true achievement is an abstract idea, and since no test is perfectly reliable, providing empirical evidence that can quantify exactly how much of the test score is due to true achievement, is a question that can never really be answered with 100% accuracy. Every (achievement) test score is made up of the true construct (achievement) plus some amount of error. Too much error results in an unreliable test score and an invalid representation of what a child really knows. The problem worsens when we use unreliable data to make decisions. Table 3.1 provides a place to start and questions to ask before a test is administered. If there are too many biases, teachers can raise a red flag, awareness and/or provide support for their students to 'opt out' of the assessment.

Table 3.1 Bias checklist for construct, language and culture-related validity checks

	Yes	No
Does the language proficiency level of the assessment match the student?		
Does the language of the test match the language of instruction (has the student had ample practice in this language doing similar tasks)?		
Are there cultural references in the test that will favor mainstream cultural groups? Have you asked students from different cultural groups to comment on this?		
Is the length of the test excessive? Or does the length of the test represent the amount of time the students typically read and write in English (or whatever the language of the test)?		
Are multiple languages an asset for successfully completing the assessment? Or is multilingualism not taken into consideration (e.g. with prompts and open-ended responses)?		
Does the assessment contain colloquials and regionalisms? Were experts (parents, teachers, students) invited to review the content of the items for linguistic appropriateness (colloquialisms, regionalisms) and appropriate use?		
Do the test items represent the construct? Are they more narrow or more broad?		

Reliability

The concept of reliability is integral to validity because if test scores are unreliable, how can they be valid? However, the reverse could be true (it is possible to have reliability without validity). Reliability is measured as a coefficient (a number between 0 and 1), which informs us empirically (with data) of how much contamination (or error) is part of the overall test score. No test is 100% reliable, but technically sound tests have a reliability coefficient of 0.85 or higher, indicating that at least 85% of the test score is due to actual achievement (for example); the other 15% is due to measurement errors, which for MLs usually take the form of language factors. For example, in one large study (sample size approximately 200,000) conducted by Jamal Abedi, reliability coefficients were consistently higher for fluent English proficient (FEP) students than for limited English proficient (LEP) students. In reading, the coefficient was 0.86 for FEPs and 0.75 for LEPs; in math, 0.90 for FEPs and 0.80 for LEPs; in language, 0.80 for FEPs and 0.68 for LEPs; and in science, 0.78 for FEPs and 0.53 for LEPs (Abedi et al., 2004). This means, for example, that 22% of the science test score for FEPs is due to error and 47% of the test score for MLs is due to error! These coefficients are very revealing about how (un)reliable the data test scores can be. This is important to know because some people assume wrongly that test scores are 'objective' and not susceptible to subjectivity (or error or noise). Reliability is also discussed in Chapter 7.

Unfortunately, those who interpret student test scores (students, parents, teachers, school leadership, for example) often fail to understand the role that measurement error should play in interpreting scores. Measurement error is often overlooked or ignored. If Student 1 scored an 80 on a test and Student 2 scored a 72, interpreters of this test may assume that this is concrete evidence that Student 1 has higher ability than Student 2, when it is not. This assumption may be wrong because the difference in test score may be due to error. True achievement could be the same.

Use and Interpretation is the Most Important Concept in Validity

Good validity takes into account how a test will be used, the consequences of using it in those ways and for whom the test was intended. It also includes empirical evidence, with external checks, that the intended use of the test does work as it should for MLs. According to standards from the measurement community, this should be done on a case-by-case basis, meaning each and every test-use for MLs should be 'tested'. It takes longer to 'test the test' but it's worth it, because when you increase validity you strengthen accountability in a meaningful way. We are still in an era that favors accountability over validity. That means we are holding schools and teachers accountable, but often with the use of invalid data.

As mentioned above, each use of the test must be considered for validity on a case-by-case basis. Common ways we interpret/use test scores for MLs are as follows: give grades, decide program, decide promotion, ML classification or SPED classification, to name some important uses. Particularly controversial is the question of whether achievement tests should be used to evaluate teachers. During No Child Left Behind (NCLB) in New York state, 20% of a teacher's annual performance reviews (APRs) was derived from state-mandated standardized test results. When considering validity, the consequences of test-use are critical. Consider the consequences of labeling a teacher as needing improvement because the MLs in his or her class were mostly new to the English language and generated low test scores (some did not finish the test). The consequences of inappropriate test-use could include: (1) the teacher may decide to move to a school with fewer MLs or quit, (2) the parents begin to doubt the teacher's ability and request to place their student in another class or (3) the teacher is put on a teacher improvement plan and becomes discouraged. The blueprints for these tests did not intend for student achievement test scores to be used for evaluating teacher effectiveness; this statement is supported by Chapter 1 in the 2014 standards for testing (APA, NCME). Luckily, as of the 2019/2020 school year, New York state test scores no longer have to be included in teacher ratings.

The measurement community – American Educational Research Association (AERA), American Psychological Association (APA) and the National Council on Measurement in Education (NCME) (2014: 23) – makes very clear the importance of test designers establishing intended uses and interpretations as shown by the following standards (for a full review, read Chapter 1 in the standards document called 'standards for validity'):

1.1 The test developer should set forth clearly how test scores are intended to be interpreted and consequently used. The population(s) for which a test is intended should be delimited clearly, and the construct or constructs that the test is intended to assess should be described clearly.
1.2 A rationale should be presented for each intended interpretation of test scores for a given use, together with a summary of the evidence and theory bearing on the intended interpretation.
1.3 If validity for some common or likely interpretation for a given use has not been evaluated, or if such an interpretation is inconsistent with available evidence, that fact should be made clear and potential users should be strongly cautioned about making unsupported interpretations.
1.4 If a test score is interpreted for a given use in a way that has not been validated, it is incumbent on the user to justify the new interpretation for that use, providing a rationale and collecting new evidence, if necessary.

Achievement Test Results Used the Wrong Way

Test score results should not be used to evaluate teachers and principals. We have better ways, which researchers have studied for years, to measure teacher and principal effectiveness. One is the National Board Certification, which includes explanations, data and reflections about its extensive methods for measuring teacher effectiveness. Some of these include observation, videotaping and methods to demonstrate integrating a culturally responsive pedagogy that matches the local community.

Academic achievement tests measure the academic achievement of a group of students for whom the test was designed. Along the same lines, language proficiency tests are designed to measure language proficiency among a certain group of students. Each instrument is intended to be used in a certain way, as outlined in the technical manual. Academic achievement test results are meant to measure student academic achievement against a set of standards, not to evaluate teachers. This is an example of not using test scores the way they were intended to be used. Because of policies that required teacher evaluation using student test scores, teachers were reluctant to work in schools with many MLs and alternately sought employment at schools with lower numbers of MLs in order to improve their teacher rating. Students who were known to score low on tests were not wanted in classrooms where teachers were threatened with their APR. In a New York state high school that the author visited, one teacher who felt stuck, deterred a beginner English speaker with lower English proficiency from enrolling in her English language arts (ELA) class, but allowed the student to audit the class, thus avoiding having the low test score attached to her APR. The student in such a case receives no credit for taking the class. This is an example of a negative unintended consequence of high-stakes testing.

SNAPSHOT: THE VALIDITY OF USING STANFORD ENGLISH LANGUAGE PROFICIENCY (SELP) RESULTS FOR RECLASSIFICATION?

This is a true story. A requirement of NCLB was that all states select one English language proficiency (ELP) test and use it across the entire state. In response, the State Department of Education in Arizona purchased a commercial test off the shelf called the Stanford English Language Proficiency Test – the SELP. At the time, Arizona state code regulated that the test publisher's recommendation for when a child is 'ready for a mainstream' class be used as the cut-off score to reclassify MLs. In other words, in this case, the publisher (Harcourt Brace) determined when MLs were ready to be mainstreamed (based solely on their SELP test score), and by law all Arizona schools needed to comply. In 2006, after using the SELP for reclassification purposes, many teachers felt that the SELP was 'too easy' as many students were placed in mainstream classes before they were ready. Unfortunately, the teachers who spoke up were accused by the state superintendent, as quoted in a newspaper article, of wanting to keep students classified as MLs to raise more money for their school (Ryman, 2006). This accusation was founded on the fact that a school is awarded a certain amount of money per student when they are classified as MLs and the superintendent implied teachers wanted to keep students classified, for the money.

Teachers began to call me and my colleagues at Arizona State University. Tom Haladyna, Jeff MacSwan and I began a study of the validity of using the publisher-recommended cut-off for reclassification using achievement (as measured by Arizona's Instrument to Measure Standards [AIMS]) as an external proxy for success – a study that should have been conducted before the state adopted the test (if we concern ourselves with validity before accountability, that is), before the publisher suggested a cut-off score and definitely before this became state code. We asked: How does a testing company from another state know when MLs in Arizona are ready for mainstream classrooms? This is a critical question that ML teachers with many years of experience struggle with, yet a test maker from another region was able to determine this with precision (via a cut-off score). What evidence is presented by the publisher with this score to ensure that we're making good educational decisions? How are MLs in Arizona doing after being reclassified by the SELP? These are all case-by-case validity questions mentioned as a heading earlier in this chapter. When the study was complete, it showed that teachers were correct; using the SELP for reclassification exited students too early. This conclusion was verified when a large percentage of students did not meet state academic standards after reclassification. We knew this because we looked at the evidence of success after classification.

Had a validity study been conducted before the test was adopted, thousands of students would not have been misclassified that year. This study was conducted using Samuel Messick's (1990) Unified View of Validity as a framework to highlight the need to examine validity on a case-by-case basis. (See Mahoney *et al.* [2009] for the full validity study.)

We must slow down accountability regulations until we're able to study valid ways of using results from tests for MLs. We need better assessments, not more assessments.

Discussion questions

- What part of validity was ignored by policymakers in this example?
- What can teachers do when they judge a test-use to be invalid?

What is a Unified View of Validity?

In 1985, major measurement organizations recognized validity as a unified concept (APA, AERA, NCME, 1985). The unified view of validity is an integrated evaluative judgment of the degree to which empirical evidence and theoretical rationales support the adequacy and appropriateness of inferences and actions based on test scores (Messick, 1989), which is a mouthful but here is how to break it down. A unified view of validity matters for MLs because the actions we take based on test scores and test interpretation are critical in making the appropriate educational decisions. If you find yourself asking questions focusing on the meaningfulness and appropriateness of using test scores for MLs, these are validity questions. The following is a list of validity questions you may have considered:

- How do we know what test scores for MLs really mean?
- What does it mean if a ML student scores a level two on the state's mathematics exam?
- What does it mean if a student scores at the advanced level on the state's English proficiency test? How should we use these scores?
- How was it determined that students were ready for reclassification?
- Do we have evidence to show that students scoring below proficiency are not ready to participate meaningfully in the classroom outside of English as a new language (ENL)?
- What evidence has been presented to show that these cut-off scores work accurately to inform these critical educational decisions?
- How does the test publisher know how to make recommendations for student placement?
- Have the recommendations been investigated empirically (with data)?
- Have test publishers considered the social and educational consequences of using the test scores based on their recommendations?

These are examples of important validity questions that we need to ask (and find answers to!) to increase validity for MLs. The following example shows how to investigate validity use in an empirical (using data) way. Two researchers decided to investigate the validity of language proficiency test results by comparing them to other tests designed to measure and use results in the same way. Jeff MacSwan and Kellie Rolstad (2006) conducted a study in which 150 elementary school MLs took three language assessments to see if they led to similar results. They used two common language proficiency assessments, the Language Assessment Scales-Oral (LAS-O) and the Idea Proficiency Test I-Oral (IPT-Spanish), along with one natural language measure. The results of the LAS-O identified 74% of the students as not proficient in their primary language and the IPT-Spanish identified 90%, whereas the natural language sample found only 2% of the sample to have high morphological error rates (remember – this was the same group of students given different instrumentation). The authors of this study argued that using test results such as these to make important educational decisions, partly leads to a disproportionate representation of MLs in SPED and other serious consequences.

Part science, part ethics

The most important question for MLs, however, is how test scores *should be used* – the *should* question. Examples of should-questions surrounding MLs under the current testing accountability climate include:

- Should ML results of achievement tests in English be used to judge how much content they have learned?
- Should scores be used to evaluate programs?
- Should one score on a language proficiency test determine whether a student receives language services?
- Should scores be used to judge whether a school or neighborhood is good?
- Should these scores decide whether a principal or teacher is effective?

Some of these questions highlight the social consequences of using (or not using) the test score as part of the validation process. Who is accountable for social consequences? We have had more accountability since the year 2000 than ever before in US schools, scrutinizing teachers and students; however, we have had little to no accountability for the measurement community or the policymakers who should be scrutinized more for test score use. For example, the measurement community suggests that they cannot control the conditions of assessment, so their involvement ends with the publication of assessments. Local administrators and policymakers make policies regarding test-use, at times unchecked using data. These ethical concepts should be part of the accountability system. Just as students and teachers are accountable to local, state and federal policymakers, it is time for policymakers who govern test-use to have equal or more scrutiny and accountability (No Administrator Left Behind [NALB] perhaps?). A true understanding of validity involves giving science and ethics equal consideration. Figure 3.1 depicts the delicate balance strived for between science and ethics.

Let's use a pharmacy analogy to better understand the consequences of testing. Federal policies and procedures ensure that a new drug is not used with the general

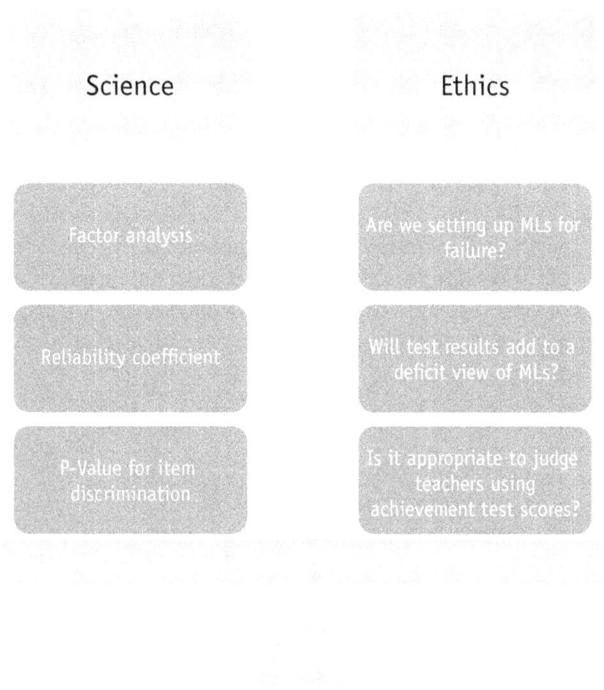

Science

- Factor analysis
- Reliability coefficient
- P-Value for item discrimination

Ethics

- Are we setting up MLs for failure?
- Will test results add to a deficit view of MLs?
- Is it appropriate to judge teachers using achievement test scores?

Figure 3.1 Balancing science and ethics in validity

public until it and its side effects have been studied over a period of time. To use a test score without a thorough (and empirically driven) understanding of its meaning is as dangerous as trusting a drug to work without knowing what it intends to treat and its potential side effects. The social consequences of test score-use are viewed as the 'side effects' of testing and are very important in the consideration of testing MLs in English; in reality though, the actual appraisal of social consequences is a difficult task. One side effect of testing MLs that is often heard through personal communication with ML teachers, is the amount of crying, fear and disappointment that occurs during 'testing season'. Many teachers describe the sense of helplessness they and their students feel when given a high-stakes test that they can't read well. These types of side effects contribute to a negative schooling experience that often spirals downward over time. If the results of assessments make students feel hopelessness, this assessment may not be a high-quality assessment, for the simple reason that it may do more harm than good (Stiggins, 2017). Although assessment is most often performed with a view to helping children acquire language and learn content, by providing students and teachers with feedback on knowledge gained and ways to improve, assessment can become an intimidating practice and cause anxiety, otherwise known as test anxiety (Popov *et al.*, 2019). Specific types of anxiety that MLs may experience are foreign language anxiety (FLA), feelings of worry and fear-related emotions associated with learning 'foreign languages' (Britton, 2021). Another type of anxiety most people are familiar with is test anxiety, over-excessive worry and fear associated with the consequences of poor results on tests and assessments in general.

Table 3.2 presents a list of some of the potential negative educational and social consequences, or potential 'side effects', in the appraisal of the appropriateness, meaningfulness and usefulness of test scores. There could be a parallel table showing the positive consequences and casting each of these ideas in a promising light (e.g. placement in a gifted program or feelings of achievement or increased numbers of bilingual schools); however, these happen much less frequently. Schissel (2019) asks the question, do the results of tests, and the consequences of tests, reflect social inequities, or do they reproduce them? Then, through a historical narrative review, Schissel (2019) illustrates that ML populations faced repeated, often severe, consequences which have both exacerbated existing inequities and introduced new ones. Table 3.2 shows possible examples of the negative and social consequences of testing just for further clarification.

Table 3.2 Negative educational and social consequences of testing MLs (in English)

	Bilingual program de-emphasizes languages other than English
	Home language is used less in instruction
	Placement in a remedial track of schooling
	Exit from ML status too early
	Overrepresentation in special education
	Access to less-qualified teachers
	Unequal opportunity to learn (OTL)
	Grade retention
	School/community maintains deficit perspective of MLs
	Disinterest in school
	Feeling of low achievement
	Low graduation/high dropout rate
Social/political	
	Devaluation of languages other than English in society
	Unemployment, lack of job opportunities
	Lower-paying jobs
	Salary gap between dominant and non-dominant
	Overrepresentation of non-English speakers in prisons
	Lack of bilingual people in high political positions

The role of ideology (language and culture)

Ideology and (cultural) values also play a role in validity. Because of national and state policy, schools are mostly concerned with measuring achievement and language proficiency (in English or another dominant colonial language) for accountability purposes. Because accountability tests are administered mostly in English in the United States, this gives a great advantage to English-speaking students and teachers of English-speaking students. At the same time, testing what students can do in their home languages or additional languages goes undetected, feeding a deficit perspective of MLs and ignoring the great value that multilingual children are, and offer. Many important constructs, in addition to achievement and language, such as acculturation and motivation, go unnoticed for MLs. Acculturation is when a student is confronted with new norms and a new culture; this is known to directly impact learning. Because of the connection between acculturation and learning, it is important to assess acculturation with MLs new to school culture (Adelman Reyes & Kleyn, 2010). Assessing acculturation is usually done through the methods of assessment such as interview with a checklist. The checklist may focus on the amount of time in a country, district and school. It may also focus on proficiency in the home language, new language and whether there are people in the school who share the home language or culture.

Constructs such as achievement and language, which are broad and difficult to define/measure, leave room for other factors such as ideology and cultural values to become part of an unintended or irrelevant construct. In the context of schooling in the United States, the values of the dominant culture (white, English-speaking middle class) have become intimately intertwined with the concept of evidence, interpretation and the meaning of test scores. The very nature of norm-referenced testing (comparing students to one another to see who is better) is embedded in the competitive values of the middle class in a way that gives advantage to those already dominant in the United States. What this means is that tests inherently represent one culture, the dominant culture, or white norms, in the United States. One of the prime tensions with implementing a culturally sustainable pedagogy in Indigenous education, such as creating a Native-centric curriculum, is the need to address 'white norms' from the federal government (e.g. the Every Student Succeeds Act [ESSA]). These federal mandates do not require assessment of important values such as level of wellness, strength of cultural identity and commitment to community, for example (Lee & McCarty, 2017).

A classic study conducted by Rhodes (1988) offers an example of how culture and values can significantly affect test score. In studying the very low achievement test scores of Hopi and Navajo students in the Southwest region of the United States, Rhodes points out that tests require quick answers, guessing, risk taking and the elimination of options in the selection of only one response. This contradicts what is taught in some Native American cultures in which decisions are made slowly and surely. Therefore, Hopi and Navajo children may be at a disadvantage in demonstrating achievement not because they are so-called low achievers, but because the construct of achievement, as measured through a standardized and timed test, may require cultural values not aligned with Hopis and Navajos.

Further, the constructs of achievement and language proficiency are largely influenced by language ideology. Language ideologies are the assumptions, interpretations and judgments about vocabulary, grammar, accent and so on, that are based upon political, religious, class or other views. In the United States, a strong language ideology is expressed by the 'English Only movement' – that is, a view that supports the idea that language homogeneity is beneficial to US society and is evidenced by the requirement to take and pass standardized achievement tests in English. We know these ideologies exist in assessment; however, as Samuel Messick (1980) pointed out 30 years ago, exposing the value assumptions of a test construct and its more subtle links to ideology – possibly to multiple cross-cutting ideologies – is a daunting challenge. For MLs, potential cross-cutting ideologies embedded in the constructs of achievement and language proficiency include, for example, political ideologies (English is the language of power), sociocultural and sociolinguistic ideologies (middle-class language and culture is normal) and race ideologies (white privilege). To be direct, one cultural group may use tests to control other cultural groups.

This idea can be used to explain the history of misuse that was presented in Chapter 2. Using very broad constructs for testing may also support a system of cultural hegemony, whereby one cultural group (English speaking and white) can manipulate the system of values in order to create a world view favoring its authority over other cultural groups (non-white and non-English speaking). Cultural hegemony is the domination of a diverse society by one world view, instead of multiple world views. Holding MLs and teachers of MLs accountable to standardized tests in English and not holding them accountable for home language development promotes this sort of cultural hegemony. An area of study called critical language testing (CLT) (Shohamy, 2017) emerged from Messick's work and the realization that tests are powerful tools in education and society, which may lead to unintended consequences that need to be examined and evaluated.

SNAPSHOT: MISSED OPPORTUNITY

During the NCLB era, I visited a bilingual school that has had problems recruiting and maintaining bilingual teachers. In the hallway, I was surprised to run into a new fourth-grade teacher – Ms Rodriguez, the daughter of a well-known bilingual teacher who has been a very effective teacher of MLs over the years. When I mentioned that I hadn't seen her name on the teacher list for the bilingual program and wondered if she had changed her name, she replied, 'I am not certified in ESL or bilingual'. She then explained to me that her mother and other teachers had warned her how difficult teacher evaluations are for teachers with large numbers of MLs and advised her to approach teaching through a mainstream teaching certificate, and she heeded their warning. Owing to an evaluation system that put teachers with large numbers of MLs at an unfair disadvantage, we lost some of our best. This was a case of a missed opportunity.

Discussion questions

- Why was Ms Rodriguez reluctant to join the field of bilingual education?
- What positive incentives do districts offer for teachers to become bilingual educators?
- Why was it more difficult for teachers with high numbers of MLs to receive positive evaluations?

Two major validity concerns are shown through the previous and following snapshots, both of which are based on true stories. The previous snapshot is an example of a serious negative consequence (good teachers deterred from the profession) of using tests scores for teacher evaluation. The next snapshot is an example of two things: a negative effect (narrowing of curriculum) and the misuse of academic achievement results to evaluate the quality of teaching.

SNAPSHOT: THE HIGHER THE TEST SCORE THE BETTER THE TEACHER?

Teacher A: Cathy spent all of her time preparing students for the ELA test. She reduced the time spent teaching Spanish language arts, science and social studies, and she cancelled the field trip to the city's art museum so she could have more time to prepare for the test. Every day, she talked about the importance of the test, practice items were reviewed again and again and test-taking strategies became a very important topic. Students memorized a song about doing well on the test, and a letter was sent home to parents indicating the importance of their children being ready for the test. Cathy spearheaded a school initiative to invite students to come early to school to jog and exercise during the weeks of testing (this initiative ended as soon as state tests ended) to help stimulate their brains during test week.

Teacher B: Despite pressure to drop traditional subjects and focus only on math and English, Roberto decided to continue teaching all subjects in school with a heavy emphasis on biliteracy. He spent time at the beginning of each school year assessing each student and increasing his cultural competency so that the instruction was culturally relevant – a method coined by Gloria Ladson-Billings to denote a pedagogy where teachers focus on cultural competence, high expectations and raising social consciousness. To teach social studies, mathematics and an ELA project, Roberto launched a community project in which his students mapped all the abandoned buildings within two square miles of the school and wrote a report to the City Development Department citing the negative impact these buildings have on youth in their community and proposing solutions to the excessive number of such buildings. The report included the community consequences of multiple abandoned buildings and how they affect children and their learning; it also suggested productive ways to renew these buildings. At state testing time, Roberto spent the two weeks before the test preparing the students for the test. However, he made it a point not to overwhelm students with anxieties about the test because they should be as comfortable as possible on test day, and outside factors were already making them nervous.

Result: The students in Cathy's classroom scored much higher on the test than in Roberto's. Roberto is being considered for a teacher improvement plan; if he doesn't raise test scores within a certain time frame, he might not receive tenure. Cathy was evaluated as a highly effective teacher and was recognized at the district level as a good mentor for new teachers. Unfortunately, in this example, it might be the case that the weaker teacher was labeled as effective and the stronger teacher was labeled as ineffective.

Although policies promoting higher test scores intended to reward highly qualified teachers while weeding out the ineffective ones, in some instances it may achieve the exact opposite. Thus, we must always ask the most pressing question: What does a high test score really mean? Does a test score represent true achievement? A high score may mean, in part, that the teacher narrowed the curriculum to focus on test preparation; thus, in some cases it may be that a higher score might actually indicate a less effective teacher. These are validity concerns.

Discussion questions

- Whose students benefitted more?
- Who has an advantage under this accountability system? Who is benefitting from a system of accountability like this?
- Do higher test scores mean better teachers?

END-OF-CHAPTER ACTIVITIES (Instructors: see advice at the end of the book)

By completing Activities 1–4, the reader will be able to:

(1) Write your own definition of validity as a unified concept.
(2) Identify key 'unified validity' vocabulary terms and use them in a sentence related to MLs.
(3) Shift thinking about test validity from whether *tests* are valid to whether *how we use test scores* is valid.
(4) Agree or disagree with the following statement and provide evidence: *Testing MLs in the United States using broad constructs may support a system of cultural hegemony.*

Activity 1

Write and say your own definition of validity as a unified concept. In small groups, students brainstorm a list of qualities that help define the unified view of validity. After 20 minutes, be prepared to share the group's definition of a unified view of validity. Afterward, students write their own definition of validity on an index card and submit it to the instructor for evaluation.

Activity 2

Identify key 'unified validity' vocabulary terms and use them in a sentence related to MLs.

Play 'vo-back-ulary' with the whole class. The instructor projects a list of key vocabulary words related to the unified view of validity (use the list at the beginning of the chapter) and provides a brief review of each term. One student stands in front with his or her back to the class, and the instructor places a large sticky note or index card/tape on the student's back with one of the key words. The standing student must guess what the word is and use it in a sentence related to MLs. The next person at the table gives clues, being careful not to give too many clues or any that lead directly to the key vocabulary word. Even if the list of words is smaller than the number of students, reuse the words until all students have a chance because many of the concepts are difficult and a review may be necessary. Since the concepts in this chapter are difficult, perhaps play vo-back-ulary with a team of two guessing the term.

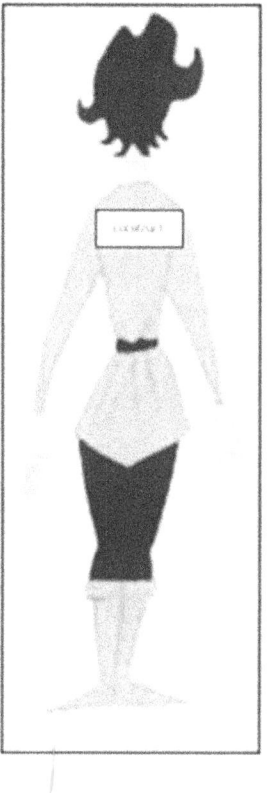

Activity 3

Shift thinking about test validity away from whether tests are *valid* to whether *how we use test scores* is valid.

Review the law in your state about teacher evaluation. Ask one small group to review teacher accountability (teacher's perspective), another group to review principal accountability (principal's perspective) and a third group to review state policy regarding the consequences of low test scores for schools and districts (school/district's perspective). Review the policies as a whole group. Give each group 45 minutes to prepare an advocacy statement to a board of education about how test scores are used for schools with large numbers of MLs and whether or not the state-mandated use of test scores is fair. Are these test scores valid for all students? Is the State Department of Education using test scores in a valid way?

Activity 4

Agree or disagree with the following statement and provide evidence: Testing MLs in the United States using broad constructs may also support a system of cultural hegemony. Be prepared to use a value line, where 1 is strongly disagree and 10 is strongly agree. In the United States, a strong language ideology is expressed

> by the English Only movement – that is, language homogeneity is beneficial to US society. Exposing the value assumptions of a test construct and its more subtle links to ideology – possibly to multiple cross-cutting ideologies – is a daunting challenge (Messick, 1980). For MLs, potential cross-cutting ideologies embedded in the constructs of achievement and language proficiency include, for example, political ideologies (English is the language of power), sociocultural and sociolinguistic ideologies (middle-class language and culture is normal) and race ideologies (white privilege).

Note

(1) A construct is a hypothetical (or constructed) idea not easy to observe. Constructs can be supported by theories, frameworks or expert judgment. Important constructs for MLs are achievement, language proficiency (home and new language), motivation and acculturation, to name a few.

References

Abedi, J. (2003, April) Impact of Linguistic Factors in Content-Based Assessment for EB Students: An Overview of Research. In M. Alkin (chair) Linguistic modification in the assessment of English language learners. Paper presented at the American Educational Research Association, Chicago, IL.

Abedi, J., Hofstetter, C. and Lord, C. (2004) Assessment accommodations for English language learners: Implications for policy based empirical research. *Review of Educational Research* 74 (1), 1–28.

Adelman Reyes, S. and Kleyn, T. (2010) *Teaching in 2 Languages: A Guide for K-12 Bilingual Educators*. Thousand Oaks, CA: Corwin Press.

APA, AERA, NCME (1985, 2014) *Standards for Educational and Psychological Testing*. Washington, DC: American Psychological Association.

Britton, M. (2021) *Assessment for Learning in Primary Language Learning and Teaching*. Bristol: Multilingual Matters.

Green, A. (2014) *Exploring Language Assessment and Testing: Language in Action*. New York: Routledge.

Haladyna, T. and Downing, S. (2004) Construct-irrelevant variance in high-stakes testing. *Educational Measurement: Issues and Practice* 23 (1), 17–27.

Kahneman, D., Sibony, O. and Sunstein, C. (2021) *Noise: A Flaw in Human Judgement*. New York: Little, Brown Spark, Hachette Book Group.

Lee, T. and McCarty, T. (2017) Upholding Indigenous education sovereignty through critical culturally sustaining/revitalizing pedagogy. In D. Paris and S. Alim (eds) *Culturally Sustaining Pedagogies: Teaching and Learning for Justice in a Changing World* (pp. 61–82). New York: Teachers College Press.

MacSwan, J. and Rolstad, K. (2006) How language tests mislead us about children's abilities: Implications for special education placements. *Teachers College Record* 108 (11), 2304–2328.

Mahoney, K., Haladyna, T. and MacSwan, J. (2009) The need for multiple measures in reclassification decisions: A validity study of the Stanford English Language Proficiency Test. In T.G. Wiley, J.S. Lee and R.W. Rumberger (eds) *The Education of Language Minority Immigrants in the United States* (pp. 240–262). Bristol: Multilingual Matters.

Messick, S. (1980) Test validity and the ethics of assessment. *American Psychologist* 35 (11), 1012–1027.

Messick, S. (1989) Meaning and values in test validation: The science and ethics of assessment. *Educational Researcher* 18 (2), 5–11.

Messick, S. (1990) Unified View of Validity. Research Report RR-90-11. Princeton, NJ: Educational Testing Service.

Popov, S., Prošić-Santovac, D. and Radović, D. (2019) We scare because we care: Young learners and test anxiety. In D. Prošić-Santovac and S. Rixon (eds) *Integrating Assessment into Early Language Learning and Teaching* (pp. 69–84). Bristol: Multilingual Matters.

Rhodes, R.W. (1988) Standardized Testing of Minority Students: Navajo and Hopi. Paper presented at the annual meeting of the National Council of Teachers of English, St. Louis, MO.
Ryman, A. (2006, March 2) Teachers, state at odds over whether test should pass or fail. *The Arizona Republic*.
Schissel, J. (2019) *Social Consequences of Testing for Language-minoritized Bilinguals in the United States*. Bristol: Multilingual Matters.
Shohamy, E. (2006) *Language Policy: Hidden Agendas and New Approaches*. New York: Routledge.
Shohamy, E. (2017) Critical language testing. In E. Shohamy *et al.* (eds) *Language Testing and Assessment, Encyclopedia of Language and Education*. Cham: Springer International Publishing.
Stiggins, R. (2017) *The Perfect Assessment System*. Alexandria, VA: The Association for Supervision and Curriculum Development (ASCD).

4 Methods

Source: L.L. Kopf. In Teaching about testing in K. Swope and B. Miner (eds) *Failing Our Kids: Why the Testing Craze Won't Fix Our Schools* (2000: 53). A Special Publication of Rethinking Schools Ltd., Milwaukee, Wisconsin.

THEMES FROM CHAPTER 4

(1) Selecting an appropriate method of assessment is directly related to aligning with the purpose of the assessment.
(2) Rubrics and checklists can be made easily from standards and criteria (purpose).
(3) Main categories of methods are one-to-one communication, written response, selected response and performance.
(4) Interviews, portfolios, storytelling and teacher observation are all very popular methods of assessment with multilingual learners (MLs). Which one you should use depends on your purpose.

Key Vocabulary

- Formative and summative assessments.
- Assessment for Learning (AfL).

- Four categories of methods: selected response, written response, performance and one-to-one communication.
- Four categories of modalities: one to group, one to one, group to group or self (examples: teacher to student, student to student or peer assessment, student to group, student to family or teacher to family).
- Peer and self-assessment (PASA).
- Content or language target.
- Oral interview.
- Portfolio.
- Role play.
- Rubric.
- Story retelling.
- Teacher observation.

PUMI Connection: Purpose, Method and Instrument

This chapter focuses on the M (Method) and I (Instrument) in PUMI. And, of course, you wouldn't know what method or instrument to use if you haven't articulated the P (Purpose). Identifying your target (purpose), picking the best method and creating or finding an instrument to support the assessment are integral ideas to good assessment. Readers are invited to explore a variety of methods and create checklists and rubrics to support the method chosen.

This chapter is designed to introduce the reader to the basics of selecting appropriate methods of assessment for MLs. Later in the chapter, popular methods of assessment are introduced, and examples are given showing specific language or content targets. When possible, share and discuss a rubric with students before the assessment takes place. The teacher decides what modality (one to group, one to one, group to group or to self) is best for each of the methods, depending on the individual needs of the students and class. Choosing self or peer assessment for modality shifts the 'agency' to the students and will also shift the classroom toward being less teacher centered (and more student centered).

Formative and Summative

There are two popular ways to use data, formatively (forming what students know) or summatively (summarizing what students know). Formative and summative assessment has to do with how we *use* the results of the assessment. Formative assessments (FAs) help us respond to the instructional needs of the student and can be thought of as the instructional steps we (both teacher and student) do after instruction occurs. Did my students comprehend the lesson? Does the teacher need to provide more support, like visuals or connections to home language and culture?

Summative assessments can also be important but may have been overvalued in the past, especially standardized tests that are mandated and not very useful for classroom instruction. On the other hand, FAs are where teachers can really impact student learning. According to Chappius and Stiggins (2016), the power of a FA lies in its ability to guide teacher and student actions, to keep learning on a successful track and to maintain student belief that success is within reach (Chappius & Stiggins, 2016). Put simply, after a student responds to an assessment, then the teacher provides feedback to nudge students along the continuum of learning, toward success. The feedback that teachers give students must be formative. This means that teachers should give feedback that is an appraisal of how the student performed in relation to the standard or criteria, as well as suggestions about how to move closer to achieving the standard or criteria. During FAs, the student has many opportunities to receive formative feedback, which may include feedback from the teacher, peer or self. After many opportunities for FA, then using assessment results for summative reasons is appropriate. Summative assessment should not happen too soon, allowing the student and teacher multiple opportunities to provide guidance and scaffolding for comprehension and opportunities to form as a teacher or learner. If too many summative assessments are given too soon, students will begin to feel anxious and lose motivation about assessments and school in general. Teachers in general need to make space for students to grow. See Table 4.1 for instructional questions to ask (as self-reflection for teachers) about formative and summative assessments.

It's easy to remember the difference between formative and summative assessment if you focus on the base words 'form' and 'sum'. Teachers use FAs to gather information in order to 'form' or shape student learning; another way to think about it is teachers are still 'forming' their professional judgment of what students can do. FA is ongoing and happens most often in classrooms and many times throughout the day.

It is increasingly common for districts to adopt and purchase benchmark assessments (otherwise known as interim or common assessments) to basically answer the question, 'which standards are my students struggling to master?'. The problems with benchmark assessments purchased from a mega-publisher like Pearson are many. For example, the content and language may include a disconnection with the home language and culture of the student; assessment methods may not be sensitive to linguistic levels; and these commercial benchmark assessments come with a very high price tag, which would be better spent if used to purchase literature relevant to the demographics of the school.

Table 4.1 Self-reflection questions for teachers regarding formative and summative assessment (the key difference is how you want to *use* the data)

Formative	Summative
What content standards are my students struggling with? Are they struggling with content or language or both? Do all of my students comprehend my instruction? How much?	How can I communicate student strengths during this quarter to parents?
If I provide closed caption translation and other translations into the home language, will this increase learning and motivation?	Are there certain standards all MLs are struggling with? Why? Language or content?
Am I providing appropriate scaffolding so that my student has access to content?	Which content standards have my students mastered and what grade should I give them?
What lesson comes next in my student's learning? What lesson will further the development of language? Content?	How do I best provide evidence of growth in two or more languages showing change over time?

Benchmarks, which are mini goals set to scaffold a student to reach an end goal, can guide FAs. Visualize a long walk (toward a goal) and stopping on a bench to rest and see how much farther there is to walk until the finish. Most assignments/assessments used in classrooms are meant to show how students are progressing toward language and content goals throughout the year. The results of FAs also help shape and form the teacher's instruction. Good FAs should lead to better summative outcomes. Summative assessments are intended to 'summarize' the progress of a program or a child after a long period of time such as a marking period or an academic year. Conversely, summative assessments often look like grades, final exam scores, regents tests, a research project or a language proficiency (LP) test score. Typically, test scores (summative) used for accountability purposes are of very little use if any to teachers/instruction. Teachers are required to do both, but both are more meaningful when embedded in classrooms and communities where culturally sustaining pedagogies (CSP) are supported (Paris & Alim, 2017). Culturally sustaining practices allow, invite and encourage students to not only use their cultural practices from home, in school, but also to maintain them. See Table 4.2 to better understand the difference between formative and summative assessment practices, which are best used within a CSP schooling environment.

Table 4.2 Examples of formative and summative assessment practices (this is aligned with how we *use* assessment results)

New York State Education Department requires all MLs to take the NYSESLAT every April.	Summative
A teacher finished a bilingual unit called 'What is a Family?' and needs to document a language arts score for report cards.	Summative
At the end of a lesson about transition words, a teacher and student must decide whether the lesson objectives have been met.	Formative
A teacher records a natural language sample and interprets these data to realize he needs to design targeted instruction on infinitives and future tense verb use.	Formative

How Should I Use FA Results?

The general goal of FA should be giving feedback to students. The feedback should focus directly on FA results and should lead students to understand where they are, relative to the language or content learning objective and what steps they can take to get closer to their learning goal. The feedback to give students should be descriptive and focus on the key attributes of their work and the content standard they are striving to meet. That way, students can understand where they are in relation to the content or language standard. The descriptive feedback that students receive should describe for them how to do better next time (examples of descriptive feedback are shown in Table 4.3). The descriptive feedback should also include time for revision. The descriptive feedback should also be used instead of grades or judgments being made (remember, you are forming your judgments in FAs, so don't make them yet). And ideally, it is appropriate to give examples of poor work and work that meets or exceeds the standard.

Table 4.3 How formative assessment results can motivate MLs, or not

Leads to promising schooling		Leads to deficit schooling
You answered all of the questions on the area of a triangle and rectangle correctly. لقد أجبت على جميع الأسئلة المتعلقة بمساحة المثلث والمستطيل بشكل صحيح. You knew that 8 + 8 = 20 was incorrect but you had some trouble writing the reason why. Try to write your response in your home language or English or tell me why you know this is incorrect. This will help you practice explaining your reasoning. You cited textual evidence to support your argument, but please cite at least two more. আপনি আপনার যুক্তি সমর্থন করার জন্য পাঠ্য প্রমাণ উদ্ধৃত করেছেন, কিন্তু অনুগ্রহ করে অন্তত আরও দুটি উদ্ধৃত করুন	Examples of descriptive feedback	You did that wrong. You cited textual evidence to support your argument, but please cite at least two more. Your grade is a C–. Your scores indicate that you fell below the English language arts (ELA) grade-level standards. You are a 'transitioning' student.
Calm feeling about school. Optimism. Desire to be present.	Effects this might have on the learner	Panic feeling about school. Hopelessness. Anxiety and fear of all assessment results.
I belong here. I can do this. I know what I need to do next. I can make sense of difficult content. I'm good at school. I know how to improve. Students like me are successful. My languages are a gift.	Thoughts the student might have based on formative feedback	I'll never learn English. I don't know what to do next. I'm so bad at English. I can't do this. I don't understand this test/results. This is so embarrassing. I don't feel safe/accepted here. I give up.
Volunteer to lead. Enjoy learning. Take responsibility for actions leading to meeting/exceeding standards. Ask for help.	Actions that might follow those thoughts	Hide from the teacher. Give up. Identify with failure. Avoid school and difficult academic tasks. Find easy things to do. Get by with minimum. Stay home.
Graduate high school. Strong sense of cultural/linguistic identity. Become a local leader for a mentor program. Graduate college. Achieve teacher certification for bilingual education. Become a bilingual teacher and serve as a role model.	Educational/life outcomes	Dislike of school. Tell your friends and family that school was never 'for you'. Just 'get by' in high school and tell yourself you are not smart enough to go to college. Accept a low paying, service-oriented job.

The feedback should model the use of key vocabulary targeted in the content area and encourage the use of two or more languages when meeting content goals. The full linguistic repertoire should be drawn from in order to access content and provide feedback. The use of translanguaging, especially in the content areas, should be a two-way street, broadening the breadth and depth of communication in the classroom, and at the same time highlighting the asset of being multilingual. This type of feedback on FAs allows students to have a clear pathway to success, plus it shifts responsibility to the students so that they can become an important agent of their school experience (self and peer assessment modalities are welcome here). Students should not have to guess at what success looks like; they should have a comprehensible pathway to success with a formative description about how far they are from success and steps to take to get there. The teacher becomes the facilitator of success and the student becomes the lead agent. An analogy for the clear pathway to success for formative assessment is the use of a GPS while driving across the United States from New York City to Cody, Washington. Suppose your phone dies and you no longer have a GPS guiding your way[1]; you may have feelings of hopelessness, not knowing how to get there, or what road to turn down. You might even wonder if and how to continue forward toward your goal of reaching Washington state without the assistance of a GPS. Just like most people need to 'see' a pathway using a GPS to successfully reach their destination, ML students need to see a clear pathway to academic success. With a GPS, we can see approximately how long it will take to reach our destination, choose multiple pathways, notifications of potential obstacles like traffic or construction (and suggestions of how to overcome them), recommended speed limit, etc. The process of formative assessment can offer similar clarity for students. The main idea behind Table 4.3 is that the quality of feedback that teachers give can have a lasting impact. When students are left to guess about how they are doing, this can result in deficit-type thoughts, actions and consequences. When students don't understand how to navigate the gap between where they are now and success, this leaves room for negative feelings like failure, self-doubt and anxiety. On the other hand, meaningful feedback that students can comprehend and act upon can lead to promising educational outcomes. Table 4.3 and this section was inspired by Chappius and Stiggins (2016).

Assessment for Learning

The term Assessment for Learning means supporting student growth by using the assessment process to keep them in touch with the development of their own academic capabilities as they learn. AfL can play a significant role in creating equity and the development of students who see themselves as lifelong learners (Heritage & Wylie, 2018). The effect of using an ongoing feedback system in AfL is to keep students believing that ultimate success is within reach if they keep trying (Chappius & Stiggins, 2016); therefore, the primary function of AfL is formative. Some teachers use the terms AfL and FA synonymously. Another acronym used in similar contexts is Assessment of Learning (AoL), which includes assessment methods used primarily for summative purposes. According to Chappius and Stiggins (2016), there are two different reasons we assess in schools: to support learning (AfL) or to report on the sufficiency of the learning (AoL), very similar to how formative and summative assessments were described in the previous section. Traditionally, schools have placed far greater emphasis on AoL and there is still a strong belief among educators that the primary purpose of classroom assessment is to generate a grade, when really the main purpose of teachers and where they can make the most impact, is with AfL. We use assessment results to assign grades, yes, but there are hundreds of other ways to use assessment results.

Further, AfL doesn't require additional tasks or tests but is an integral part of teaching and learning and can be enacted through the usual lesson activities (Britton, 2021). After an extensive literature review on the definition of AfL and FA, Britton (2021) decided that for pragmatic purposes, AfL and FA can be used interchangeably, and that complicating assessment discussions by trying to differentiate between AfL and FA might distract from what is truly at the heart of AfL: the for-learning purpose of assessment (Britton, 2021). Developing teacher knowledge in AfL is an important consideration for implementing AfL. Chappius and Stiggins (2016) categorize AfL into three categories that are easy to understand: (1) Where am I going? (2) Where am I now? and (3) How can I close the gap?

Similarly, Heritage (2018) articulates specific features of co-regulations that demonstrate/lead to AfL:

(1) Goal orientation – a focus on learning to be achieved.
(2) Scaffolding – the assistance the teacher provides to achieve a goal that is currently beyond the student's unassisted efforts.
(3) Intersubjectivity – a shared understanding based on a common focus of attention.
(4) The active construction of knowledge by students, rather than the transference of knowledge from teacher to student.
(5) Temporary support, provided through scaffolding and the extended supports that students can ultimately appropriate as their own.

As the previous section provides examples for using assessment results in formative or summative ways, some assessment methods lend themselves to summative or formative uses. The way we use results determines if it is formative or summative, not the assessment method. Table 4.4 demonstrates how formative and summative assessments can be used for either formative or summative purposes.

Table 4.4 Examples of methods of assessment that can be used in formative or summative ways

Formative assessment	Summative assessment
Anecdotal records	Selected response items
Observation with rubric	Observation with rubric
Performance with rubric	Performance with rubric
Questioning	Portfolio

Note: Many assessment methods can be used in both categories.

Assessment Methods Used in the Sheltered Instruction Observation Protocol (SIOP) Model Assessment Component

The SIOP has been a popular model in the United States for delivering content and language instruction in English. Translanguaging strategies can be and should be used in the sheltered English environment as a key component of delivering high-quality instruction and assessment. We tend to focus on sheltered instruction, but really we are focusing on sheltered instruction and assessment. Visualize a person seeking shelter from the rain using an umbrella – the teacher provides the 'umbrella' to protect or shelter the student from not comprehending the lesson. The general rule in assessment is whatever we shelter for instruction, we must also shelter for assessment. Table 4.5 lists fun interactive SIOP strategies (techniques) used by many teachers to deliver sheltered assessment. The techniques for assessment in a sheltered environment are drawn from the SIOP model (Vogt & Echevarría, 2008, 2022; Vogt *et al.*, 2015). An effort is made in Table 4.5 to suggest multilingual ways to use these assessments, even if the teacher is not multilingual.

In General, How are Methods Broadly Categorized?

This section is mostly written for readers who like categories. The introduction of these categories is meant to increase understanding of assessment methods. However, if this section is confusing, please skip to the next section of this chapter. There is no crystal-clear way to categorize assessment methods broadly. For the purposes of this book, all methods will be placed loosely into four categories. It is less important to know what category of assessment method you are using than to pick an appropriate individual method. Each example from Table 4.6 is listed so that you can see how these categories work. Table 4.6 shows how to begin aligning assessment methods while lesson planning.

(1) **Selected response: Any method where a student has to choose from predetermined responses** (no examples in Table 4.6, but true/false and multiple choice are popular methods).
(2) **Written response: Any method where a student has to write the response** (example method: essay with rubric, written short responses).
(3) **Performance assessment: Any method where a student is doing, completing or performing something, action oriented** (example methods: reading, speaking, oral presentation, observation with checklist, anecdotal records, think aloud with rubric).
(4) **One-to-one communication: Any method where the student and teacher, for example, are working together one to one** (example methods: discussion with rubric, interview, questioning).

What's Your Purpose?

If you want to hit the bull's eye, you need to know exactly what the target is. The single most important concept in assessing MLs is to have a clear purpose for the assessment. For example, if a teacher is using a story retell as an assessment method, the purpose could vary greatly. The purpose could be a variety of things such as (1) to assess reading – focus on reading cues; (2) to assess oral language – focus on speech output; or (3) to assess a certain skill such as using the present tense – focus on oral language form, or other measurable factors. Good assessment practice requires knowing your purpose and sharing it with students before the assessment begins. Purpose can also be called targets, achievement targets, language targets, standards, anchors or objectives, among other terms.

Each state has an approved set of standards to which schools must adhere. These standards dictate what content targets teachers are required to use; these come in the form of knowledge and associated processes such as analyzing, producing, constructing, reasoning, defining, developing and using. To develop language targets for instruction and assessment, educators use the required set of Language Proficiency

Table 4.5 Low-tech and interactive techniques for assessment from the SIOP model

Name of assessment technique	Category or method of assessment	Modality	Notes on multilingue use
Share Bear: In small groups the student with the stuffed bear answers the open-ended question posed by the teacher. Then the bear is passed to another student and they answer an open-ended question.	Performance assessment (oral language)	Student-to-group assessment	Teachers can look for patterns in language use to design new instruction. Can be used to assess oral language objectives and content. For pre-K to Grade 2. Teachers can encourage mixed language answers for a full view of language skills.
Numbers 1–3 for self-assessment of objectives: This is a quick and easy way for students to self-assess the degree to which they think they met the objective. The teacher articulates the learning objectives (content or language) and at the end of the lesson, the students assess how they did when compared to the learning objective.	Teacher observation Performance assessment	Self-assessment	1 = I didn't meet the objective; 2 = I didn't meet the objective but made progress toward it; and 3 = I fully met the objective. At the end of the lesson, students hold up 1, 2 or 3 fingers. The teacher can ask students to explain and use this information to plan new instruction. Encourage explanations in any language. For self-assessment especially with older children, they can tell you exactly what they are struggling with. Saves time and energy to use self-assessment, in some cases.
Find someone who: Students are given a review sheet with content-based questions and circulate around the room finding students who can answer the questions on the sheet. Walk around the room circulating until all answers are completed.	One-to-one communication Written response	Peer assessment	They approach each other and ask a content review question. If a student knows the answer, she writes it down and signs her initials. Each student may give information to no more than one question on another student's paper. Students may seek out other students who share the same home language.
Response boards: Boards can be laminated file folders or paper in plastic sleeve or store-bought whiteboards. One board per pair or small group.	Performance assessment Written response	Small group to whole class	Teacher poses a question and the pair or small group conferences on the answer. Students can hold up or stand up with response board and explain their answer. The teacher can assess whether students are ready to move on to more content. A student can explain in their home language, say Bengali, and another bilingual student in the class can translate for non-Bengali speakers in the class.
Find the Fib: Sometimes called Two Truths and a Lie. The teacher reads three statements and the students identify which one is the lie.	Performance assessment	Whole class to teacher	Allows the teacher to assess understanding of content. Students work alone, in pairs or small groups. Use fingers or cards to identify the 'fib'. The cards should read '1 is the fib', '2 is the fib' and '3 is the fib'. This type of selected response doesn't require language output.
Mystery Word: This is to review vocabulary previously used. Students will try to guess the mystery words by listening to clues. Gives clues one at a time.	Performance assessment	Whole class to teacher	Students stand up when they know the mystery word (and should write the mystery word on a dry erase board). Call on one student, then move on to next word. Another version of this is 'vo-back-ulary' where a student stands with her back to the rest of the class and an index card with the mystery word is taped to her back. One student gives her clues about the mystery word. Word banks can be available for scaffolding. The teacher can use a translator application speaker (like Google Translate) to translate clues (this creates meaning and comprehension), but target words can remain in English (or other target language).

(Continued)

Table 4.5 (Continued)

Name of assessment technique	Category or method of assessment	Modality	Notes on multilingual use
Bingo[a]: Have students fold a piece of paper into nine equal pieces (fold in three, then in three again). Students write nine predetermined content words in any spaces so each student has a unique bingo board.	Selected response	Whole class to teachers	Make a master sheet with clues for definitions to read to the students. Be careful not to make the clues too easy. Read the clues. To win, students need three in a row. Winner yells 'bingo'. Check answers. You can ask the winner to explain some of her answers. Continue playing to find the next winner. Assess content. Encourage clarification of clues in home language.
Dice Talk: Partners. Give handout with six questions. Allow students to skim through the questions and answer stems/word bank first. Partners take turns rolling the dice and one asks the question and the student rolling the dice answers. Switch.	Teacher observation One-to-one communication	Peer	Scaffolding can be used with sentence frames. Take turns rolling, asking and answering questions.

Source: Vogt and Echevarria (2008, 2022) and Vogt et al. (2015).
Note: All of these can have multilingual components.
[a]Mahoney's favorites.

Table 4.6 Sample lesson plan considerations: Pick an appropriate method

	Select key practices from core standards	Methods of assessments to consider and why
ELA	Analyze complex texts	*Discussion with rubric* because this allows the students to think aloud and the teacher to document analysis of text.
	Produce clear and coherent writing	*Essay with rubric* because this generates a writing sample and the rubric can articulate clarity and coherence.
	Construct arguments	*Graphic organizer with checklist* because students can practice building arguments visually and the checklist will guide students and teachers into building a solid argument.
Math	Solve problems	*Observation with checklist* because it is most authentic to watch students solve a problem. Questioning and think-aloud methods also work very well for assessing problem-solving.
	Reason abstractly	*Think aloud with rubric* because students can think aloud to express reasoning. Written responses (if writing proficiency is available) with rubric also work well.
	Use appropriate tools	*Observation with checklist* because it is most authentic to watch students use appropriate tools.
Science	Ask questions	*Anecdotal records* because scientific questions will emerge naturally throughout the learning process. Self-assessment using a rubric can guide students to ask better questions and more frequently.
	Define problems	*Written response with rubric* because students will define problems based on real-world factors. Questioning or oral presentation of problems provides nice scaffolding for key principle.
	Analyze and interpret data	*Graphic organizers (table, figure, etc.) with checklist* because the graphics will assist the teacher to focus student work on analysis and interpretation. Short oral or written responses can help assess interpretation of data.

(LP) standards chosen by your area. In your LP standards, language targets should represent communicative activities such as language use (student and teacher) and language tasks, as well as different modalities and registers of the classroom (Valdés & Lee, 2013). The English language proficiency (ELP) standards[2] in your area should articulate an academic discourse quite different from everyday discourse to allow teachers to focus on content and language targets toward school success. Some states or regions do not adopt LP standards; they use the content standards to identify linguistic demands – these demands become language targets. With academic standards, it is recognized that MLs must have access to core standards from the first day of school. An assumption that most educators of MLs know (but is perhaps not known to others) is that MLs can master content before they acquire native-like performance in English. There is no need to wait for students to develop English fully before teaching rigorous content.

To view standards more conceptually, career- and college-ready standards cover a small fraction of the total universe of content and language. Having said that, the language and content targets suggested in this book represent the content and language that educators are accountable for – the required content and language in schools today. The language targets of your area LP standards should reflect the language expectations and underlying language practices embedded within the state content standards. Keep in mind that content and language targets found in standards documents are not representative of all; hidden/suppressed discourses, socio-emotional, family interests, translanguaging and other important targets are rarely included in these documents but are still critically important.

Home languages are not included in the state-level standards, but educators should not underestimate the importance of knowing where (assessing) a child is in his or her home language and how this can be used for promising practices in the classroom.

SNAPSHOT: HOW MUCH HOME LANGUAGE LITERACY?

Mrs Caruso is a fifth-grade teacher who has new students from the Dominican Republic, Puerto Rico, Burma and Bangladesh. Her district has conducted many English assessments but no home language assessments, and Mrs Caruso wants to know where students are with their home language writing ability because she wants to design some instruction to transfer writing ability from the home language to the new language plus study the languages side by side. Assessing the home language will also allow her to use a variety of translanguaging strategies. She also wants to know if any of her students are not able to write in their home language because she will refer to a specialized framework[3] for students with low home language literacy. Mrs Caruso knows Spanish but has to find people who know Karen and Bengali. A writing assessment can be very authentic, is not very time-consuming and can help guide teachers in explaining how students are responding to the curriculum and instruction in their class. The General Home Language Writing Assessment Rubric can be used as a stand-alone general measure of home language literacy, or combined with another test of home language to see if the results match (and confirm valid results). A quick PUMI study shows this (Table 4.7).

Table 4.7 General home language writing assessment rubric

P (Purpose)	U (Use)	M (Methods)	I (Instrument)
To assess writing ability in home language.	To assist instruction (can the teacher use the home language to help teach English and content?)	Written response.	Prompts, rubric.
	To help decide if a special framework or program may be necessary to provide appropriate programming, early.		

Teacher prompts: Ask students to write either (1) a memory they have of a special person in their lives (encourage students to write the steps of the story first using a timeline or other graphic organizer) or (2) an informative text about their life in their home country (give students ideas about what they might include, such as information on food, clothing, holiday traditions, school, free time and activities, friends and family and home).

Student name:		Grade:		Date:
Criteria	4	3	2	1
Response to prompt	Student fully responds to writing prompt given.	Student mostly responds to writing prompt given.	Student vaguely responds to writing prompt given.	No response given.

Student name:		Grade:		Date:
Criteria	4	3	2	1
Details in writing	There are details to support and enhance the response.	There are some details to support and enhance the response.	There are few details to support and enhance the response.	There are no details to support and enhance the response.
Organization	Response is well organized.	Response is somewhat organized.	Response is poorly organized.	Response is not organized.
Mechanics of writing	There are less than six errors in spelling and that distract the reader from the content.	There are less than six errors in spelling and grammar that distract the reader from content.	There are less than eight errors in spelling and grammar that distract the reader from the content.	There are eight or more errors in spelling and grammar that distract the reader from the content.
Use of transition words	Student uses transition words to create a cohesive writing piece.	Student uses one or two transition words to create a cohesive writing piece.	Student does not use transition words, but sentences follow a somewhat logical sequence.	Response is disjointed. Sentences do not follow logical sequence. No transition words used.
Total score (out of 20)		Comments:		
Writing fluency				
16–20		Average LOTE home literacy		
13–16		Low home literacy. Needs this framework		
8–12		Low home literacy. Certainly needs this framework		
5–7		Very low home literacy. Needs an intensive program		

This General Home Language Reading Assessment Rubric can be found in a book called A CUNY-NYSIEB FRAMEWORK for the Education of Emergent Bilinguals with low home literacy: 4–12 grades García,O., Herrera, L., Hesson, S., and Kleyn, T. (https://www.cuny-nysieb.org/wp-content/uploads/2016/05/CUNY-NYSIEB-Framework-for-EB-with-Low-Home-Literacy-Spring-2013-Final-Version-05-08-13.pdf). The rubric can be found in Appendix A.

Discussion questions

- How does Mrs Caruso use PUMI to decide if this assessment is appropriate for her students?
- How will Mrs Caruso use the results of the assessment to improve instruction for MLs?

Some Assessment Methods Highlighted

Whether teachers are selecting assessments from prescribed curriculum or designing their own, keep these key principles in mind.

(1) Make sure the assessment method is appropriate for the purpose of the assessment (this represents the P and M in PUMI – it is integral to the assessment that the purpose and method are aligned. This step requires teacher judgement).

(2) Use multiple assessments and make sure that multiple points of evidence are saying the same thing before making any big decisions about the target (like student achievement).
(3) The assessment must be of high quality. That means the items are written straightforward and in a way that students will understand them. And yes, teachers have a right to review test items and have a say. Same for scoring.
(4) Be on the lookout for and minimize/protect students from sources of bias, especially biases based on the amount of and language they know.

The following sections highlight assessment methods that have been very popular over the years. The purpose of this section is to introduce the reader to ML-friendly assessment methods; however, specific targets are not given. And really, a method such as interview could possibly have 100+ different purposes. The first five methods (interview, retelling, portfolio, teacher observation, role play) are typically used as instruction and assessment practices leading to promise, which is to say that they embrace student-centered participation in authentic contexts. In addition to selecting the method, the role of the educator is to use his or her expertise to select modality, content and language objectives, appropriate differentiation, classroom methods, non-academic targets, and to make instruction and assessment culturally relevant to the particular class.

Interview or questioning (one-to-one communication)

This method is categorized as one-to-one communication because it requires the interaction of two people to complete it. This method is considered by many to be authentic because interviewing someone is an authentic experience (it will really happen throughout one's life in a variety of contexts). Within this method of assessment, educators can ask questions (input) and evaluate answers from MLs (output). Such interviews can be time-consuming because they are administered one on one. Questions to ask might depend on the level of English or home language and could include: What is your family like? What is your favorite activity with friends? Do you like English? Do you like school? Tell me about your experience on the first day of school. What is the easiest part of school for you? What is difficult about school? These questions can lead to further questions, yielding a high-quality, authentic language sample to assess (depending on your purpose), not to mention a deeper understanding of factors that affect second language acquisition such as motivation and experience with English. The purpose of an interview could be to measure motivation, to measure attitude, to measure speaking complexity (among others). Educators can assess while the child is speaking, immediately following the interview, or the interview can be recorded and assessed later. Interviews can be conducted in the new or home language and in the following modalities: teacher to student, student to student (peer assessment), student to family or teacher to family.

Tables 4.8 and 4.9 show two examples of how educators might use the method of interviewing to measure two distinct purposes. Table 4.8 is an example of using interview to measure speaking complexity and Table 4.9 is an example of using interview to measure language use in content area.

Table 4.8 Example of using an interview to measure speaking complexity

P	U	M	I
To assess speaking (complexity).	To design appropriate instruction for content areas.	Interview (one-to-one communication).	Interview prompts. Rubric.

Interview questions	
	Who is in your family?
	What do you do with friends?
	Tell me about your experience on the first day of school. How did you feel?
	What is the easiest part of school for you? Do you like English?
	What is difficult about school?

Rubric below: After reviewing student responses to the questions above, put an X through the box

Level 1	Level 2	Level 3	Level 4	Level 5
Single words, short phrases, chunks of memorized speech.	Speaks with short sentences or phrases.	Speaks with expanded sentences or phrases. Responses show some detail.	Speaks with a variety of sentence lengths with varying complexity. Speech is emerging as clear and cohesive.	Extended discourse – organized and supported with details.

Table 4.9 Example of a math interview to measure language used for academic purposes in math

P	U	M	I
To assess communication during math.	To design appropriate language objectives for instruction.	Interview (one-to-one communication).	Interview prompts, checklist.

Interview questions: These questions are designed to measure the language used for academic purposes in math during a unit on triple digit subtraction using exchanges. The student has a set of base 10 blocks and has been asked to solve two problems. This interview takes place after the student has had time to solve the problem. (Note: Some may call this assessment method questioning.)

	Tell me about how you solved your problem. What steps did you take?
	Is this a good solution?
	Why is this a good solution?
	Now explain to me in words why this is a good solution.
	How are these two problems similar and how are they different?
	Can you show me on paper how to solve these two problems?

Checklist for language used for academic purposes (*answer yes or no*)

	Summarizes steps taken to find a solution.
	Uses sequential language to describe steps in solution in a logical order.
	Uses formal math terms (exchange, subtract, trade, tens, ones, etc.) and symbolic notation to defend her solution.
	Describes similarities and differences between two problems.
	Gives evidence to support/defend solution.

Table 4.10 shows an actual interview between a teacher and a student, about his interests in schooling. The student is from Puerto Rico and was enrolled in an 'English-only' program. The results of this interview provide evidence for the teacher to introduce translanguaging pedagogy, or at least provide access to the

Table 4.10 Informal interview with Roberto

Teacher question	Student response
What is your favorite subject?	I like science, it is my favorite.
Do you like math class?	It is okay, sometimes it is really hard for me. I like when we go to the computer lab.
What is difficult for you in math class?	There are a lot of numbers and sometimes I don't know what to do. It is hard when the questions are long and you have to do a lot of things. Sometimes I forget what the questions want me to do.
What could I do to help you in math?	Um I don't know. Sometime it helps me when I can talk to Yolanda or Maeva in Spanish, but we aren't supposed to use Spanish. I like English better, but sometimes I don't know what the question wants me to do. It helps me when I can ask questions.
Did you like math class in Puerto Rico? Can you teach me how to say some of these words in Spanish?	No, I don't like math class in Puerto Rico. I liked science and playing soccer. I know how to say these in Spanish, but I'm not supposed to talk in Spanish.

math content by translating the directions into Spanish (audio and written). A more holistic and promising view of Roberto is necessary to prevent thoughts and the effects of hopelessness and deficit. Interviews can provide powerful insight into what a learner is experiencing.

Story retelling (performance)

What is authentic about assessments? This method is considered authentic because storytelling is familiar to many students in some form from a young age. Talking or speaking can be categorized as performing, or performance assessment. MLs read or listen to text and then retell the main ideas and some details. This type of assessment usually has two purposes: (1) to assess something in English language arts (ELA) and (2) to assess something in ELP. Through story retelling, educators can assess a variety of targets, like how the student describes the events in a story (ELA), or assess signifiers such as fluency, grammar or tense usage (ELP). For ELP, the language functions used to retell a story usually include summarizing, describing details and giving information. Story retelling, along with other performance and one-to-one communication, provides ample opportunity for translanguaging, even if the teacher does not know the home language. For example, students can retell a story and create a short audio recording in the home language retelling the story. Students can retell the story in Spanish, for example, then retell in English. Alternatively, students can retell the story to one another in their home language and then retell in English. To make the assessment more culturally relevant, have the child retell a personal story or one that is popular in his or her family or community. If your purpose is to assess oral language proficiency the actual story choice does not matter, but will yield more valid results if it is culturally relevant.

The general directions for a story retell are to read the story to the child or play a recorded reading of the story. Ask the child to retell the story, but avoid having it feel like an interview – one of the true strengths of a story retell is the opportunity that the student is given to talk. The teacher documents the assessment by using a rubric or checklist. This method of assessment can be easily aligned with a standard like the one in Table 4.11.

Table 4.11 A speaking and listening standards K–5

Presentation of knowledge and ideas: Grade 3

(1) Report on a topic or text, tell a story or recount an experience with appropriate facts and *relevant, descriptive details, speaking clearly at an understandable pace.*

Example checklist used with story retelling

P	U	M	I
To assess ability to tell a story.	To guide instruction.	Story retell (performance).	Story, checklist.

Checklist

	Student initiates.	*Responds to teacher prompt.*	*Comments or details.*
Important factors in story retelling:			
Uses chronological order to recall events.			
Identifies major events.			
Uses appropriate and relevant facts from the story.			
Uses details to describe main character.			
Uses details to describe setting.			

Portfolio assessment (may include all or a mix of assessment methods)

Portfolios are sometimes misunderstood as one assessment method. Portfolio assessment may include a *profile* of assessment methods and therefore does not fall into only one category of methods. It may contain a mix of selected response, written response, performance assessment and one-to-one communication. Traditionally, portfolios are associated with the arts; the word evokes the image of artists carrying their best work in a portfolio to demonstrate their talents. However, a portfolio can be created and maintained for any student to showcase growth through time and a whole body of work. Usually, it contains samples of student work, selected by the student and the teacher systematically and purposefully to show evidence that the student is learning core standards. Unlike a single test score that documents one point in time, the portfolio is multidimensional and charts student growth across multiple points throughout the school year; it can therefore reveal much more about what students can actually do. The teacher uses the portfolio to integrate the results of individual assessments and make instructional decisions based on this evidence. The key is to make portfolio building an important part of instructional time and to make students the agents of their own assessments.

In the digital age, portfolios can be much more compact; they might be digital with audio and video components, or they can be presented in a simple three-ring binder with plastic sleeves to organize and hold the content. For an example of digital portfolios built around the theme of Howard Gardner's multiple intelligences, see the work of Evangeline Stefanakis (2002) also in the Recommended Readings section at the end of the chapter.

Getting started with a portfolio entails the following steps, remarkably similar to PUMI: (1) articulate the purpose of the portfolio; (2) articulate how the results of the portfolio will be used; (3) set criteria (usually content and ELP standards selected by state) and pick or make tools in the form of checklists or rubrics to help document the criteria; and (4) review the contents to make sure they match Purpose and Use. It is very common to have a portfolio that addresses both language and content goals, as well as other goals.

One strength of the portfolio is that it supports a holistic classroom in which instruction is student centered, meaningful and authentic. Teachers may choose to allow students to select the contents of the portfolio and also take part in evaluating their own work. The act of self-assessment is critical; many educators believe that it is important to allow students to be active learners who construct their own knowledge, set their own goals and check their own progress. Most teachers who practice portfolio as assessment report that students become more responsible about their learning. One way in which MLs can reflect on their own work is to ask them to review their work and set some goals to improve it. The feedback can be combined with peer and teacher assessment to show three points of view of the student's work. See Table 4.12 for suggestions for self-assessment.

Table 4.12 Suggested questions for portfolio self-assessment

Look at your writing sample that describes important characters from the story called 'Father Hawk' and answer the following questions:
(1) What did you do well in this writing sample?
(2) What do you need to do better?
(3) Write one thing you will do better when writing the next draft.

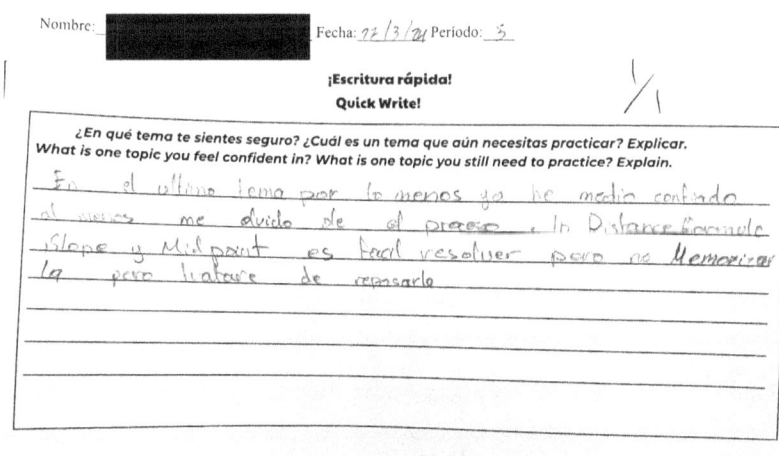

Figure 4.1 The combination of self assessment and translanguaging can reveal a lot about what students know. This is a 10th grade student from Integrated Geometry class in Brooklyn, NY. (Source: Gabrielle Bonello for the image and assessment idea)

The teachers switched from English-only Quick Writes to using translanguaging in Quick Writes because the students were always translanguaging in class; they explain things to each other and discuss Mathematics concepts using English and home language, so it just made sense to the teachers to switch from English-only.

This roughly translates like this: *In the last topic at least I feel a little confident at least I forget about the process. In **distance formula**, *slope* and **midpoint** it is easy to resolve but not to memorize it but I will try to review it".*

This student used Spanish language proficiency and English mathematical terms to show what he knows. This also demonstrates how students will learn new vocabulary in the language they are taught. Assessments like this Quick Write is a great scaffold to allow students who are still developing English to access and develop in Mathematics. Instead of spending so much money and time on assessments to find out what students know, why not ask them? They know. Self-assessment is a powerful assessment tool.

Another powerful aspect of the portfolio as assessment is its direct alignment with instruction. Usually, the portfolio assessment process includes a conference between the teacher and the child and perhaps a presentation to parents. MLs can prepare for the conference by completing some reflective questions, as shown in Table 4.13.

Table 4.13 Suggested questions to prepare for the portfolio conference

Please review your entire portfolio.
(1) What does this portfolio tell about you as a student in English and math?
(2) What are you good at? Where is evidence of this in the portfolio?
(3) What goals will you continue to work on?

Margo Gottlieb and Diep Nguyen (2007) describe a pivotal portfolio that has worked well in dual and transitional bilingual education programs. The pivotal portfolio is a hybrid of both a working portfolio (contains work in progress) and the showcase portfolio (contains display of best work), with three main distinctions: in the pivotal portfolio, each teacher gathers what the teachers collectively consider evidence of essential student learning and achievement; all of the teachers use common assessments of that essential student work; and it follows the student for the length of his or her career in the language education program. In fact, in Schaumburg School District 54, this portfolio follows each student from year to year and becomes the student's graduation present at the end of eighth grade. For more detail on this particular model and on portfolios, see Gottlieb and Nguyen (2007).

Figure 4.2 shows a rubric for a poetry portfolio from Adelman Reyes and Kleyn's (2010) book *Teaching in 2 Languages: A Guide for K-12 Bilingual Educators*. The authors warn that although portfolios are relatively common, the danger is that they turn into nothing more than a folder of mandated assignments, rather than a collection of work that students select which showcases their progress and learning over time. Figure 4.2 is an example of a rubric used to assess a poetry anthology that connected the genre of poetry with the topic of identity (Adelman Reyes & Kleyn, 2010).

Language portfolio

The language portfolio has been developed in Europe over the past 10 years, with each country creating its own versions, accredited by the Council of Europe (Celic & Seltzer, 2012). Celic and Seltzer review the language portfolio and offer links and directions on how to create a language portfolio in your class, or even school- or district-wide. The language portfolio is an example of how to encourage

	4–Exceptional	3–Proficient	2–Developing	1–Beginning
Content	Student has written more than 5 poems. They may include • 1 identity poem • 1 family poem • 1 culture experience poem • 1 object poem • 2 or more poems of his or her choice	Student has written 5 poems. They may include • 1 identity poem • 1 family poem • 1 culture experience poem • 1 object poem • 1 poems of his or her choice	Student has written 3 or 4 poems. They may include • 1 identity poem • 1 family poem • 1 culture experience poem • 1 object poem • 2 poems of his or her choice	Student has written 1 or 2 poems. They may include • 1 identity poem • 1 family poem • 1 culture experience poem • 1 object poem • 1 poem of his or her choice
	Poems have many poetic elements, including metaphors and similes	Poems have some poetic elements. including metaphors and similes	Student attempts to use poetic elements, including metaphors and similes	Poems do not have any poetic elements, including metaphors and similes
	Poems include many concrete and sensory images	Poems include some concrete and sensory images	Student attempts to include concrete and sensory images	Poems do not include any concrete and sensory images
	Student's identity is clearly reflected throughout all poems	Student's identity is clearly reflected in most poems	Student attempts to reflect identity through poems	Student's identity is not reflected through poems
Process	All steps of the writing process are turned in: draft, revisions, and final copy	Most steps of the writing process are turned in: draft, revisions, and final copy	Some steps of the writing process are missing	Few steps of the writing process were followed
	Student edited paper independently and with partner	Student edited paper with help from teacher	Student relied on teacher to edit work	Student did little or no editing

Figure 4.2 A rubric for a poetry portfolio (topic identity)

(Source: Created by Elizabeth Silva, Surky Mateo, Jaqueline Rodríguez and Wenn Siak. From Adelman Reyes, S. and Kleyn, T. (eds) *Teaching in 2 Languages: A Guide for K-12 Bilingual Educators*. Thousand Oaks, CA: Corwin Press. Reproduced with permission)

an environment that celebrates languages and cultures and also raises multicultural competence for all students. Students keep the language portfolio with them as they proceed through grade levels. The language portfolio has three sections: language biography – to record experiences emphasizing intercultural understandings; language passport – includes rubrics and checklists to document what students know and can do in different languages; and language dossier – where multilingual academic work is showcased and includes setting future goals. Canada also uses a portfolio-based language assessment (PBLA) aligned with Canadian language benchmarks (CLB) to replace standardized language assessments and also recognize the language proficiency of adult immigrants (language.ca/resourcesexpertise/on-pbla/).

Teacher observation (performance assessment)

Since the teacher is observing students 'performing' something, teacher observation is categorized as a performance assessment. Teacher observation is an assessment method used by all teachers, but not all teachers consider it a 'serious' method. Whether teaching young children or college students, all good teachers will change their instruction – perhaps even mid-lesson – based on what they observe the students to be doing. For example, if a teacher sees that most of the students are off-task and unsure about how to start an activity, he or she will adjust the instruction by modeling the directions better, or by having a student paraphrase the instructions for a second time, using the home language. The teacher continues to observe and make instructional decisions based on what he or she sees. The following Spanish as a second language (SSL) rubric (Table 4.14) was created by faculty in a dual language program to create an assessment using teacher observation to document performance in SSL from K–6 (Gottlieb & Nguyen, 2007). Table 4.14 shows the rubric for first grade only as an example of observation as an assessment method. However, the full K–6 checklist can be found in Gottlieb and Nguyen (2007: 202).

Role play (performance assessment)

Since students are acting out to demonstrate something, role play is categorized as performance assessment. Role play as a pedagogic tool can be used to engage and motivate learners as well as support the language learning process (Courtney, 2019). Look for opportunities during role play to assess language or content. Checklists and rubrics can be used to document the results of role play. Role play is often overlooked but can be quite valuable as an assessment method with MLs due to its reliance on physical movement and comprehension (other versions of role play are sometimes referred to as improvisations or simulations). Role play invites students to speak or act through the identity of others. This type of dramatic activity can make the classroom an exciting place. At the same time, it can provide an authentic context for students to learn language and content, and for teachers to assess it. When preparing a lesson, survey the whole lesson to see if there are opportunities to role play (ORP[4]). Almost every lesson offers ORPs, yet ORPs in instruction and assessment are underutilized. For example, students can act out the problems and needs of their community in a human rights lesson, or a dinner party with Beyoncé, Bad Bunny, Cardi B and Lady Gaga for a language arts lesson. If you are teaching New York state history, role play (host) a meeting between Seneca Indian President George Heron and US President John F. Kennedy to discuss an alternate location for the Kinzua Dam that would not flood ancestral lands, for example. The students then study their role and dramatize an event. Role play offers an authentic setting for MLs to practice natural language use, such as facial expressions, hesitations and repetitions. In addition, many important language functions can be practiced during role play, such as

Table 4.14 Example of first-grade Spanish as a second language (SSL) checklist (Beginning, Developing and Secure are three levels of performance)

P	U	M	I
To measure SSL development overtime.	To evaluate and show the effects of dual language program to parents and administrators.	Observation (performance assessment).	Checklist.

Checklist			
Oral performance indicators	Beginning	Developing	Secure
Initiates, responds to greetings appropriately for time of day.			
Uses familiar phrases and simple sentences in appropriate context.			
Lists vocabulary words according to specific categories.			
Actively participates in routine oral language activities (songs, shared reading, calendar, daily routine).			
Reading performance indicators			
Recognizes the letters and sounds of the Spanish alphabet.			
Demonstrates interest in Spanish books.			
Reads aloud controlled vocabulary with understanding (colors, numbers, etc.).			
Reads aloud simple picture books and matches text to picture with teacher guidance in order to demonstrate comprehension.			
Actively participates in shared reading and demonstrates comprehension by retelling in English.			
Uses cognates to guess meaning of words.			
Demonstrates comprehension of key vocabulary from a story with prompting.			
Writing performance indicators			
Writes short familiar phrases and sentences using sentence starters.			
Spells familiar words correctly in writing activities (journal, dictation).			
Grammar usage performance indicators			
Uses the present tense in the following verbs in the first-person singular (estar, ser, tener, ir, gustar).			
Vocabulary knowledge performance indicators	0–20 words	20–35 words	35–50 words
Demonstrates comprehension and usage of new core, targeted vocabulary words.			

Source: Adapted with permission from Gottlieb and Nguyen (2007) © Caslon, Inc. All rights reserved.

agreeing/disagreeing, giving or evaluating an opinion, persuading and so on. It also offers an authentic situation to use translanguaging and home languages to increase meaning and comprehension. According to Courtney (2019), it is clear that data from role play tasks can provide a window into the linguistic development of learners. It is also possible to focus on only one aspect of language development such as vocabulary or verb tense. Teachers and/or students can record role plays to return to the recording again for possible focus on language or content targets.

To get started with role play, as with all assessments, identify the purpose. Allow students time to practice their roles. Make sure any reading or cue cards are at the students' level. Differentiate the activity by language level – for example, more advanced students will agree/disagree and evaluate, while beginner students will be cued to ask simple questions or supply one or two word utterances to the other players. Before using role play as an assessment, be sure that the students have sufficient time to practice in school. If the purpose is to assess oral language skills, a rubric or checklist can be used to systematically document the assessment. Share the rubric to help students prepare for the assessment. Videotaping the role play is another way to allow for self-assessment or peer assessment. This method of assessment can align with content standards.

Table 4.15 shows a popular rubric used for some role play assessments in history. Don't forget to use the same supports (scaffolds) for MLs in assessments that are used in instruction. Table 4.15 shows a rubric with the purpose of measuring history content and presentation skills; however, the purpose may also be to measure speaking skills in history class by simply changing the purpose (and content) of the rubric. In summary, teachers tend to think of role play as appropriate in early childhood, but this author sees the applicability of role play with older adolescents and young adults, using a culturally relevant topic for role play.

Standardized test (selected response)

Selected response means just that – someone writes a list of **responses** and you have to **select** the right one (usually there is only one *right* answer). Most textbooks do not talk much about standardized tests as a method of assessment for MLs, but the stark reality is that they are very high stakes, used often and regularly. The reason selected response methods are used so much is because of the large number of students tested in annual state, national and sometimes international assessments, the costs of test development and scoring are high. The most efficient/economical assessment method for these large-scale groups is selected response (for example, they can be quickly scored by a machine). Keep in mind that these may be the most economical, but not the most valid or appropriate method. Because selected response is not good at measuring things like reasoning or problem-solving, or metalinguistic awareness, for example, assessments made of only or mostly selected response are severely limited in content, language and other learning targets. This limitation is simple to understand, yet school leaders continue to place 'high stakes' on the very tests we know to have these limitations. Many important decisions are made on the basis of standardized test results. Unfortunately, and unlike the other popular methods (interview, observation, role play), teachers typically do not design these; in fact, they usually cannot see the high-stakes tests until moments before the test begins.

There are many downfalls to selected response when used as a high-stakes assessment, but when selected response assessment is not used as a high-stakes assessment (low-stakes), this assessment can yield quick and accurate data to inform instruction (Table 4.16). Now with Artificial Intelligence (AI) teachers can create selected response quizzes from PDFs or video with transcripts, and simplify the language within minutes (for example, see integrated AI feature in Quizziz, quizziz.com). Using PUMI as a decision-making process becomes critically important to assure alignment in AI generated assessments.

Table 4.15 Key design considerations

Students adapt their communication in relation to audience, task, purpose and discipline; they set and adjust the purpose for reading, writing, speaking, listening and language use as warranted by the task. They appreciate nuances, such as how the composition of an audience should affect tone when speaking and how the connotations of words affect meaning.

P	U	M		I
To measure history content and presentation skills.	To contribute to 30% of history marking period grade.	Role play (performance assessment).		Rubric, props.
	Example of role play rubric			
	Excellent (4)	Good (3)	Adequate (2)	Needs improvement (1)
Works cooperatively with group.	Always willing and focused during assigned talk.	Usually willing and focused during assigned talk.	Sometimes willing and focused during assigned talk.	Rarely willing and focused during assigned talk.
Presentation of perspective.	Convincing communication of character's role, feelings and motives.	Competent communication of character's role, feelings and motives.	Adequate communication of character's role, feelings and motives.	Limited communication of character's role, feelings and motives.
Use of non-verbal cues (voice, gestures, eye contact, props, costumes).	An impressive variety of non-verbal cues in an exemplary way.	Good variety (three or more) of non-verbal cues were used in a competent way.	An acceptable variety of non-verbal cues were used in a competent way.	Limited variety of non-verbal cues were used in a competent way.
Historical accuracy.	Historical information appears to be always accurate.	Historical information appears to be usually accurate.	Historical information appears to be sometimes accurate.	Historical information appears to be rarely accurate.

Table 4.16 Examples of selected response assessment

Multiple choice	What causes night and day? (a) The earth spins on its axis. (b) The earth moves around the sun. (c) Clouds block out the sun's light. (d) The earth moves into and out of the sun's shadow. (e) The sun goes around the earth.
Matching	Match the word to the definition: (1) __tradition (a) To ask for something politely or formally. (2) __enable (b) To allow someone to do something. (3) __maneuver (c) To say something excitedly. (4) __request (d) Something special done for a long time. (5) __exclaim (e) To move or turn skillfully.
True/false	(1) Many food chains make a good web. (2) An empty lot is a habitat. (3) All food chains start with the sun. (4) Plants can survive without light. (5) A habitat can recover from flood.

Incorporating Multiple Languages in Assessment Products

Using multiple languages in instruction and assessment is not just for bilingual programs. English as a new language (ENL) teachers, bilingual teachers and monolingual teachers can encourage more than one language in a variety of settings to better match the student. Table 4.17 suggests ideas for translanguaging for a final assessment product. Many teachers don't discourage use of the home language; however, they don't often encourage it either. Some view the integration of the home language as a waste of time. To represent the child more holistically, try to find more creative ways to use and value home languages in your final assessment products.

Table 4.17 Example of translanguaging with a final assessment product

Final product	Add translanguaging
Write persuasive reviews about local restaurants.	Write one in English and one in the home language to target more audiences.
Write about causes/effects of World War II.	Create a short audio recording summarizing causes/effect of World War II in the home language.
Research a country of their choice.	Take notes in the home language and English. Read research on the internet from home language websites and English websites.
Write a document-based question (DBQ). A DBQ is a type of essay that provides the writer with documents to serve as sources of information for the writing.	Write a DBQ in the home language. Include one sentence in English and English key vocabulary words.
Write a story.	Use the home language and English to write a story.
Create a campaign advertisement.	Create one advertisement in the home language and one in English.
Critique a poem.	Choose a poem in the home language and create a PowerPoint in English to explain the poem to peers. Include a comparison of English to the home language. Give oral presentation in English.

Bilingual rubrics

The Literacy Squared project (Escamilla *et al.*, 2014, 2018) was a biliteracy model designed to develop literacy skills in bilingual children (Spanish and English). Figure 4.3 shows an example of a bilingual rubric that allows the teacher to evaluate both

Spanish Score	Level of Discourse	Language Structures and Conventions	Vocabulary Development and Word Choice	Collaborative Participation	English Score
4	Produces sustained, articulate expressions of complex ideas, adapting language for the task, audience and purpose	Fluently uses a variety of appropriate language structures and demonstrates and command of language conventions	Incorporates an expanding range of grade-level academic vocabulary while speaking, using the words in ways that reveal a deep conceptual understanding	Expresses complex ideas, asks relevant questions, provides detailed responses and takes a leadership role in class discussions and small-group conversations	4
3	Produces sustained expressions of ideas, with an awareness of task, audience and purpose	Incorporated learned language structures and shows an increasing understanding of language conventions	Incorporates learned academic vocabulary while speaking, using the words in ways that reveal a growing understanding of word meanings	Expresses ideas, asks questions, and participates actively in class discussions and small-group conversations	3
2	Produces sentences that express ideas about topics	Uses provided language structures to express ideas and shows some understanding of language conventions	Incorporates learned vocabulary words while speaking, in ways that reveal a basic knowledge of the words	With some support, expresses ideas and answers questions in class discussions and small-group conversations	2
1	Uses gestures and produces words and phrases to convey basic ideas about a topic	Uses simple sentence frames to express basic ideas and feelings	Incorporates basic learned words while speaking	With support, expresses basic ideas in class discussions and small-group conversations	1

Figure 4.3 Bilingual rubric example (From ReadyGEN *Biliteracy Pathway Handbook*, Pearson)

languages at the same time. Please note, the furthest left column is for Spanish scoring and the furthest right column is for English scoring. Any two languages can be substituted.

Introduction to Rubrics and Checklists

Broadly speaking, rubrics and checklists count as Instruments (I) in PUMI; they can be thought of as 'instruments of documentation'. In good assessment, there is a fine line between instruction and assessment, but what distinguishes the two is the way student progress data are recorded or documented. Checklists and rubrics are the most popular instruments to collect data in a reliable manner. They can be used in different modalities, perhaps by the teacher, the student or even a parent, to make the assessment process less teacher centered and to generate multiple perspectives of data. The rubric is not the assessment method – it is a tool to keep the data collection systematic and focused on the same purpose or target (usually content or language standards, for example). Rubrics are an important part of good assessment because they increase predictable (or reliable) results and allow for less judgment or 'noise' in the assessment results.

If teachers judge a curriculum appropriate for MLs, they should use existing rubrics and checklists from the curriculum already used at their school. However, curriculum-based checklists and rubrics may align with the curriculum, but they may not be aligned with core content and language standards documents. In addition, curriculum-based rubrics and checklists (and all assessments) are usually designed for native English speakers and therefore need to be differentiated the same way that instruction is differentiated. Table 4.17 shows a math standard.

The following paragraphs and tables demonstrate how to create your own checklist from a set of standards. From Table 4.17, the ML educator designs content and language objectives such as those shown in Table 4.18 using LP standards and expertise as guidance. Many educators create language and content objectives aligned with the content standards to support a sheltered learning environment for MLs, which further promotes language learning in a meaningful academic context. Remember: Standards tell teachers what to teach, not how to teach (or assess). Moving from the standard in Table 4.17 to the content and language objectives in Table 4.18 is the first step toward appropriate standards-based assessment.

Table 4.18 Math standard example

Number and operation, fractions
Build fractions from unit fractions by applying and extending previous understandings of operations on whole numbers.
Decompose a fraction into a sum of fractions with the same denominator in more than one way, recording each decomposition by an equation. Justify decompositions, e.g., by using a visual fraction model.
Examples: 3/8 = 1/8 + 1/8 + 1/8 3/8 = 1/8 + 2/8 2 1/8 = 1 + 1 + 1/8

Checklists collect dichotomous data; this means that there are only two choices in responding, such as yes/no, complete/incomplete, present/not present. Because checklists generate dichotomous data, their usefulness to illustrate growth is limited. However, checklists are quick and easy to carry around on a clipboard while the teacher is observing students and asking questions. Usually, the data are in the form of checkmarks (√). Checklists are easy to make – simply use Microsoft Word to create a table with the objectives in the first column and the names of students in the remaining columns (Table 4.19).

Table 4.19 Teacher-designed checklist for MLs aligned with math standards

	Student #1	Student #2	Student #3	Student #4	Student #5
Place a check next to student's name when he or she completes the task. Check means complete √. Blank means the student did not complete.					
Student will be able to (SWBAT) match the equation 5/8 = 1/8 + 4/8 to the appropriate visual model (using Cuisenaire rods).					
SWBAT produce short phrases to explain why the matched Cuisenaire rods model 5/8 = 1/8 + 4/8.					
SWBAT sort pattern blocks by denominator 1/2, 1/3, 1/6 and show two different ways to make an equation with the same denominator (e.g., 1/3 + 1/3 = 2/3 or 1/6 + 3/6 = 4/6).					
SWBAT write two equations with the same denominator in more than one way with visual models (Cuisenaire rods or pattern blocks), writing it in symbols and saying the equations aloud to peers.					

Making a checklist for the whole class, a small group or one student (the teacher decides the modality of assessment) from the content and language objectives is relatively easy using the Microsoft Word table feature (see Table 4.18). The checklist can be carried by the teacher and used while sitting next to students and watching them learn, or it can be used in a different modality, such as one to group, one to one, group to group or to self, with slight or no modifications.

Using a checklist like this is convenient for observing large or small groups of students and documenting at the same time on the same sheet of paper. The checklist can be easily turned into a holistic rubric (see Table 4.20 for an example) for one student showing whether he or she is developing, meeting or exceeding this target. In addition to a check mark, there is room for anecdotal information (notes) to help provide evidence for this level or note what the student can improve upon. The data become more cumbersome when there is a rubric for each student v. one checklist for the whole class. However, both are useful in different contexts. Table 4.20 shows this type of rubric. Creating a good rubric is more time-consuming than creating a checklist, because the teacher has to unpack the levels of performance and the

Table 4.20 Teacher-designed (holistic) rubric for MLs aligned with math standards

	Developing (1)	Meeting (2)	Exceeding (3)
Place a check next to student's name when he or she completes the task. Check means complete. Blank means the student did not complete. Add anecdotal information where possible.			
Student will be able to (SWBAT) match the equation 5/8 = 1/8 + 4/8 to the appropriate visual model (using Cuisenaire rods).			
SWBAT produce short phrases to explain why the matched Cuisenaire rods model 5/8 = 1/8 + 4/8.			
SWBAT sort Cuisenaire rods by denominator 1/4, 1/3, 1/2, 1/8 and show two different ways to make an equation with the same denominator 6/8.			
SWBAT write two equations with the same denominator in more than one way with visual models (Cuisenaire rods), writing it in symbols and saying the equations aloud to peers.			

categories of the construct being measured. If creating a rubric from scratch, Chappius and Stiggins (2016) recommend the following steps:

(1) Establish your knowledge base.
(2) Collect samples of student work and sort them according to levels of quality.
(3) Identify the key characteristics that differentiate levels of quality.
(4) Determine whether you will create an analytic (like a matrix or grid showing all levels broken down) or a holistic rubric (a single scale with all criteria together).
(5) Define levels of quality and identify anchor papers.
(6) Practice applying the rubric, revising as needed.

There are ways to create rubrics that are less time-consuming. Artificial Intelligence (AI) offers quick ways to create rubrics and checklists, but must be checked for accuracy, language level and PUMI alignment. The rubric shown in Table 4.21 was created in just a few minutes using RubiStar (http://rubistar.4teachers.org), a free website funded by the US Department of Education with customizable templates. It is very convenient to save the customized rubric in your free RubiStar space; you can also download it as an Excel file, then modify and save it without having to log on to RubiStar for access (also see rubric-maker.com).

Table 4.21 shows a rubric focusing on mathematical concept, explanation, diagrams and sketches, working with others, as well as mathematical terminology and notation. The selection of categories is very important because this is your target (directly related to purpose – remember PUMI) unpacked into levels (usually three to five levels).

Also, educators need to keep in mind that the categories on RubiStar are designed for native English speakers and may need to be modified in the same way that instruction is modified, to meet the needs of beginner and intermediate MLs for the language objectives only. When comparing the rubric to the checklist, you can see that the rubric has four categories and four levels of performance. This gives your data four levels of performance per category, allowing you to document much more detail than a checklist (Table 4.21). (Again, choosing the instrument [I] depends on the purpose, and often checklists are sufficient.)

Table 4.21 Teacher-designed (analytic) rubric (using RubiStar) aligned with math standards

Teacher name: Ms Mahoney

Student name:_____

Category	4	3	2	1
Mathematical concepts	Explanation shows complete understanding of the mathematical concepts used to solve the problem(s).	Explanation shows substantial understanding of the mathematical concepts used to solve the problem(s).	Explanation shows some understanding of the mathematical concepts needed to solve the problem(s).	Explanation shows very limited understanding of the underlying concepts needed to solve the problem(s) *or* is not written.
Explanation	Explanation is detailed and clear.	Explanation is clear.	Explanation is a little difficult to understand, but includes critical components.	Explanation is difficult to understand and is missing several components *or* was not included.
Diagrams and sketches	Diagrams and/or sketches are clear and greatly add to the reader's understanding of the procedure(s).	Diagrams and/or sketches are clear and easy to understand.	Diagrams and/or sketches are somewhat difficult to understand.	Diagrams and/or sketches are difficult to understand or are not used.
Working with others	Student was an engaged partner, listening to suggestions of others and working cooperatively throughout lesson.	Student was an engaged partner but had trouble listening to others and/or working cooperatively.	Student cooperated with others, but needed prompting to stay on-task.	Student did not work effectively with others.
Mathematical terminology and notation	Correct terminology and notation always used, making it easy to understand what was done.	Correct terminology and notation usually used, making it fairly easy to understand what was done.	Correct terminology and notation used, but it is sometimes not easy to understand what was done.	There is little use, or a lot of inappropriate use, of terminology and notation.

END-OF-CHAPTER ACTIVITIES (Instructors: See advice at the end of the book)

By completing Activity 1 and 2, the reader will be able to:

(1) Make a list of products that MLs can create using translanguaging strategies.
(2) Create one checklist and two rubrics aligned with the core standards and give examples of how to use with home and new languages.

Activity 1

Make a list of products that MLs can create using translanguaging strategies. Throughout this chapter, hints are given about how to use more than one language to create final products. Final products can act as formative or summative assessments but usually summative. In small groups, make a list of 10 ways that students in your class can use translanguaging methods to create final products.

> **Activity 2**
> Create one checklist and two rubrics aligned with the core standards and give examples of how to use with home and new languages.
>
> In small groups, examine the core standard in Table 4.22. Follow these steps to practice making checklists and rubrics. *Step One*: Read the standard and brainstorm content and language objectives. Write one content and one language objective on chart paper, starting with 'Student will be able to (SWBAT) …' *Step Two*: Make one checklist, one rubric, and another rubric using RubiStar – similar to the ones presented earlier in this chapter – from the content and language objectives your group wrote.
>
> **Table 4.22** Speaking and listening standards K–5
>
> | Vocabulary acquisition and use: Grade 3 |
> | --- |
> | (6) Acquire and use accurately grade-appropriate conversational, general academic and domain-specific words and phrases, including those that signal spatial and temporal relationships (e.g. 'After dinner that night we went looking for them'). |

Notes

(1) This really happened to teacher Nicholas Tay, who suggested this analogy.
(2) In the United States, according to the ESSA, each state must produce an English Language Proficiency Standards document for use across the state. According to the ESSA, this document must adhere to the following: (1) are derived from the four recognized domains of speaking, listening, reading, and writing; (2) address the different proficiency levels of English learners; and (3) are aligned with the challenging state academic standards.
(3) A framework (for students with low home literacy) and the General Home Language Writing Assessment Rubric used in this snapshot can be found in A CUNY-NYSIEB Framework for the Education of Emergent Bilinguals with Low Home Literacy: 4–12 grades by Garcia *et al.* (Spring 2013) and can be found at http://www.nysieb.ws.gc.cuny.edu/files/2013/05/CUNY-NYSIEB-Framework-for-EB-with-Low-Home-Literacy-Spring-2013-Final-Version-05-08-13.pdf. The rubric is in Appendix B.
(4) Opportunity to Role Play (ORP) acronym was invented by Kate Mahoney. There are ORPs in many of our lessons. It's a good idea to scan your lesson to look for ORPs. Great for all students, especially MLs. Use props!

References

Adelman Reyes, S. and Kleyn, T. (2010) *Teaching in 2 Languages: A Guide for K-12 Bilingual Educators*. Thousand Oaks, CA: Corwin Press.
Britton, M. (2021) *Assessment for Learning in Primary Language Learning and Teaching*. Bristol: Multilingual Matters.
Celic, C. and Seltzer, K. (2011) *Translanguaging: A CUNY-NYSIEB Guide for Educators*. New York: CUNY-NYSIEB, The Graduate Center.
Chappius, J. and Stiggins, R. (2016) *An Introduction to Student-Involved Assessment for Learning* (7th ed.) New York: Pearson.
Courtney, L. (2019) Role plays: A versatile tool for assessing young learners. In D. Prošić-Santovac and S. Rixon (eds) *Integrating Assessment into Early Language Learning and Teaching* (pp. 155–169). Bristol: Multilingual Matters.

Escamilla, K., Butvilofsky, S. and Hopewell, S. (2018) What gets lost when English-only writing assessment is used to assess writing proficiency in Spanish-English emerging bilingual learners? *International Multilingual Research Journal* 12 (4), 221–236. https://doi.org/10.1080/19313152.2016.1273740.

Escamilla, K., Hopewell, S., Butvilofsky, S., Sparrow, W., Soltero-Gonzalez, L., Ruiz-Figueroa, O. and Escamilla, M. (2014) *Biliteracy from the Start: Literacy Squared in Action*. Philadelphia, PA: Caslon.

Gottlieb, M. and Nguyen, D. (2007) *Assessment and Accountability in Language Education Programs: A Guide for Administrators and Teachers*. Philadelphia, PA: Caslon.

Heritage, M. (2018) Assessment for learning as support for self-regulation. *The Australian Educational Researcher* 45, 51–63.

Heritage, M. and Wylie, C. (2018) Reaping the benefits of assessment for learning: Achievement, identity, equity. *ZDM Mathematics Education* 50, 729–741.

Paris, D. and Alim, S. (eds) (2017) *Culturally Sustaining Pedagogies: Teaching and Learning for Justice in a Changing World*. New York: Teachers College Press.

Valdés, G. and Lee, O. (2013) English language learners and the next generation science standards: Using the English language proficiency development (ELPD) framework (PowerPoint). A webinar hosted by the Council of Chief State School Officers.

Vogt, M. and Echevarría, J. (2008) *99 Ideas and Activities for Teaching English Learners with the SIOP Model*. Boston, MA: Pearson.

Vogt, M. and Echevarría, J. (2022) *99 Ideas and Activities for Teaching English Learners with the SIOP Model*. Boston, MA: Pearson.

Vogt, M., Echevarría, J. and Waham, M. (2015) *99 More Ideas and Activities for Teaching English Learners with the SIOP Model*. Boston, MA: Pearson.

Recommended reading

Britton, M. (2021) *Assessment for Learning in Primary Language Learning and Teaching*. Bristol: Multilingual Matters.

This book provides a detailed account of the practical use of assessment for learning (AfL) in primary language classrooms. There is a detailed account of eight experienced primary language teachers and how they incorporated this type of assessment into their practice.

Gottlieb, M. (2006) *Assessing English Language Learners: Bridges From Language Proficiency to Academic Achievement*. Thousand Oaks, CA: Corwin Press.

The main topic of this book is how to appropriately assess language proficiency and content learning. It includes many tools to help educators organize, interpret and report data for educational decision-making. In addition to including evaluation instruments, the author guides readers in understanding the pros and cons of different types of assessments.

Stefanakis, E. (2002) *Multiple Intelligences and Portfolios: Window into the Learner's Mind*. Portsmouth, NH: Heinemann.

In this book, Stefanakis provides practical tips, guidelines, teacher anecdotes and examples of digital portfolios that can guide teachers from kindergarten through high school toward documenting a child's progress in school through multiple intelligences.

Stefanakis, E. and Meier, D. (2010) *Differentiated Assessment: How to Assess the Learning Potential of Every Student*. San Francisco, CA: Jossey-Bass.

In this book, Stefanakis and Meier provide detailed and practical tools to implement a classroom portfolio program. It includes real-world examples of model assessment programs from five school environments containing multilingual students and large numbers of underperforming students. The authors emphasize student portfolio assessments and personalized learning profiles.

Stiggins, R. and Chappuis, J. (2011) *An Introduction to Student-Involved Assessment for Learning* (6th edn). New York: Pearson.

This introductory text on assessment is written for teacher candidates who have little or no classroom experience. It provides an initial and thorough orientation to classroom assessment.

5 Content and Language

THEMES FROM CHAPTER 5

(1) When assessing *content*, minimize or simplify the language so you can focus on content (you can never eliminate language, but there are ways to reduce it, without reducing content).
(2) *Language* is best assessed in context and over time. Language is not assessed well out of context (decontextualized) and at one point in time.
(3) The *environment* of language assessment should be integrated, natural and authentic, but the *purpose* should be articulated, isolated and clear.

Key Vocabulary

- Content categories.
- Knowledge.
- Reasoning.
- Key practices.
- Dispositional.

- Formative assessment.
- Summative assessment.

PUMI (Purpose, Use, Method, Instrument) Connection: Purpose and Use

This chapter focuses on the Purpose (P) and Use (U) of assessing school-related content and language, broadly defined. A variety of purposes and assessment methods are explored in relation to content and language.

Introduction to Chapter

The photograph at the opening of this chapter is typical in classrooms with multilingual learners (MLs) where the teacher articulates how language and content are separated and practices translanguaging by connecting content and language to the home language (in this case, Karen – a popular language in Burma). This chapter emphasizes the importance of separating language and content in assessment and knowing whether the purpose of the assessment is language or content.

The first half of this chapter covers content and the second half language, that is, content and language typically found in schools.[1] Most of this chapter focuses on logically thinking about your purpose in order to pick the right method of assessment for content and language. Because content and language are never completely separate constructs, there is a discussion of the relationship between content and language in the middle of the chapter, which transitions the reader into the second half on language. Both formative and summative assessment examples are provided for language and content.

How to think about writing a lesson plan with PUMI

Regardless of what lesson plan format you use, somewhere in the plan is a place to articulate the assessment method. When planning for assessment, you should create a PUMI table, or at least think through the PUMI framework for each objective to guide you in selecting the appropriate assessment. It's not feasible to assess every learning objective, so teachers use their judgment after considering the purpose and use of an objective, then select an appropriate method and instrument. If the language demands of an assessment are too high, then the assessment and results become less meaningful and therefore less valid. Does the assessment require a rubric and if yes, how is that related to the purpose? Before introducing assessment external to the lesson, look inside your instruction for authentic pieces of student work that can be assessed; this leads to more authentic assessment practice. And finally, the assessments of a lesson plan should happen in natural places; assessing every objective is too much. Strive for meaningful assessments that won't disrupt instruction. The best assessment practice looks almost exactly like instruction (the only difference sometimes is the presence of a rubric or checklist)!

Types of Content

The different types of content used in schools are oftentimes highlighted in content standard documents. Drawing from various content standards, this author will organize and explain content in the following ways: *knowledge, reasoning, key practices* and *dispositions*. As discussed in Chapter 4, knowing what kind of content you are targeting is required to pick the appropriate assessment method. Please note that these categories are not mutually exclusive; they are used to help organize the different types of content. For example, it takes *knowledge* and *reasoning* to perform the *key practices*.

Knowledge

Knowledge can be defined in many ways, but within a school setting it is usually defined as subject matter content that teachers want MLs to master. Every discipline or content area has a set body of *knowledge* that defines it. For example, mathematics *knowledge* may consist of measurement, geometry, number sense and algebra. In science, *knowledge* may consist of life, earth, space and physical sciences. *Knowledge* of content typically means that teachers ask students to learn important content as defined by the standards. Teachers design instruction and give notes and study guides to help them master *knowledge* in their content areas. Students then study the content and attempt to memorize it by test time. Examples of *knowledge* include knowing the parts of a cell, knowing multiplication facts or knowing the dates of the Revolutionary War. *Knowledge* can easily be assessed by using selected response type assessments (multiple choice, true/false or matching). A base of *knowledge* is a prerequisite to move into other types of content targets such as *reasoning* and *key practices*.

Table 5.1 presents suggestions for assessing *knowledge*. In order of preference, selected response, one-to-one communication and written responses are recommended. Performance assessment is not recommended for assessing *knowledge*. Keep in mind, since the main purpose is to measure content, then any of these assessments can be administered (input) or responded to (output) in the home language or using a translanguaging pedagogy (both home language and new language).

Table 5.1 Appropriate assessment methods for *knowledge*

Category	Method	Comment
Selected response	True/false, matching or multiple-choice test	If items are written simply (linguistic simplification) – see Chapter 7: this can be a quick and efficient way to assess *knowledge*. Selected response can be translated or read to student in home language.
One-to-one communication	Questioning, survey, conference, interactive journal	Can assess *knowledge* but may be too time-consuming. Home language can be used if student prefers.
Written responses	Essays, written reports, short or extended responses, etc.	*Construct-irrelevant variance (CIV)*[a] *warning*: Written responses sample *knowledge* but depend on student writing ability. Other two methods preferred.

[a]CIV was discussed in depth in Chapter 3: Validity. For example, if you are trying to measure *reasoning* (construct), you don't want writing ability (irrelevant construct) to interfere. CIV is a validity threat to many assessment results for MLs and is also known as 'bias'.

Reasoning

Most people think *knowledge* gives rise to *reasoning*, and some think *knowledge* and *reasoning* grow together. *Reasoning* means that students will think, understand and form judgments using logic. Students should be able to use their *knowledge* to figure things out, relate *knowledge* to other *knowledge*, critique information based on *knowledge* and more. *Reasoning* usually includes skills such as classifying (e.g. sort from smallest to largest), comparing (e.g. compare political systems of the United States to Mexico) and synthesizing (e.g. what do two stories have in common?), to name a few examples. Just as all content areas are defined by a certain base of *knowledge*, they are also defined by the ways that students reason within the discipline. For example, *reasoning* could include comparing and contrasting presidents, debating opposing political views or explaining why an amount becomes smaller as the denominator becomes larger.

Note that while *reasoning* is tied to higher levels of thinking, it also entails a type of language-use often referred to as academic language, or language used for academic purposes, which is a separate construct[2] needed to *express reasoning*. English language proficiency (ELP) standards in the United States have shifted to focus more sharply on language used to access core standards, a requirement that started with the No Child Left Behind (NCLB) federal policy and still remains in the current Every Student Succeeds Act (ESSA) policy. Just like other aspects of language, language proficiency used in academic areas develops across a continuum of the second language acquisition (SLA) process. For educators, developing students' language skills used to express *reasoning* in content areas is now a major priority.

Table 5.2 presents suggestions for assessing *reasoning*. In order of preference, performance, one-to-one communication and written response are recommended. Selected response is not recommended for assessing *reasoning*.

Table 5.2 Appropriate assessment methods for *reasoning*

Category	Method	Comment
Performance assessment	Observation with checklist. Teacher observes *key practices* (analyzing, producing, constructing, building, asking, etc.). For example, teacher observes student as they think aloud.	Natural context; students can reason without high levels of literacy (nice for language beginners). Students can use new language or home language.
One-to-one communication	Questioning, survey, conference, interactive journal. Questioning: Teacher asks questions to probe *reasoning*.	These methods provide a window into *reasoning* without relying on literacy (nice for language beginners). Teacher can ask student to respond in new language or home language.
Written response	Essays, written reports, short or extended written responses, etc.	*CIV warning*: Students can explain their *reasoning* through writing; however, beware of CIV – make sure the writing doesn't interfere with students' ability to express their *reasoning*. Keep the constructs of writing and *reasoning* as separate as possible. Students can write in new language or home language.

Key practices

Practices or procedures (what we do with content) are sometimes called *key practices*; see Table 5.3 for a sample of popular *key practices* across some content areas (drawn from current core standards documents). The idea of *key practices* within a content area can be thought of as 'things we do with the content' or otherwise thought of as the application of content.

Table 5.3 *Key practices* across content standards

English language arts • Analyze complex texts • Produce clear and coherent writing • Construct arguments
Math • Solve problems • Reason abstractly • Use appropriate tools
Science • Ask questions • Define problems • Analyze and interpret data

Table 5.4 provides suggestions for assessing *key practices*. In order of preference, performance and one-to-one communication are recommended. Selected response is not recommended as a method for assessing *key practices*. Since the purpose is assessing content, flexible combinations of the home and new language are welcome.

Table 5.4 Appropriate assessment methods for *key practices*

Category	Method	Comment
Performance assessment	Teacher observes *key practices* (analyzing, producing, constructing, building, asking, etc.) project.[a]	Performance assessment is best for less literacy-based *key practices*; this method can demonstrate 'practice' or 'performance', 'doing' or 'creating'[a] something. Home or new language can be used.
One-to-one communication	Questioning, survey, conference, interactive journal.	Very strong match if key practice involves assessing oral communication (such as asking questions, constructing explanations). Home language encouraged.
Written responses	Essays, written reports, short or extended written responses, etc.	Very strong match if key practice involves assessing written communication (such as producing clear and coherent writing and written explanations of problems). Home language encouraged.

[a] As projects such as posters, inventions and models are categorized as performance assessment in this book, it is suggested that performance assessment should be used as one method to assess proficiency in creating things as well as assessing the attributes of the product itself. Even though 'performance' and 'product' are different, they are both very appropriate for *key practices*.

Dispositional

The final category when discussing content, and an especially important one to MLs, is *dispositional* targets (otherwise known as affective targets). *Dispositional* targets are important to MLs because they include the measurement of important factors that we know add to or subtract from students' experience with second language acquisition (SLA). Rarely are dispositional targets required by school policy/leaders, but they can provide important insight into how to provide culturally relevant pedagogy and other information important to the learning environment in the classroom. Specific examples of affective targets are values, attitudes, interests, aspirations and sense of academic efficacy. *Dispositional* targets help educators understand factors affecting SLA such as motivation, attitude and negative and positive experiences with immigration or English or school. *Dispositional* factors contribute to what Stephen Krashen calls the 'affective filter' (a filter that may accelerate or slow down SLA), which focuses on factors such as anxiety, motivation and self-confidence. All educators know how important it is to monitor these factors because, on the one hand, if any of these dispositions are 'too high', this may negatively impact SLA. On the other hand, when these factors are kept 'low', SLA is more apt to typically develop. Other examples of *dispositional* targets may include MLs' attitudes toward reading, how confident they are in joining a whole-class discussion and how their family contributes to their success in school.

Table 5.5 presents suggestions for assessing *dispositions*. All four categories of assessment approaches are recommended (one-to-one communication, written responses, selected responses and performance assessment). Choose the method that will lead to more meaningful answers. If the teacher does not have the home language skills to use the home language, *seek someone who does*. Please ask peer teachers, teacher aides, parents, other students or interpreters, in addition to using technologies such as Google Translate. Google translate and applications like it can be used for conversation, transcription, and sometimes the camera feature works to translate hand written documents.

Table 5.5 Appropriate assessment methods for *dispositions*

Category	Method	Comment
One-to-one communication	Questioning, conference, interactive journal, questionnaires.	Educators can talk with students and families about dispositions toward content, school, home and community.
Written responses	Questionnaire with open and written responses.	If appropriate to student's writing level, open-ended responses can show window to dispositions.
Selected response	Questionnaires with selected response.	Simple and quick questionnaires can access student feelings. Closed responses good for beginners.
Performance assessment	Teacher observes *key practices* (analyzing, producing, constructing, building, asking, etc.).	Weaker than the other three, but teachers may be able to assess and infer feelings based on observations of behavior at school, home and community.

The remainder of this chapter shifts from assessing school-related content to school-related language. The transition from content to language starts with a discussion of the relationship between content and language, where content and language are narrowly defined as the content and language used in schools.

Language Plays a Role when Measuring Content

All assessments – no matter what the subject area – depend upon language for their administration and for the ways in which students provide their responses. For example, when a teacher gives a content area assessment, the directions are typically administered orally or in writing (most of the time in English only) and therefore depend on language. Even in a mathematics test, students more than likely have to read the item to discern what the answer is, and often must write extended responses to show what they 'know'. Hong Kong researchers Lo and Fung (2020) studied the interplay of the cognitive and linguistic demands of content and language integrated instruction (CLIL) assessments. CLIL is a pedagogical approach that integrates the teaching, learning and assessment of content and new or foreign languages. After analyzing over 4900 test questions, they found that as (productive) linguistic demands increased, the students' performance on CLIL declined (Lo & Fung, 2020). This shows that if the language of an assessment is too complicated, students cannot access the content as much, resulting in lower scores. The low scores do not necessarily mean the student knows less content.

Using translanguaging assessment practices offers teachers ways to access and assess rigorous content with MLs. Celic and Seltzer (2011) list the numerous benefits to planning for instruction and assessments using many languages. The two points in the following list most relevant to the assessment of content are in bold, but all should be considered important.

(1) Scaffold MLs' development of academic content, language and literacy abilities in English.
(2) Help MLs better understand the content by utilizing their home language as a vehicle for learning.
(3) Help MLs develop language and literacy abilities in their home language.
(4) **Provide an opportunity for MLs to best demonstrate what they know and can do.**
(5) **Help teachers more accurately assess MLs' knowledge and understanding of both content and language.**
(6) Help MLs think critically and at a higher level by asking them to create something in multiple languages and for multiple purposes and/or audiences.
(7) Help MLs engage with the *knowledge* they bring from home.
(8) Help MLs affirm and build their multilingual identities by encouraging them to use their home language practices at school.

Figure 5.1 is a content assessment example. How much language is necessary to show what the student knows in math? To translate the student responses into English, see Table 5.6.

Content and Language 113

Figure 5.1 Content assessment example

Table 5.6 Interpreting student responses from Figure 5.1

Item	Student response	Interpretation in English
2a	No written response – just a circle.	No interpretation needed.
2b	Yo cogiel metro poques es mas largo.	I chose the meter because it's larger.
2c	2 + 5 = 7	2 + 5 = 7
	Bill trow jis bin bag 7 meters	He threw his bean bag[a] 7 meters.
2d	Por que ella tiro la bin bag lego que Bill.	Because she threw the bean bag farther than Bill.

[a]When Mahoney used this activity with graduate teaching English to speakers of other languages (TESOL) students, we discovered that the two international students (India, Saudi Arabia) had never thrown a bean bag and were unfamiliar with any games related to bean bags. But the 14 domestic students had all thrown a bean bag previously. These types of cultural referents may make the assessment more comprehensible to students from mainstream US culture. These types of cultural constructs that lead to test bias many times go unnoticed.

That's a lot of language for a math assessment. Most assessments like Figure 5.1 are filled with both content and language – it's never just a content assessment. The following paragraph reviews the format of responses and the general language demands found in Figure 5.1. The first item (2a) uses selected response, which requires the student to read, comprehend and circle the answer. The second item (2b) uses open-ended response, which requires the student to read, comprehend and explain her answer in writing. The third item (2c) requires the student to read, comprehend and draw. And the fourth item (2d) requires the student to explain her answer in writing. Table 5.7 shows a summary of the language and content required for the assessment in Figure 5.1. A PUMI study further clarifies what this looks like as a content area assessment.

P	U	M	I
To assess understanding of distance using meters.	To provide formative feedback, to inform future instruction.	Selected response, written response.	Worksheet downloaded from engage.org.

Table 5.7 Breaking down the content and language required in Figure 5.1

Content	Language
Knowing how to use measuring tools	Reading for understanding
Knowing what a meter is	Reading language for math
Thinking abstractly about a bean bag that was thrown even further (pre-algebra)	Comprehend the sentence using superlative 'farther'
Reasoning about who won the contest	Writing to explain *reasoning*

The student answered incorrectly for 2c, but why? Is the reason related to language or content? At first glance, an error analysis of 2c shows that this student was able to use English to answer the questions, but the mathematics was incorrect. The correct answer is 'Samantha threw her bean bag three meters and the correct equation is $5 - 2 = 3$'. It is likely that the student is able to do the math – add and subtract (the correct subtraction is shown in Figure 5.1: 2c), but if the student does not understand the English word 'farther[3] than' then language (English) may have led to the error. Probably language was the source of the error, not the math. Because this is a formative assessment, her teacher will use these responses to design a mini lesson on comparative adjectives and how to write comparative adjectives as math equations.

Because the purpose of the assessment shown in Figure 5.1 was to measure content, the language of the responses can be in English or Spanish or a combination of both. This student used translanguaging in her responses by choosing to answer 2b in Spanish, 2c in English and 2d in Spanish. She also used English (la bin bag) in the Spanish sentence (2d). This is encouraged because allowing students to use their full linguistic repertoire in content area assessments provides an opportunity for MLs to best show what they know, *when the purpose is assessing content*.[4]

In content assessment, it is also critical to modify the language demands of the content area learning and assessment – *but not the content itself*. In other words, MLs are due the same rigor of content as non-MLs but with reduced language demands. Reducing the language demands of content area assessment increases the chances for MLs to reveal their strengths because they can more directly access content. It might help to think of the language of content assessments as *input* and *output*. The input can be a set of instructions, a prompt for an essay or a reading/video excerpt. These 'assessment inputs' need to be at a language level appropriate so that the student has full access to the content. The 'assessment output' is how students are expected to respond and can be reading and selecting the right response (selected response), constructing a short utterance (constructed response) or constructing a narrative (extended constructed response). How a teacher modifies the input and output of an assessment can make an important difference in students showing what they know. Opening up assessments to include multiple languages will better support MLs. Conversely, content area assessments with too much language interference or in English-only can cover up or disguise content area strengths.

SNAPSHOT: ASSESSING CONTENT OR LANGUAGE?

Mrs Weiss was frustrated by the district-level math tests because they seemed too wordy and her ML students were guessing or leaving blanks on their tests because it appeared that the language was too difficult for them. Mrs Weiss knew that many of her students were unable to show what they really knew about math because of the way the items were written. Of her own will, she typed into Google search the terms 'simplify language', 'test items', 'English as a second language (ESL)' and 'strategies', and she found two documents to help guide her. One was a recent chapter in the *Handbook of Test Development* by Jamal el Abedi (2015) titled 'Language Issues and Item Development'. This researcher studies the language that gets in the way of assessing content (linguistic features that may hinder student understanding of test items). Mrs Weiss followed his advice and made changes (called 'linguistic simplification') like those below the test items:

Original #1: A certain reference file contains approximately 6 billion facts.
Revision #1: Mack's company sold 6 billion hamburgers (replaced unfamiliar words with familiar ones).
Original #2: The weight of three objects was compared.
Revision #2: Sandra compared the weight of three suitcases (replaced verbs in the passive voice with verbs in the active voice).
Original #3: If X represents the number of newspapers that Lee delivers each day…
Revision #3: Lee delivers X Amazon packages each day (replaced conditional 'if clause' with sentence and replaced newspapers with a more relatable term (Amazon packages).

Mrs Weiss anticipated that the other math teachers in her department might suggest that she was dumbing down the test or changing the math content in some way to make it easier. So, she documented the linguistic modifications she made and cited Abedi (2015). Then, she circulated the items and asked her peer teachers to judge whether the content was changed. Overwhelmingly, they agreed that by deleting the 'language that gets in the way', she had not changed the difficulty level of the content (math). She also found an article on translanguaging strategies and decided to implement translanguaging assessment strategies in her math class: (1) students were permitted to answer open-ended questions in their home language if they chose and (2) the directions to every section and subsection were read to the students in their home language and their new language. After implementing the linguistic test item modifications and the translanguaging assessment strategies, Mrs Weiss observed an increase in math scores, self-esteem, interest and motivation in math. This was worth the extra time and work. Her colleagues began to take notice.

Discussion questions

- Do you think Mrs Weiss made the content easier? Why or why not?
- Can you ever fully separate language from content? Explain.

The remainder of the chapter now turns to ways of assessing language in school.

Method Suggestions for School-Related Language

When assessing school-related language, special consideration should be given to selecting the appropriate method to match the language target. Table 5.8 suggests methods. With language assessments, obviously you should stay focused on the target language, whether it is the new language (English) or the home language (Spanish), for example. Translanguaging is acceptable within language assessments.

Table 5.8 Matching purpose to method (PUMI): Good and bad choices

Assessment method[a]	Bad choices		Good choices	
Speaking	*Multiple-choice test:* Method doesn't match language target.	*Written essay:* Method doesn't match language target.	*Teacher observation* (with checklist) of student speaking in social studies debate.	*Interview or questioning:* Provides lots of opportunity for assessing language in context.
Listening	*True or false test:* Not preferred. Other language constructs such as literacy may interfere.	*Short essay:* Doesn't match language target.	*Teacher observation* of student responding to commands/requests.	*Interview or questioning:* Teacher can ask questions and evaluate answers.
Writing	*Matching test:* Language target doesn't match method.	*Role play:* Language target doesn't match method.	*Written science lab:* Can provide highly authentic sample of writing.	*Interactive journals:* A written conversation between teachers and student.
Reading	*Multiple-choice test:* Usually decontextualized; therefore, not a good language assessment.	*Extended written response:* Language target doesn't match method.	*Running record[b]:* Provides a natural context thorough documentation.	*Interview or questioning:* Teacher can ask questions and evaluate answers in a natural setting.

[a]To make any language assessment 'standards based', suggested methods should be used with a rubric or checklist designed from standards such as your state ELP standards.
[b]See figures showing examples of running records in current chapter.

This can be done by creating instruction and assessment using the target language, but encouraging students to use both languages to expand meaning-making opportunities.

Bilingual vs Monolingual Writing Assessments

When writing ability is underestimated, expectations may be lowered. Escamilla *et al.* (2017) examined the writing skills of 44 bilingual fourth and fifth graders. Writing outcomes were compared on a monolingual English-only test to bilingual Spanish and English test, then outcomes were considered holistically. Overall, these researchers found that when students' Spanish and English outcomes are considered holistically, the general writing ability is not underestimated. And when assessed in English only, writing ability is underestimated, which may lead to instruction targets that are too low. Figure 5.2 shows how English and Spanish writing samples are interpreted together side by side, to create a more holistic view of Victoria.

To Integrate or Not?

Despite the presentation in Table 5.8 of language as four distinct areas, that's not really how language works. Instead of separating language into reading, writing, listening and speaking, Bachman and Palmer (2010) suggest that designers of assessment should define language ability in a way that is appropriate for each particular language-use situation. Examples of these situations in schools are reading for gist, writing for reasoning in math, speaking for science presentations or listening in the

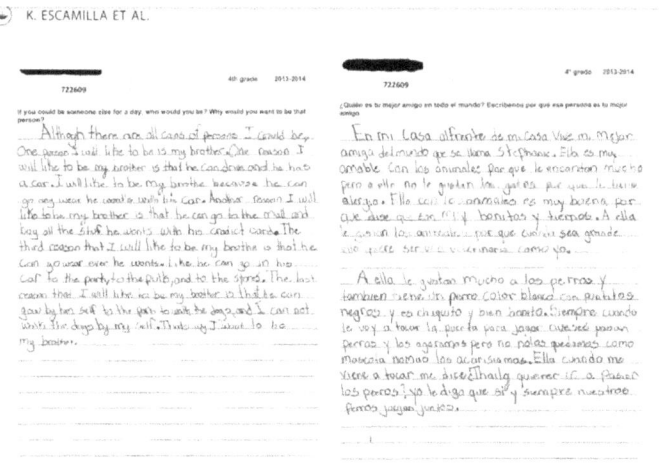

Figure 3. Victoria's fourth-grade biliterate writing samples.

English Translation: Prompt: Who do you consider to be your best friend in the whole world? Write about why that person is your best friend. *In my house across from my house lives my best friend in the whole world and her name is Stephanie. She is very kind to animals because she loves them so much but she doesn't like cats because she is allergic to them. With the animals she is very nice because she says that they are very nice and affectionate. She likes animals because when she grows up she wants to be a veterinarian like me. She really likes dogs and she also has a dog that is white with black spots and it is little and very pretty. Every time I get to her front door to play at times dogs will pass by and we grab them but we don't keep them as pets we just pet them. When she comes to my how she says Thaily do you want to walk the dogs? And I say yes and our dogs always play together.*

Figure 5.2 Victoria's biliterate writing samples (From Escamilla *et al.*, 2017)

science laboratory. Integrated assessment (language, literacy and content) creates a more authentic environment to collect assessment data. The environment should be integrated, natural and authentic, but the purpose of the assessment should be articulated, isolated and clear. Since real language practice is not segmented, the practice of separating language in assessment erodes the authenticity (and validity) of assessment results. Integrated assessment involves finding a meaningful way to develop language, literacy and content learning over an extended period of time. Don't overlook the multiple opportunities for MLs to hear, speak, read and write within meaningful content instruction. Integrated instruction and assessment within a culturally relevant environment that supports translanguaging is ideal for MLs – the type of environment that may be captured using portfolio assessment. This is the main reason portfolio assessment was and continues to be so popular among educators. Portfolios are a practical assessment used in schools today that show change over time and integrate language in authentic ways. Plus, the format is flexible and allows for the integration of language, literacy and content.

As an example of different ways language is integrated in educational contexts, the next section demonstrates how WIDA organizes and integrates language in their teacher resources. WIDA organizes their resources by integrating speaking/listening for their 'Can Do' resources, but WIDA organizes resources for performance definitions by expressive domains (speaking and writing) and receptive domains (listening and reading) for resources and materials for teachers (https://wida.wisc.edu/resources/performance-definitions-expressive-domains). Forty-one states in the United States participate in WIDA resources to assess ML students (sorry New York State readers – NY chose NYSESLAT over WIDA). WIDA is now celebrating 20 years since they formed as an important assessment leader in the United States. Since at least 2012, WIDA has provided 'Can Do' booklets to support teachers of ML students. As the name implies, the Can Do descriptors are designed to communicate with all teachers what language ML students are able to understand and produce in the classroom. Teachers not trained in language acquisition and development also really like these. Below are examples of how WIDA organizes speaking/listening for Can Do descriptors for Grades 9–12 (Figure 5.3) and WIDA performance definitions for listening and reading (receptive domains of language) (Figure 5.4). These are just meant to show examples of popular ways to integrate language in educational contexts. For full resources and explanations, please visit wida.wisc.edu/resources. There are many ways to organize the interaction of language.

Although this is somewhat artificial (not integrated) the next sections are separated by speaking, listening, reading and writing.

Speaking

Speaking and listening naturally interact; despite this, they are usually assessed separately. What is clear from research studies on SLA is that speaking, also referred to as oral language development, almost always continues to develop among MLs in two or more languages, even if they do not have exposure to languages other than English for instruction and assessment. Students continue to speak and acquire all of their languages during school and outside school with family, friends and the community. This can be a huge benefit for educators who can use multiple language abilities as a classroom asset.

Content and Language 119

KEY USE OF EXPLAIN

By the end of each of the given levels of English language proficiency English language learners can...

		ELP Level 1 Entering	ELP Level 2 Emerging	ELP Level 3 Developing	ELP Level 4 Expanding	ELP Level 5 Bridging	ELP Level 6 Reaching
LISTENING		Process explanations by • Ordering events or stages of phenomena from oral statements • Identifying words and phrases related to sequence	Process explanations by • Sequencing steps in processes or procedures described orally • Comparing information, symbols, or icons on charts or tables described orally	Process explanations by • Recognizing relationships in a series of oral statements • Identifying causes for particular events or phenomena in short oral presentations	Process explanations by • Identifying components of systems from multimedia • Interpreting cause and effect from oral discourse	Process explanations by • Identifying effects and consequences of events and phenomena from class discussions • Identifying interdependence of different parts of systems from multimedia presentations	Process explanations by • Recognizing specific language used to enhance clarity and precision • Recognizing and following language related to the same event or phenomenon throughout presentations
SPEAKING		Explain by • Ordering events or stages of phenomena with sequential language (e.g., *first, next, step 1*) • Using words and phrases to identify visually supported phenomena	Explain by • Naming properties, characteristics or features of illustrated content-related topics • Posing and responding to Wh-questions that relate to phenomena	Explain by • Connecting causes to effects in a series of statements • Sequencing processes, cycles, or procedures in short extended discourse	Explain by • Describing components of systems in small groups and class discussions • Providing precise words and phrases to provide details, descriptions, classifications, comparisons, causes/effects, or procedures	Explain by • Presenting information using an objective, neutral tone in extended discourse • Using nominalization to compress information and maintain coherence (e.g., "*This expansion...*" "*Weathering....*" "*An implication....*")	Explain by • Providing precision and accuracy in classifications, procedures, processes, and accounts using abstraction, technical language, and a variety of active/passive verb forms • Following discipline-specific organization (e.g., *orienting the reader, details, conclusion*) and supporting presentations with graphs, formulas, quotes or other media

Except for Level 6, for which there is no ceiling.

Figure 5.3 An example of Can Do descriptors organized by listening/speaking for Grades 9–12 (WIDA, 2016)

WIDA Performance Definitions - Listening and Reading Grades K-12

Within sociocultural contexts for processing language...

	Discourse Dimension	Sentence Dimension	Word/Phrase Dimension
	Linguistic Complexity	Language Forms and Conventions	Vocabulary Usage
	Level 6 - Reaching		
	English language learners will process a range of grade-appropriate oral or written language for a variety of academic purposes and audiences. Automaticity in language processing is reflected in the ability to identify and act on significant information from a variety of genres and registers. English language learners' strategic competence in processing academic language facilitates their access to content area concepts and ideas.		
	At each grade, toward the end of a given level of English language proficiency, and with instructional support, English language learners will process....		
Level 5 Bridging	• Rich descriptive discourse with complex sentences • Cohesive and organized, related ideas across content areas	• A variety of complex grammatical structures • Sentence patterns characteristic of particular content areas	• Technical and abstract content-area language • Words and expressions with shades of meaning across content areas
Level 4 Expanding	• Connected discourse with a variety of sentences • Expanded related ideas characteristic of particular content areas	• Complex grammatical structures • A broad range of sentence patterns characteristic of particular content areas	• Specific and some technical content-area language • Words or expressions with multiple meanings across content areas
Level 3 Developing	• Discourse with a series of extended sentences • Related ideas specific to particular content areas	• Compound and some complex grammatical constructions • Sentence patterns across content areas	• Specific content-area language and expressions • Words and expressions with common collocations and idioms across content areas
Level 2 Emerging	• Multiple related simple sentences • An idea with details	• Compound grammatical structures • Repetitive phrasal and sentence patterns across content areas	• General content words and expressions, including cognates • Social and instructional words and expressions across content areas
Level 1 Entering	• Single statements or questions • An idea within words, phrases, or chunks of language	• Simple grammatical constructions (e.g., commands, Wh- questions, declaratives) Common social and instructional forms and patterns	• General content-related words • Everyday social, instructional and some content-related words and phrases

Figure 5.4 An example of Performance Definitions organized by listening/reading for grades K-12 (Retrieved from https://wida.wisc.edu/sites/default/files/resource/Performance-Definitions-Receptive-Domains.pdf).

The assessment of speaking should involve interactive and two-way communication in which one person conveys a message and the other person interprets the message. Speaking can be measured more holistically, as a whole conversation, or by some of its components (grammar, vocabulary, pronunciation, fluency). Educators regularly listen to oral language samples in their classrooms, but most teachers do not have a systematic way to document and analyze oral language proficiency to record growth over time. Oral language proficiency is an important step in scaffolding MLs into reading and writing, but it is most often overlooked in instruction and assessment.

Table 5.9 is an example of an assessment for the purpose of measuring listening and speaking. The method is called observation with a checklist because the teacher is observing and listening and using a checklist to document the results. This checklist was modified from Genesee and Upshur (1996) to include a classroom context and core ideas. The language assessment can take place in a very natural (authentic) classroom setting, where students are engaging with academic tasks. Teachers can use this as a checklist by marking a check for yes and leaving a blank for no. Alternatively, a rating scale (1 = low, 2 = average and 3 = high) can be used to generate slightly more descriptive data. A PUMI study is shown below.

P	U	M	I
To assess listening, comprehension and speaking during classroom instruction.	To differentiate instruction based on individual language needs and share with other content teachers.	Teacher observation.	checklist.

Table 5.9 Example of a listening/speaking assessment: Observation with checklist

Listening during content instruction	Speaking during content instruction
1 Understands simple directions.	1 Pronounces vowel sounds correctly.
2 Understands simple sentences.	2 Pronounces consonant sounds well.
3 Understands simple yes/no.	3 Pronounces blends correctly.
4 Understands plurals.	4 Uses word stress correctly.
5 Understands content vocabulary appropriate to age.	5 Uses tone correctly.
6 Understands adjectives appropriate to age.	6 Gives one-word responses.
7 Understands several related sentences.	7 Produces simple sentences/questions.
8 Understands contractions and other common shortened forms.	8 Gives simple directions.
9 Distinguishes tones and understands their meaning.	9 Uses tense markers correctly.
10 Understands meaning of difference intonation patterns.	10 Uses prepositions correctly.
11 Understands more complex directions.	11 Forms complex sentences.
12 Understands rapid speech.	12 Gives descriptions.
13 Understands language in content area activity.	13 Uses vocabulary appropriate to age.
14 Understands language when peers speak to them.	14 Uses classroom language easily.

Listening

Whereas classroom instruction usually involves meaningful interaction with the teacher and peers, large-scale assessments of listening are generally restricted to a paper and pencil test simultaneously administered to a large group of MLs. Theoretically, test constructors design the listening items on discrete point (taken at one point in time) tests to measure only listening. An example of a discrete point listening assessment popular in schools, is measuring phonemic discrimination through a task such as recognizing minimal pairs (a minimal pair comprises two words that differ only by a sound, or phoneme). Figure 5.5 shows a decontextualized listening assessment (selected response) measured at one point in time. And there is no meaningful two-way interaction (e.g. the assessment is not administered in a communicative-based manner). Assessing discrete listening skills introduces many challenges.

As discussed earlier in this chapter, it is nearly impossible to separate listening from content in a school context. For example, if a student is asked during a listening assessment to sequence events in a story using story pictures, they must have listening comprehension, knowledge of the story and the ability to sequence events, each of which is a construct outside of listening. It is important to recognize the many constructs. This is called confounding constructs (when strong constructs get mixed, like language and content) and are considered a validity threat.

Figure 5.5 Listening assessment (phonemic discrimination). Directions: In each row ask students to circle the word the teacher pronounces.

The need to keep language constructs such as listening from confounding with other language or content constructs has been a challenge for psychometricians (measurement scientists) and educators. It may seem feasible on paper to separate languages, but the reality is that no one item measures only listening. It is more meaningful and natural to assess listening in a communicative-based manner, such as questioning with a rubric. Teacher observation is also an appropriate method for a communicative-based listening assessment. A teacher can observe a ML student performing many classroom-based listening activities. A rubric or checklist can easily be developed (see Chapter 4 for how to construct a rubric or checklist) to document how well a student listens within academic contexts and what progress he or she makes. For example, teachers can observe and document how MLs respond when they are asked to follow simple directions (put away the book, line up at the door), construct maps or figures from oral directions (identify symbols on a map, places from models) or sequence a series of events or illustrations using hands-on material from oral directions.

Reading

Educators assess reading for a variety of reasons. They might want to assess prior *knowledge*, decoding skills, reading comprehension strategies, interest and family practices in reading or many other reading measurables. The key, again, is to identify the purpose of the reading assessment and align the instruction and assessment with it. Often, reading assessments are done by mixing reading with productive language skills, like speaking and writing. However, when a teacher asks a student to retell a story (for the purpose of assessing reading comprehension), this is also an assessment of speaking. In the same way, asking a student to write about the story he or she just read can be an assessment of writing and speaking. It is important for educators to be aware of this natural confounding of variables when measuring constructs like reading, and to find ways to isolate skills when appropriate and necessary – but it's also important to understand that confounding language is a natural and authentic classroom use of language.

Another very natural way to read texts with MLs is to read content area texts in the home language, where available; this allows MLs to build more background *knowledge* and understand the English text more. This type of translanguaging method can be used during assessment and instruction. Also, consider running records when assessing reading; these are an in-depth way to observe a student's reading performance, and have been used for many years by reading experts. They allow the teacher to quickly assess strengths and weaknesses and to identify reading strategies used by the student, as well as those not used. Briceño and Klein (2018) studied how to use assessments such as running records to support ML students, students who are emerging in both language (new language in general) and literacy or multiliteracies. The researchers reframed 'error' as asset-based language related (LR) approximations. According to Briceño and Klein (2018), LR approximations are reading errors that are attributable to reader's language (the way they speak, the language structures they use and the vocabulary they know, e.g. 'he say' instead of 'he said'). This study shows that sometimes what teachers think are errors are linguistic features bound to the student's speech community (not errors).

For reading, it is important to draw from the whole linguistic repertoire (home languages and new languages) in decoding and retelling (Noguerón-Liu *et al.*, 2020). When using miscue analysis with MLs, it's important to identify miscues that are LR (due to the natural development of an additional language) from miscues that are reading related. Miscues related to reading include inserting words or changing words that impact the meaning of the text. For example, if a student reads 'villain' instead of 'village', this will change the meaning of the text and should be coded as a substitution miscue.

Ascenzi-Moreno (2018) studied how teachers can provide more equitable reading assessment practices. Adding two more categories to the traditional miscue analysis, related to language (L) and pronunciation (P), opens up spaces for translanguaging (Chapter 7 provides more detail about this as an accommodation for formative reading assessment). This is different from a monolingual administration of a formative reading assessment. Further, Noguerón-Liu *et al.* (2020) cautions against the three-cueing system because by expanding the formative reading assessment called miscue analysis to include LR perspectives (like translanguaging), teachers and families understand how MLs draw from their multiple language and literacy resources in decoding and retelling. Espinosa and Ascenzi-Moreno (2021) differentiate miscue analysis in this way by creating this differentiated miscue analysis form and through their ML framework (shown below in Figure 5.6) they guide teachers into articulating the language-based and reading-based miscues in a way that highlights the strengths of a developing ML reader. Figure 5.6 shows a strength-based framework for formative reading assessments.

Noguerón-Liu (2020) studied reading assessment sessions, audio recordings, home visits and interviews to discover more about how ML first graders use multiple linguistic resources during reading. To capture a fuller repertoire, the study was designed so that children used English and Spanish to retell the same text. Then they used the home language to retell to their mothers. Insights from this study highlighted the complexity of the pooled language resources of young children's repertoires.

Writing

As with reading, students write for a variety of purposes and utilize a number of different genres. Writing to share knowledge and give information and details on a topic is called informative or expository writing, whereby MLs rely on existing knowledge to integrate new ideas or analyze or synthesize ideas. Autobiographies or creative types of writing are based on observations that students have made in their lives; this is called expressive or narrative writing. Persuasive writing, which is evaluative in nature, combines some background knowledge with the author's view or opinion. Danling Fu (2009) emphasizes the following to develop writing skills and other language skills among MLs:

- Provide plenty of writing opportunities.
- Teach writing across content subject areas.
- Understand and guide students through writing stages.

Step	Responsive Adaptation	What is the Purpose of this Adaptation?
Introduce the Assessment	• Introduce story structure to students • Make culturally relevant connections/position difference • Introduce and revisit vocabulary	• To clarify themes or topics in the story which may be unfamiliar to students • To ensure that students are reminded of new vocabulary prior to reading
Listen to and Document Student Reading	• Create and use a column for language features	• To provide teachers with a way to determine whether miscues are reading- or language-related
Have Students Retell and Answer Comprehension Questions	• Rephrase questions • Invite students to retell or answer questions, using any features from their language and social resources	• To provide students with alternative wordings of comprehension questions that target their level of understanding • To provide students with opportunities to use their entire linguistic repertoire as they read
Determine Reading Level	• Calculate reading level, taking into account language learning (excluding language-based miscues)	• To determine whether miscues are language related and therefore should not be counted toward total number of miscues
Give Feedback to Students	• Focus on both language and reading teaching points	• To provide guidance to students that target both their language learning and reading

Figure 5.6 Strength-based framework for formative reading assessments (Espinosa & Ascenzi-Moreno, 2021)

- Give students the freedom in their language choice for expression.
- Allow students to move back and forth from their native writing to English writing.
- Urge bilingual, ESL and regular classroom teachers to collaborate on their curriculum for ML literacy and language development.

The next two figures (Figures 5.7 and 5.8) show a pre-assessment to a writing unit. Pre-assessments occur when teachers collect 'data' before a unit starts, then adjust the unit based on the results of the pre-assessment. Teachers in this NYC dual language bilingual program conducted writing responses (extended and short responses) to assess the way students in this class were languaging. These writing samples are culturally relevant because they are writing about their own family practices with food.

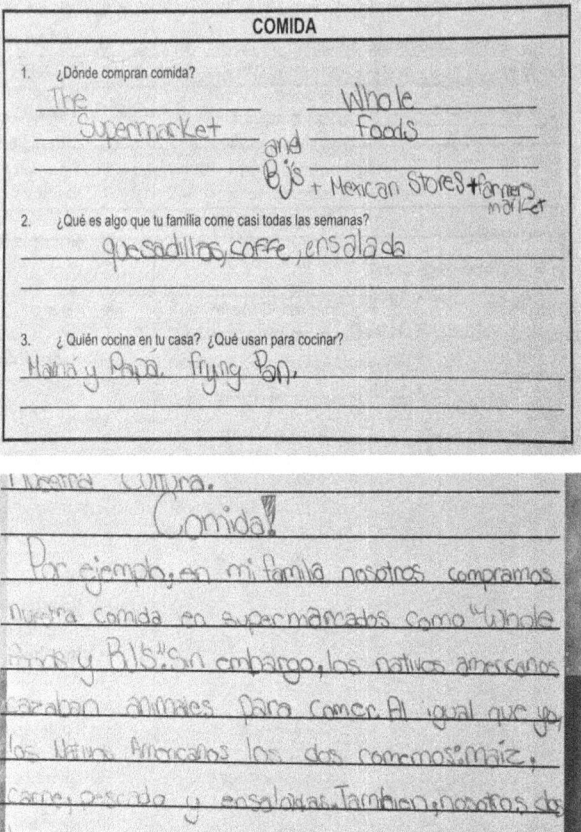

Figure 5.7 Contextualized writing samples showing how to use translanguaging with writing assessment (From Solarzo et al., 2019: 46–50)

Figure 5.8 shows how students are using both languages in this context. Based on language observations (data) the teachers collected (as shown in Figure 5.7), including vocabulary, compare/contrast language and past imperfect verbs, the teachers modify the curriculum and instruction to meet the exact needs of this group of students. This is student centered and contextualized (in-context) language learning.

The opposite of student-centered contextualized language learning is when schools choose to assess language out of context, as shown in the next example. This chapter ends with a snapshot of a situation where a summative language assessment was causing students to be labeled as non-nons, or not knowing any language. This demonstrates the danger of assessing language out of context and at one point in time (see assessments leading to deficit in Chapter 1), then using the results to make program and student-level decisions that negatively impacted students and families. At the time, most people didn't question the test; unfortunately, they trusted the test and questioned the children. This is further explained in the snapshot.

Week 1 Pre-Assessment: Language Observations

Basic Needs Vocabulary	Compare/Contrast Language	Natural Resources Vocabulary	Past Imperfect Verbs
Day 1 Comida *carnicería* *bodega* farmer's market *restaurante* street fair *vendedor de frutas* hot dog stand *supermercado* pizza *tamales* (Carlos) rice beans *pollo arroz* *estufa horno* Hogar *bildin* *edificio* building *casa de dos familias* *cobijas* *casa privada* *mantas* heater *calentador estín* radiator *ladrillos* *madera* *cemento* siding panels	Day 1 *también* also *ambos* (Pedro & Lisa) *y* *pero* too *tampoco* *igual que* (Yacely) neither both and *los dos*	Day 2 *(Gracias te damos)* trees wood *madera* *agua* *bayas* reindeer fish *plantas* squash Day 3 fur (not *pelaje*) *botes* *barcos* reindeer tipl	Day 3 Objectivo: "*usaban ___ para ___*" "used to" - Lucas translated incorrectly "*usaban de hacer*" (then Joseph repeated) Ryan, Sara, Samantha spoke in present tense "*usan*"

Figure 5.8 As a pre-assessment, Dual Language Bilingual teachers make language observations to determine instructional focus. Please note: This pre-assessment was done through a TLG lens. The roman words are in English and italic words are in Spanish.

SNAPSHOT: MOST PEOPLE QUESTIONED THE CHILDREN NOT THE TEST

The research study described here was launched by Dr Jeff MacSwan of the University of Maryland to investigate reports of large numbers of 'non-nons' (MLs who allegedly have no language) in states throughout the United States. The Individuals with Disabilities Education Act (IDEA) proficiency test (IPT)-Spanish and other Spanish language instruments were leading districts and state departments to conclude that students – who were known to be dominant Spanish speakers – did not know Spanish and were limited speakers of their primary language. These children were also not proficient in English; hence, they were labeled as semilingual or 'non-non'. The educational consequences of this label were severe. Students were often denied ESL or bilingual services and instead were mainstreamed. Some students were placed in special education (SPED) programs, contributing to the overrepresentation of MLs in SPED. Instead of questioning the instruments that measured language, most people questioned the children. MacSwan launched a major convergent validity study to investigate the (construct of many Spanish language proficiency) tests.

MacSwan, as reported in MacSwan and Mahoney (2008), investigated approximately 150 Spanish-dominant students who had been assessed in Spanish using the IPT-Spanish. The purpose of this test, as articulated by the test manual, was to measure Spanish oral language proficiency. Only 17 students were determined by the IPT-Spanish to be fluent in their native language. Upon further inspection, it was discovered that four items that required students to respond in a full sentence skewed the results. As the directions outlined, children who missed all four of the items shown in Table 5.10 were told to stop after that section and were consequently labeled as limited speakers of their native language. Many features of these items go against what we know to be good assessment practice for MLs: the items were decontextualized, the students must respond in a full sentence or their answer was wrong and the content of the items was peculiar and confused many students. It didn't help that at the time of this study, the Disney movie *Dumbo* was re-released and some students answered that yes, elephants can fly (see Item #22).

Even more troubling was a curve reminiscent of a bell shape that was formed by the results (Figure 5.9), which highlighted how strong test design (normal referencing) over (language) theory or conceptual framework can be. Keep in mind that the bell shape does not occur naturally; it is manipulated during test construction, and the pilot study in particular, when the measurement scientists select the items that behave properly (discriminate well) to create a 'normal' curve (on a norm-referenced test). This introduced many problems because first language acquisition does not function like a bell curve – nearly all students learn their first language orally, fluently and without much effort. This is in direct opposition to the assumptions of the bell curve.

The authors argued that requiring speakers to respond in complete sentences reflected a naive view of language proficiency, inconsistent with linguistic research, and characterized the requirement as 'academic bias' – that is, a prejudice that results from confusion between academic content knowledge related to language arts and actual linguistic ability. Consequently, the result produced arbitrary favoritism toward members of the education classes (MacSwan & Mahoney, 2008).

Discussion questions

- Should the IPT-Spanish be used for Spanish language assessment with Spanish-speaking children?
- How can language assessments using decontextualized items lead to invalid test scores?
- What were the consequences of using invalid test scores for MLs?
- What do you notice about the test items commonly missed by students in Table 5.10?

Table 5.10 Four items on the IPT-Spanish that skewed results

Item #17 *Qué está haciendo el niño?* (What is the boy doing?) Correct answer is *'El (niño) está leyendo/ estudiando'*.
Item #18 *Cuántas manos tengo yo?* (How many hands do I have?) Correct answer is *'Usted tiene dos manos'*.
Item #21 *Pueden correr los caballos?* (Are horses able to run?) Correct answer is *'Sí, pueden corer'*.
Item #22 *Vuelan los elefantes como los pájaros?* (Do elephants fly like birds?) Correct answer is *'No, los elefantes no vuelan'*.

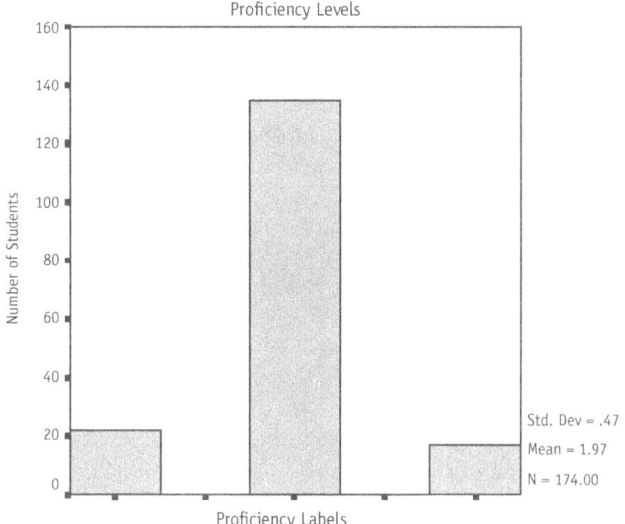

Figure 5.9 An example of how norm-referenced tests, by design, produce the bell curve; NSS: non-Spanish speaker; LSS: limited Spanish speaker; FSS: fluent Spanish speaker (From MacSwan & Mahoney, 2008)

END-OF-CHAPTER ACTIVITIES (Instructors: see advice at the end of the book)

By completing Activities 1–4, the reader will be able to:

(1) Sort eight clue cards into four content categories (*knowledge*, *reasoning*, *key practices* and *dispositional*) and describe one method of assessment that aligns best with this type of content.
(2) Choose the most appropriate assessment method for a given objective and instruction by completing an alignment table.
(3) Use ELP standards and PUMI to design assessment for MLs.
(4) Differentiate a language assessment by five levels.

Activity 1

Sort eight clue cards into four content categories (*knowledge*, *reasoning*, *key practices* and *dispositional*) and describe one method of assessment that aligns best with this type of content.

The instructor will give each table 10 clue cards to sort. At your table, sort the clue cards into the five content target categories (*knowledge*, *reasoning*, *key practices*, *products* and *dispositional*) and discuss with your group why you think it belongs in that category. After 15–20 minutes of practice, the instructor will ask each group, one by one, to bring up one clue card and deposit it into the correct brown bag and tell the class why your group thinks it belongs there. Each group has the exact same clue cards, so there will be opportunity for agreement/disagreement and good discussion as a whole group.

Activity 2

Choose the most appropriate assessment method for <u>objective</u> and <u>instruction</u> by completing an alignment table.

By yourself, complete two alignment tables (Tables 5.11 and 5.12) to practice selecting an appropriate assessment method.

Activity 3

Use ELP standards and PUMI to design an assessment for MLs.

Step 1 is done for you (given below). With a partner, complete Steps 2 and 3 to design a standards-based language assessment.

Step 1: From this standards-based statement, write one language objective, then create a PUMI table to provide an overview of the assessment. Students at all levels of ELP analyze the relative length of objects.

Step 2: _____ (insert one observable and measurable language objective.)

Step 3: _____ (practice PUMI to select an appropriate assessment method.)

Activity 4

Differentiate a language assessment by five levels.

Complete Activity 4 by using the content from Activity 2 and the six levels of language development introduced by WIDA (entering, emerging, developing, expanding, bridging and reaching) or using the language levels used in your school context. With a partner choose a graphic organizer to differentiate the language assessment by five levels. How might you differentiate the assessment? Hint: Whenever you differentiate the objective or instruction, you must also differentiate the assessment to maintain good alignment.

Table 5.11 Planning for assessment

Objectives	Instruction	Assessment
Content: SW (Student will) be able to compare and contrast the attributes of a square and a rectangle.	Is a square a rectangle? TW (Teacher will) model use of blocks to identify characteristics of square and rectangle. SW use a graphic organizer to collect evidence for or against.	What is a good method to assess content (think PUMI first)?
Language: SW be able to produce a written argument for why a square is a rectangle.	TW model using graphic organizer to write arguments and how to turn those arguments into a short paragraph.	What is a good method to assess language (think PUMI first)?

Table 5.12 Planning for assessment

Objectives	Instruction	Assessment
Content: SW (Student will) be able to calculate the number of protons, electrons and neutrons in an element, given its atomic number and atomic mass.	TW (Teacher will) use clue cards which have a question side and an answer side. SW rotate cards around small circle and practice reading and answering chemistry Q&A.	What is a good method to assess content (think PUMI first)?
Language: SW be able to listen to a question and tell a partner the number of protons/electrons/neutrons in an element.	In pairs, each student will listen to their partner read a chemistry clue card and practice answering it.	What is a good method to assess language (think PUMI first)?

Notes

(1) The author recognizes that content and language are huge constructs and that studying language and content in schools in this chapter is just a small fraction of the universal concepts of content and language. For a full book on language assessment, see Bachman and Palmer (2010) referenced in the Recommended Reading section at the end of this chapter.
(2) The idea of 'construct' is also discussed in detail in Chapter 3. A construct is a complex concept such as achievement, language proficiency, motivation, readiness and creativity. None of these concepts are 'visible', like height and weight are and, therefore, cannot be measured in a simple way like height and weight.
(3) Farther and further are comparative adverbs or adjectives. They are the irregular comparative forms of far. By not comprehending 'farther than' language used in math class, she is led to create the math equation, $2 + 5 = 7$ instead of $5 - 2 + 3$.
(4) Note: If the purpose was to assess Spanish language used in math (perhaps in a bilingual program), then it would be appropriate to assess in Spanish only. Along the same lines, if the purpose was to assess academic English used in math, then it is appropriate to assess in English only. The language of instruction depends on the purpose. But when the purpose is to assess content, translanguaging is encouraged and allows for more access to content.

References

Abedi, J. (2015) Language issues in item development. In S.M. Downing and T.M. Haladyna (eds) *The Handbook of Test Development* (pp. 377–398). Mahwah, NJ: Lawrence Erlbaum Associates.
Ascenzi-Moreno, L. (2018) Translanguaging and responsive assessment adaptations: Emergent bilingual readers through the lens of possibility. *Language Arts* 95 (6), 355–369.
Bachman, L.F. and Palmer, A.S. (2010) *Language Assessment in Practice*. Oxford: Oxford University Press.
Briceño, A. and Klein, A. (2018) A second lens on formative reading assessment with multilingual students. *The Reading Teacher* 72 (5), 611–621.
Celic, C. and Seltzer, K. (2011) *Translanguaging: A CUNY-NYSIEB Guide for Educators*. New York: The Graduate Center, CUNY-NYSIEB.
Escamilla, K., Butvilofsky, S. and Hopewell, S. (2017) What gets lost when English-Only writing assessment is used to assess writing proficiency in Spanish-English emerging bilingual learners. *International Multilingual Research Journal* 12 (4), 1-16.
Espinosa, C. and Ascenzi-Moreno, L. (2021) *Rooted in Strength: Using Translanguaging to Grow Multilingual Readers and Writers*. New York: Scholastic.
Fu, D. (2009) *Writing between Languages*. Portsmouth, NH: Heinemann.
Genesee, F. and Upshur, J. (1996) *Classroom-Based Evaluation in Second Language Education*. Cambridge: Cambridge Language Education.
Lo, Y. and Fung, D. (2020) Assessments in CLIL: The interplay between cognitive and linguistic demands and their progression in secondary education. *International Journal of Bilingual Education and Bilingualism* 23 (10), 1192–1210.

MacSwan, J. and Mahoney, K. (2008) Academic bias in language testing: A construct validity critique of the OPT I Oral Grades K-6 Spanish Second Edition (IPT Spanish). *Journal of Educational Research and Policy Studies (JERPS)* 8 (2), 86–101.

Noguerón-Liu, S. (2020) Expanding the knowledge base in literacy instruction and assessment: Biliteracy and translanguaging perspectives from families, communities, and classrooms. *Reading Research Quarterly* 55 (S1), S307–S318.

Noguerón-Liu, S., Shimek, C. and Bollinger, C. (2020) 'Dime De Que Se Trató'/'Tell me what it was about': Exploring emergent bilinguals' linguistic resources in reading assessments with parent participation. *Journal of Early Child Literacy* 20 (2), 411–433.

Solorza, C., Aponte,G., Leverenz, T., Becker, T. and Frias, B. (2019) *Translanguaging in Dual Language Education: A Blueprint for Planning Units of Study*. New York: CUNY NYSIEB, the Graduate Center, CUNY.

Stiggins, R. (2017) *The Perfect Assessment System*. Alecandria, VA: The Association for Supervision and Curriculum Development (ASCD).

WIDA (2016) Can do descriptors. Board of Regents of the University of Wisconsin System on behalf of the WIDA Consortium (www.wida.us)

Recommended reading

Ascenzi-Moreno (2016) An exploration of elementary teachers' views of informal reading inventories in dual language bilingual programs, literacy research and instruction. https://doi.org/10.1080/19388071.2016.1165318.

This article is a study examining how elementary teachers in a dual language program view assessment to support their students' reading growth. This article highlights reading assessment for MLs through the perspective of dynamic bilingualism.

Bachman, L. and Palmer, A. (2010) *Language Assessment in Practice*. New York: Oxford University Press.

This book presents the fundamental theory and application of design, development and use of language assessment.

Valdés, G. (2001) *Learning and Not Learning English: Latino Students in American Schools*. New York: Teachers College Press.

Valdés highlights four Mexican children in an American school and the struggles they face. She highlights the policies/instruction/assessment surrounding their learning of English. Her book offers a comprehensive view of real issues surrounding English language learning in US schools.

Valdés, G., Capitelli, S. and Alvarez, L. (2010) *Latino Children Learning English: Steps in the Journey*. New York: Teachers College Press.

Valdés, Capitelli and Alvarez describe the challenges faced by K–3 students who currently attend segregated schools. They highlight the ways in which English language proficiencies develop in newly arrived immigrants and challenge the myth that young children learn a second language effortlessly and quickly.

6 Psychometrics

Source: Gary Huck and Mike Konopacki, Labor Cartoons Collection; WAG 264; Box 26; Folder 63; Tamiment Library/Robert F. Wagner Labor Archives, New York University. Reproduced with permission.

THEMES FROM CHAPTER 6

(1) Criterion-referenced tests (CRTs) are more popular than norm-referenced tests (NRT); however, both have drawbacks.
(2) There are many types of scores but they are all generated from the same raw score.
(3) Teachers and parents have grown to not trust test scores due to multiple public test items or scoring errors made by testing companies.

Key Vocabulary

- Criterion referenced.
- Cut score.
- Norm referenced.

- Normal curve equivalent (NCE).
- Percentile rank (PR).
- Proficiency level.
- Psychometrics.
- Raw score.
- Scale score.
- Standard score.
- Standardized.
- Stanine.

PUMI Connection: Use

This chapter focuses on the U (Use) and interpretation of test scores by explaining test score results in a way that teachers and parents can understand. When educators of MLs receive reports back from publishing companies, it can be an overwhelming experience due to the large number of test scores presented. This chapter reminds the reader that all test scores are derived from one raw score and usually from a test given at one point in time. In addition to deconstructing the meaning of test scores, suggestions are also given on how to use test scores in appropriate ways.

As outlined by the American Educational Research Association (AERA), the American Psychological Association (APA) and the National Council on Measurement in Education (NCME) (2014) in *The Standards for Educational and Psychological Testing*, the test development process is completed in four phases: (1) development of test specifications; (2) development, tryout and evaluation of items; (3) assembly and evaluation of new test forms; and (4) development of procedures and materials for scoring and administration. Designing tests for multilingual students continues to be a challenge for the test makers. De Angelis (2021) outlines an approach to testing multilinguals that is sensitive to their unique needs.

A Multilingual Approach to Standardized Testing

Conducting her research in South Tyrol, Italy, Gessica De Angelis (2021) promotes an integrated approach to testing, an approach that lies somewhere in the middle of the traditional approach (monolingual testing in the dominant language for all students) and a holistic approach (the use of multiple languages as part of the testing process). According to De Angelis (2021), an integrated approach is when due considerations are given to test taker's profiles when they are scored and interpreted. An integrated assessment approach supports the idea that all assessments can be designed in a way that is sufficiently sensitive to linguistically and culturally diverse student populations. The integrated approach refers to the process of gathering information about the knowledge, skills and abilities of MLs, using tools designed for linguistically and culturally diverse populations that may be administered in multiple modalities, scored by multilingual examiners and interpreted using data about the test takers that include information about their language background and their living environment. De Angelis (2021) provides step-by-step non-technical recommendations on writing tests for linguistically and culturally diverse student populations and provides a general framework for test development and test interpretation based on her research in a trilingual community (Ladin, English, Italian) in South Tyrol, Italy. More detail on this framework is given later in this chapter. To build some background for a framework like this, it's important to understand what standardized tests really are.

What Exactly Does Standardized Mean?

Everything is standardized (the same) about the assessment: the items, the amount of time, the responses, the directions, etc. Typically, standardized tests consist of some combination of selected response (multiple choice or true/false, for example) and open response (short constructed response or extended constructed response) and usually standardized tests are given to a large group of students at the same time. *Everything about the test is standardized, except, of course, the students.* The illustration chosen to open this chapter demonstrates this idea in cartoon form. The anxious-looking students who represent different shapes and sizes are waiting to see if they 'fit' the cut-out shape.

Even though we usually discuss standardized assessments as large-scale NRTs or CRTs, the concept of standardization can apply to assessments that are alternatives to testing, such as oral presentations, observation checklists and journals. Most people see the strengths of standardized testing as (1) an efficient way to assess things such as achievement or language proficiency, (2) the fact that many students can be tested and scored in rapid time and/or (3) standardized assessments allow for large-scale comparisons.

What is the Difference between Norm-Referenced and Criterion-Referenced Scores?

When it comes to test design, one of the major differences in tests is whether they are norm referenced or criterion referenced. CRTs are more popular in schools today because the focus is now on evaluating how students perform against standards such as English language proficiency (ELP) or core standards (the standards are the criteria). Table 6.1 shows the differences and similarities between them.

The biggest difference between NRT and CRT achievement testing is who or what the scores are compared to. With NRT scores, students' performances are compared to another group of students' performances to judge how well they learned (did they perform better or worse than other students?). The other group is known as the norming group (sometimes called the peer or cohort group). In CRT testing, students' performances are compared to a set of behaviors, usually standards (did they meet the standard or not?). Normative scores – scores derived from NRTs – are far easier to obtain and consequently have been historically the most popular. Many standardized achievement tests were designed to fit into the age-old purpose of schools as sorting students (recall Figure 2.1 in Chapter 2 of this book 'schools as sorters' and accompanying discussion). The items selected in the final version of a test are designed specifically to discriminate (or sort) differences in student achievements. One thing we don't often think of is that the items on a test that don't discriminate (or sort students) do not make the final published version of a test. Because of this, norm-referenced tests are constructed and designed to sort students; this (e.g.

Table 6.1 Similarities and differences between NRTs and CRTs

	NRT	CRT
Differences	Performance is determined based on comparison to peer group	Performance is determined based on comparison to standards
	The norm is a rank at the 50th percentile	Cut score determines the point between proficient and not proficient
	Half score above the 50th percentile and half score below	Theoretically, all students can meet the standard
	Half score above grade level and half score below	Theoretically, all students can meet the standard
Similarities	Standardized	Standardized
	Usually high stakes	Usually high stakes
	Linguistic complexity of items can introduce error for MLs	Linguistic complexity of items can introduce error for MLs
	MLs are expected to perform similarly to students who can read the test	MLs are expected to perform similarly to students who can read the test

the normal curve) does not happen naturally and would not happen if not for the items written in a way, and selected for final test assembly, as items that 'discriminate' well. Because of this, norm-referenced tests buy into the 100-year-old 'schools as sorters' myth.

Test Fairness

Fairness in testing is closely related to bias. After the 1960s, the topic of test fairness became increasingly popular and is still growing. Many test designers are extremely concerned with test fairness, especially with groups of students with unique needs such as MLs. Test fairness researchers try to determine with data whether a test favors one group of students over another (like English speakers and non-English speakers). When a test favors one group of students over another, there are test fairness concerns.

The classic validity concern with NRT and MLs is the underrepresentation of MLs in the norming group. This means that when the test was designed, it was not 'tried out' with MLs to see if the test functioned in a similar way for MLs. This also means that the group of children chosen to compare scores with 'the norm' includes an underrepresentation of MLs. These practices lead to comparing MLs to native English-speaking children; this will always lead to a low ranking of MLs. It is much more methodologically appropriate to compare MLs to other MLs; ideally, norming groups should consist entirely of MLs. One widely criticized norm in second language (L2) research is what researchers call the 'native speaker norm'. In language testing, this is the practice of measuring L2 learners' performance using native-like norms and is now associated with what is commonly referred to as the *monolingual bias* (De Angelis, 2021). There is another parallel bias called *the bilingual bias*, which refers to the tendency to establish an equivalence between a bilingual and a multilingual mind, especially seen in multilingual testing and assessment, particularly since most of the research is conducted with bilinguals and applied to the topic of multilingual testing (De Angelis, 2021). Further, multilinguals who struggle to reach language proficiency in each of their languages identical to their monolingual counterparts are always compared to them and tend to receive lower scores. This leads to multilinguals being penalized for their multilingual competencies, sending a message that multilingual knowledge is a liability (Shohamy, 2011). Plainly put, the field of multilingual testing cannot address the needs of multilingual students if the focus is on monolingual and bilingual students.

Test designers have become sensitive to norming-bias issues and use sophisticated measurement methods to construct fair norming groups and more articulated direction (in the blueprint) about who should use their instruments. Unlike in the past, they now select large groups of children to participate in norming studies, including African American, white, Hispanic, Native American and Asian, as well as affluent, middle class, poor, urban, suburban and rural. Thus, test publishers develop various kinds of 'local norms' so comparisons can be made with similar demographics. But is this enough? Can the complexity of culture and language for such a large variety of groups be represented in the functioning of a test without causing too much error? Students have different languaging profiles and use those languages differently from context to context. Hypothetical group membership and language profiles used in a test blueprint may be convenient for test designer but it contributes to the perceived 'gap' in test scores between monolinguals and multilinguals. These types of ideas can lead teachers and students to feel like the 'system' is set up against ML students.

AERA, APA, NCME (2014) views fairness as a fundamental validity issue that requires attention throughout all stages of test development and use. They also review two major concepts that have recently emerged to minimize bias and increase test fairness. The first concept is accessibility – the notion that all test takers should have an unobstructed opportunity to demonstrate their standing on the construct being measured (AERA, APA, NCME, 2014). The second new concept is universal design – an approach to test design that seeks to maximize accessibility for all intended examinees. Universal design intends to reduce construct irrelevant variance (CIV) for examinees like MLs. A detailed discussion of universal design can be found in the 'Fairness in Testing' chapter of the *Standards* (AERA, APA, NCME, 2014: Part 1 Chapter 3).

Michael Zieky (2006) discusses how fairness reviews occur when designing tests. He gives six fairness review guidelines in the *Handbook for Test Development*. A more detailed discussion of fairness can be found in the *Handbook*.

(1) Treat people with respect.
(2) Minimize the effects of construct-irrelevant knowledge or skills.
(3) Avoid material that is unnecessarily controversial, inflammatory, offensive or upsetting.
(4) Use appropriate terminology to refer to people.
(5) Avoid stereotypes.
(6) Represent diversity in depictions of people.

These fairness guidelines from 2006 seem to be more superficial and start to scrape the surface of what needs to be done with bilingual or multilingual test design. In 2021, De Angelis introduced ways of designing good quality tests for culturally and linguistically diverse student populations that adhere to the principles of validity, inclusivity, viability and accessibility (or VIVA). Table 6.2 further articulates VIVA.

Table 6.2 VIVA, a way of designing good quality tests for culturally and linguistic diverse populations that adhere to the principles of validity, inclusivity, viability and accessibility

V: Validity	A good quality test must show good construct validity, even in a translated or simplified format, which means that the test must successfully measure all the stated learning objectives by providing versions of similar difficulties in all languages. This applies to all multilingual tests, whether they are multilingual-by-translations or multilingual-by-design.
I: Inclusivity	A test should be designed for linguistically and culturally diverse student populations of learners who may have different levels of proficiency in the language(s) of testing. A test is inclusive when it is designed for the multilingual population in general, not for a subset of the multilingual population such as immigrants or minority language speakers with poor language proficiency in the language(s) of testing.
V: Viability	Viability means that the test must offer a truly workable option. Viability is one of the most difficult challenges of all, since viability and the number of languages to be included in a test have an inverse relationship with each other, that is, the more languages that must be represented in the test, the lower the viability.
A: Accessibility	A good quality test must also show accessibility. That means it should be easy to understand for all students, including those with limited proficiency in the language of instruction, and must give students the opportunity to access their knowledge resources to complete the test. These resources can be internal (personal language or content knowledge) or external (use of language support).

Source: De Angelis (2021).

Cut Scores

Within the concept of test fairness, cut scores have become increasingly controversial because important educational decisions are made about MLs (and non-MLs alike) on this basis. Cut scores are recommended by the test publisher, but oftentimes final determination is made by state departments of education. CRT is appealing to parents and teachers in general (especially those tired of NRTs) because it moves away from using one group of children as normal or standard; however, CRT design and valid implementation are not as easy as one might expect. Pitfalls include determining cut scores; specifying educational outcomes with enough clarity to measure them; using a limited range of behaviors to represent larger educational goals; the increased stakes associated with cut scores (graduating or not, advancing grade level or not, college entrance decisions, etc.); and accounting for the measurement error inherent in tests.

The process by which testing companies set proficiency levels (cut scores) for standards is largely based on judgment because test designers call upon teachers, instructional staff, community members and others to make judgments about how well students should perform on standards-based assessments. What exactly is the cut between being proficient at something or not? Imagine making the incredibly difficult judgment about when a student is proficient in a language and when he or she is not based on a number. Because language is a process, developmental and a continuum of growth, choosing a cut score for language proficiency tests is always questionable (and should be questioned!). To exasperate the problem of cut scores, we know less about language proficiency levels than we think. The state of knowledge about the stages of acquisition in L2 learning does not support precise expectations about the sequence of development of English by the group of students whose proficiency must be assessed and determined by federally mandated ELP language assessments. Because of this, constructing developmental sequences and progressions is very much a minefield (Poza & Valdés, 2017).

These issues for CRTs have never been resolved; in fact, the need to resolve them has intensified as the sanctions for not passing CRTs have increased since No Child Left Behind (NCLB). Another inherent problem with CRTs is that educators often disagree about the quality of a given set of standards. Some state standards have been criticized for including too little or too much information, for being too difficult, for undermining local curriculum and instruction and for taking sides in political and educational controversies. That said, a CRT can only be as good as the standards it is trying to measure.

How Do I Know If a Test is Norm Referenced or Criterion Referenced?

The quickest way to tell whether a test is an NRT or a CRT is to review how the results are presented. If test scores are presented through grade equivalent (GE), percentile rank or any rank score, these are associated with norm referencing – these scores are all used to compare test takers to one another, or rank. If the results are presented through some type of categorical scale (approaching, meeting or exceeding the standard), they are associated with criterion referencing. However, the most thorough way to investigate a test is to read the test manual (sometimes called a blueprint) that must be made public and must thoroughly explain the test design, standards and theories used to design it, the test construction principles and much more. Easier said than done because test manuals may be difficult to find and even more difficult to read. The test manual contains detailed information and reading the technical test manual is the best way to understand if a test is based on norms or criteria.

How Should I Interpret Test Scores?

Teachers have always struggled with interpreting results from standardized tests, in particular making results useful for the teachers, students and families. The following section intends to clarify common standardized test score interpretations, in hopes to increase the communication of assessment results. Effective communication of assessment results should be a required priority in high-quality assessment. Schools leaders should not ask teams of teachers to spend hard-to-find meeting time trying to decipher the meaning of complex and confusing test score results, when this time can be used for things like planning student-centered lessons. Instead, teachers should be given useful and immediate assessment results. The following sections cover some of the basics with test score interpretations.

Raw score

A raw score is exactly what it implies – nothing has been done to it yet or it hasn't been 'cooked' yet. For example, if you scored 20/30 on an assessment, this is the raw score; you answered 20 items correctly and 10 items incorrectly. It is not ranked or compared to groups of children. Alone, the raw score has no independent meaning. It is not appropriate to compare across subjects or across grade level. It is an independent score and not very useful. All other scores are derived from the raw score. So, if it looks like a child has five scores, it is likely the child has one score (raw) and it is dressed in five different ways (see all test score types below).

Scale score

The scale score is derived from the raw score, and it links together all test forms (different forms for different grade levels) within one content area. Therefore, it is acceptable to compare across grade levels or other forms of the test with scale scores as long as you remain in the same content area. This score is useful if you want to study change in performance over time. As with a language proficiency test, it is appropriate to compare the scale score across three or more years to see how a student is doing on English proficiency (as defined by the test). The drawback is that scaled scores cannot be compared across content areas or subjects. If you are interpreting a scale score from the ACCESS for English language learners (ELLs language proficiency test from WIDA), there are separate scale scores for reading, writing, speaking and listening; a 380 in speaking does not necessarily mean the same thing as a 380 in writing, for example. Of all the scores, scale scores are the best interpretation to show growth over time within the same area.

Proficiency level scores

Proficiency level scores are an interpretation of scale scores and they are a direct result of choosing a cut score for each language level. Remember that proficiency levels are not set in stone; it is up to the test developers to determine them, which can sometimes be an arbitrary process. This is why proficiency levels for different tests are not usually comparable. For any test, you have to dig deep to find out how proficiency levels are determined; sometimes, this is too time-consuming and frustrating for educators. But for those who really want to know what proficiency levels mean, test companies must give an answer about what theory or conceptual framework was used to develop standards or proficiency levels and how cutoffs for levels were determined. Some companies are more forthcoming than others.

One issue of accessing this important information can be the denseness of reports. For example, the WIDA Technical Reports can range from 185 pages to 683 pages long. Technical Reports provide extensive information on the conceptualization of the assessment from standards to development. Topics and evidence can range from how standards were set (remember that proficiency levels are anchored in standards) to showing the background information about the cut scores that informed proficiency levels. The total number of pages in the technical reports is enough to scare any educator away because they usually run from 100 to 350 pages.

However, if persistent, you can find technical reports by visiting a website or calling a publishing company; according to the *Standards* (AERA, APA, NCME, 2014), technical reports should be accessible. WIDA makes their technical reports available annually online. Go to the WIDA website and type in technical report in the search engine https://www.wida.us/index.aspx.

If your state participates in WIDA (more than 40 do), then the six WIDA language proficiency levels are important to you: (1) entering, (2) beginning, (3) developing, (4) expanding, (5) bridging and (6) reaching. As the results of testing, both parents and teachers receive bar graphs showing proficiency scores. Proficiency level scores for the ACCESS for ELLs test also have decimal points to show the proportion within that proficiency level. For example, 3.9 shows that the student is almost a level 4; be aware, however, that these proportions are not equal from level to level because different levels of scale scores make up different levels. Therefore, a scale score of 350 in writing may be a performance level of 4.8 for writing, but a scale score of 350 in speaking may be 4.2. Unlike scale scores, proficiency levels may be used to make comparisons between domains. As you can see, with each interpretation, we get further away from the raw score.

Composite scores

As the name implies, this is a score that combines the scale score of several domains, but with a weight to adjust for the difference in scaling by domain. The proficiency levels of composite scores are determined when scale scores from relevant domains are combined and weighted, then the scores are added together. On the ACCESS for ELLs test by WIDA, the comprehension score is calculated by 70% reading and 30% listening according to the following formula: (reading scale score × 0.7) + (listening scale score × 0.3) = comprehension scale score. Like non-composite domains, the scale score can lead to a proficiency level. They are intended to offer a variety of perspectives on student language development, but they may make test score interpretation more complicated than it needs to be. This author prefers not to use composite scores much because the results are too aggregated (combined).

Grade-level equivalent

GEs are often misinterpreted, and are being used less and less. If a sixth-grade student is learning English as her L2 and she scores 3.5 GE on an NRT that was given to her in English, this could be interpreted in a variety of ways. First, the student may have systematic errors caused by not fully knowing the language of the test. Therefore, it is difficult to make any judgments about how much content she actually knows. In this case, more authentic language assessments should be used to make educational and instructional decisions about the student. In his book *Put to the Test*, Gerald Bracey (2002) decoded some of the myths around grade-level equivalents:

> Mischief often occurs when a child in, say, the fourth grade, brings home a test report declaring that she has a grade-equivalent in reading of 7. Why, the parents are likely to wonder, is my child not in seventh grade, at least for her reading, since she is reading at seventh-grade level. But she is not reading at seventh-grade level. The

seventh-grade level for seventh-graders is the score that the average seventh-grader would score in seventh-grade material. When a fourth-grader gets a grade equivalent of 7 on a test, it represents what the average seventh-grader would score on fourth-grade reading material. Of course this would be true only if any seventh-graders had ever taken the fourth-grade test. But they haven't. Test publishers cannot afford too much out-of-grade testing, such as giving the fourth-grade test to seventh-graders. Mostly, they give the fourth-grade test to some sample of third-graders and fifth-graders. The projection of how a typical seventh-grader would score is a statistical extrapolation based on the scores of third-, fourth- and fifth-graders. We have no idea how valid it might be in reality. (Bracey, 2002)

In addition, GEs do not hold equal intervals – the distance between ranks can vary widely. A student who was ranked with a PR of 95 may have scored 625, whereas a student who ranked 94 may have scored 595 (a difference of 30). This will not hold equal intervals because a student who scored a PR of 49 may have scored 450 and someone who was ranked 48 may have scored 449 (a difference of 1). Bracey (2002) uses the analogy of house addresses. In a rural area there might be long distances, perhaps a half-mile, between houses, yet the house numbers may be 6005 and 6007. In an urban area, however, house numbers 6005 and 6007 may be only a few feet apart. These house numbers (ordinal) do not hold equal interval and it would make no sense to average them or add them for any reason. Because GEs do not hold equal intervals, it is not appropriate to average them; newspaper writers sometimes do this and it can be very misleading. The GE test score is more misunderstood than it is useful, and therefore it is discouraged for use with students in general.

Percentile rank

PR tells where a student stands in regard to other students. PR is similar to GE because PRs are related to the normal curve and NRTs. Most people think that if a student learning English as an additional language receives a PR of 51, he or she performed better than 51% of the students at his or her school or the students in the nation who took the test that year. However, this is not correct. The norming group is ranked from 1 to 100, and the student is compared to the norming group. Since most norming groups are made up of native English-speaking students, who have the advantage of knowing the language of the test, MLs will almost always rank low. Like GEs above, PRs do not hold equal intervals and because of that should not be averaged.

Normal curve equivalents

Like the GE and the PR, the NCE is related to the normal curve and NRTs and it carries with it the same inherent concerns. This score was designed to correct for the lack of equal intervals in GE and PR, but the only way to interpret NCE in a meaningful way is to have a normal curve line graph accessible and compare the PR scale to the NCE scale. Rarely do educators have the chart in front of them to use this test score. Conceptually, this score can be used to average and researchers will often use NCEs in effectiveness studies.

Are Tests Objective?

We, as a society, have historically placed blind trust in standardized test results that have centuries of a not-so-pleasant history (see Chapter 2). If the test says so, then it's the truth. Many people (parents, students, policymakers, school leaders, general public) place blind trust in the results of tests and take the results as 100% truth. This is not to imply that tests are useless, they are just not flawless and in some cases with MLs or others who are not from the mainstream culture, tests can do more harm than good, as the cartoon at the opening of this chapter implies.

In addition, standardized tests are typically promoted as more objective than classroom assessments, but many aspects of standardized tests are subject to human error aside from scoring, when done by a programmed machine. How to use test results, how items are worded, what items to include on the test, which answers are correct and how the test is administered are all susceptible to human subjectivity as well as human error. Tests can be just as subjective as other assessments. In all assessment, we want to remove subjectivity unrelated to the purpose of the assessment (or the construct). If we keep tests in perspective and balance them with other assessments (multiple methods or triangulation) that work in classrooms, a more balanced and promising view of students can emerge.

What Do Report Card Grades Really Tell Us?

When final report card grades are documented, the grade that is given represents a lot of information that has been condensed into one letter grade or number. We do this to make it easier to manage the information and make it easier for teachers, parents, college admissions and school leadership to use. But the amount of information that is eliminated in order to have an easy way to communicate how a student is doing may be working against the idea of efficiency. Classroom-level assessment results may document how a student progressed across a continuum of learning the content standards; however, all of this detail disappears with a report card. Because one letter or number is given per subject, all detail about students' mastery of specific learning targets is missing in a report card. To add insult to injury, teachers average the grades across content areas and years, to generate one overall average or grade point average (GPA) to represent one student. This overall average becomes critically important when applying to university and becoming eligible for academic scholarships. The same five MLs with a B+ average can have wildly different learning trajectories and strengths in their ability. Report card grades are easy to manage but how much meaningful information is lost by making it simple?

How Can We Communicate Assessment Results More Effectively?

The previous sections of this chapter showed many ways to make assessment results complicated, which frequently makes the results less useful for teachers and students. Assessment results may contain content not familiar to the recipient, they might be delivered in a language unfamiliar to the recipient, presented with complicated data displays and more. These may cause frustration for the teacher, the student and others, and may even make the time, energy and stress to make them a waste of valuable teaching time. One area in need of improvement in the assessment of MLs is the ability to communicate assessment results in a timely manner and also in a way that teachers, parents and students can understand the results and make use of them. Communicating assessment results in this way can inform educational decisions on all levels. These results should be informing us how well students have mastered the content standards and also how a student is progressing in language development. Only after timely and effective communication of assessment results can teachers determine what learning objectives come next. The only way to obtain accurate and meaningful data on student achievement is to assure the Purpose (P) is clear, the Use (U) is appropriate, the Method (M) is a good match for the purpose and the Instrument (I) is of high quality – PUMI. The results should be simple, useful and in a language the intended audience understands well. For multilingual classrooms where the teacher is monolingual, this means using interpreters, digital translators or linguistic resources from other teachers, staff, students and community members. Assessment results should be written in a simple way and in a language that gives access to many stakeholders.

Psychometricians Do Make Mistakes

Because of the increased demand for and the quantity of testing at the onset of NCLB, an unprecedented strain was put on the capacity of testing manufacturers. At times, this led to an increase in the number of wide-scale errors affecting the lives of hundreds of thousands of children (FairTest: The National Center for Fair and Open Testing, 2007). In 2003, the Harcourt Assessment Company had to apologize for 45 flaws on the Hawaii state test, which was given to thousands of Hawaiian students. That same year, Harcourt made a series of expensive mistakes in Nevada (including mistakenly informing 736 high school sophomores that they had failed the math test) for which the state fined Harcourt $425,000. In Connecticut, CTB/McGraw Hill needed to hire additional workers to re-score student writing on the Connecticut mastery test to rescue their $48 million contract with the State Department of Education. There's more. Minnesota denied diplomas to 8,000 students based on testing errors. In Illinois, 400 public schools were labeled as failures when they had actually met federal standards in 2003. Table 6.3 shows a sample of previous newspaper headlines regarding test construction errors, as found on FairTest.org.

Table 6.3 A sample of news headlines about widespread test error in the NCLB

$3 million settlement for SAT scoring error
Florida test scoring error highlights exam flaws
Suits filed over teacher test scoring error
GMAT error hurts applicants: Test takers not told of mistake for 10 months
Minnesota students win lawsuit
ETS pays $11.1 million to settle teacher test lawsuit
N.C. lawsuit charges test
Seventy percent of schools to fail

Source: Headlines from FairTest.org.

SNAPSHOT: HASTY MISTAKES ERODE PUBLIC TRUST

In New York State, after complaints about the spring 2012 tests, Pearson deleted at least 29 items due to errors such as confusing terminology (e.g. 'median' confused with 'mean'), negative signs becoming positive signs and so forth. In addition to fundamental errors, many typos were found. Needless to say, this experience eroded public support for using test scores for accountability and cast severe doubt on using test scores to evaluate students and teachers at the time. However, a panel of experts deemed that using these test scores was still valid. Negative public response, as reflected in many blogs, was directed at Pearson for being so careless and at New York State for contracting with Pearson and using test scores with known flaws to evaluate teachers, at that time. One blog response to an article about the errors read, 'You mean to tell me you make $32 million dollars on New York tests, and you can't afford to hire a proofreader?'. As a consequence, in 2015, New York cancelled its contract with Pearson, as did many other states.

Discussion questions

- Why do you think large publishing companies such as Pearson made mistakes such as these?
- What are the consequences of these mistakes?
- What can educators do to protect against these types of errors?

SNAPSHOT: THE PINEAPPLE DEBACLE

In an Old Danish fairy tale, an emperor is duped into buying 'magic' cloth that only some people can see. Believing the cloth to be real, the emperor marches in a procession completely naked, but only a small child has the courage to state that the emperor has no clothes. The phrase has come to symbolize an obvious political truth that is still denied by a majority of people. In the world of high-stakes testing, the phrase 'a pineapple has no sleeves' has much of the same meaning and was often used as a rallying cry by the anti-testing movement to symbolize the overreliance on high-stakes tests.

The roots of the phrase date back to roughly 2007, when a nonsensical passage, written by the author Daniel Pinkwater, began to appear on English language arts (ELA) tests from the Pearson Corporation. Because test items were withheld from the public and researchers, backlash was restricted to word of mouth. This changed in 2012 when New York State students began to discuss the ELA passage on Facebook and Twitter and almost overnight the news went viral. Teachers and parents were outraged; student reaction ranged from laughter to anger to disbelief and the whole affair came to be known as 'Pineapplegate'. Years later, it still serves as an embarrassment to Pearson and New York State education officials.

The passage itself is a parody of Aesop's famous 'Tortoise and the Hare' fable, but this time the hare races a pineapple. Other animals are worried that the pineapple might have a trick up its sleeve to win, but predictably the pineapple cannot move and the hare wins the race. The animals then eat the pineapple. Students were required to answer six follow-up questions, two of which were impossible to answer correctly based solely on the given passage. Those two questions were

(1) The animals ate the pineapple most likely because they were (a) hungry; (b) excited; (c) annoyed; (d) amused.
(2) Which animal spoke the wisest words? (a) the hare; (b) the moose; (c) the crow; (d) the owl.

The story went viral and was covered by national news outlets such as *The Washington Post*, *The New York Times* and *The Wall Street Journal*. Pinkwater, who wrote the passage, was 'baffled' that it was used in such a way, telling *The Wall Street Journal* that his story was 'nonsense on top of nonsense on top of nonsense'.

Pearson refused to comment on the item, citing company policy. In the wake of the controversy, then New York Education Commissioner John King decided to exclude the item from the test results; he stated that the passage was reviewed by a committee of teachers and was chosen to compare New York students to students in other states who were presented with the same item. He argued that the test itself was still valid (the outdated concept of validity), despite the discarded item. Teachers and administrators grew more alarmed and frightened that 20% of their effectiveness would be judged on such tests and test items with little regard for checks and balances. Parents were dismayed that an item such as the pineapple question could be used to make important educational decisions about their child. The fact that the item had appeared on high-stakes tests dating back at least five years seemed to be a stunning indictment of the entire test development system.

Discussion questions
- Why didn't the committee of reviewers catch this item?
- What sort of checks and balances are in place to ensure high-quality items for high-stakes tests?
- How do you think MLs negotiate items such as the pineapple item?
- How can educators be assured that the test scores being used for high-stakes testing, such as promotions or determining teacher effectiveness, are valid data?

Table 6.4 Simulated 2012 student roster report from ACCESS for ELLs[a] English language proficiency test

Student, year	Tier	Cluster	Listening		Speaking		Reading		Writing		Oral language[b]		Literacy[c]		Comprehension[d]		Overall[e]	
			Scale score	Prof level	Scale score	Prof level	Scale score	Prof level	Scale score	Prof level	Scale score	Prof level	Scale score	Prof level	Scale score	Prof level	Scale score	Prof level
Orlanny 2017	B	9–12	373	3.4	326	2.2	341	1.9	376	3.2	351	2.8	359	2.5	351	2.3	356	2.6
Orlanny 2016	A	9–12	266	1.7	347	2.8	384	4.0	375	3.2	307	1.9	380	3.4	349	2.3	358	2.7
Orlanny 2015	B	9–12	383	3.2	182	1.0	336	1.9	367	3.1	273	1.7	352	2.5	344	2.3	328	1.9
Edwin 2017	B	9–12	406	4.6	370	3.7	350	2.1	402	3.9	383	4.2	378	3.2	367	2.9	379	3.5
Edwin 2016	A	9–12	356	2.8	358	3.2	371	2.9	370	3.0	357	2.9	371	2.9	367	2.9	366	2.9
Edwin 2015	B	9–12	354	2.9	328	2.2	331	1.9	374	3.3	341	2.6	353	2.5	338	2.1	349	2.6
Leomar 2017	B	9–12	416	5.0	406	5.4	392	5.0	417	4.6	411	5.2	405	4.7	389	5.0	406	4.9
Leomar 2016	B	9–12	397	4.4	337	2.6	390	5.6	387	3.7	367	3.5	389	3.9	392	4.7	384	3.8
Leomar 2015	C	9–12	397	4.4	358	3.4	378	3.7	337	2.0	378	3.9	358	2.7	384	4.0	364	3.0

[a] ACCESS for ELLs® stands for Assessing Comprehension and Communication in English State-to-State for English Language Learners. It is a large-scale test that first and foremost addresses the English language development *standards* that form the core of the WIDA Consortium's approach to instructing and testing English language learners. *31 US states and territories* now belong to the WIDA Consortium.
[b] Oral language = 50% listening + 50% speaking.
[c] Literacy = 50% reading + 50% writing.
[d] Comprehension = 30% listening + 70% reading.
[e] Overall = 15% listening, 15% speaking, 35% reading, 35% writing.

> **END-OF-CHAPTER ACTIVITIES (Instructors: see advice at the end of the book)**
>
> After completing Activities 1 and 2, the reader will be able to:
>
> (1) Interpret test scores from language proficiency test results.
> (2) Identify nine key terms in psychometrics.
>
> **Activity 1**
>
> Interpret test scores from language proficiency test results.
> Read Chapter 6 and interpret Table 6.4 to answer the following questions.
>
> (1) What are scale scores?
> (2) What are proficiency levels?
> (3) Which scores are composite and which are not? What are the composite scores made of? What are composite scores? Do you think composite scores help or hinder what you know about a student's language proficiency? How might you use composite scores?
> (4) What are some overall trends you see in the data?
> (5) How is Orlanny doing?
> (6) How is Edwin doing?
> (7) How is Leomar doing?
>
> **Activity 2**
>
> Identify nine key terms. Use these words to set up the BINGO board: psychometrician, Norm referenced, Criterion referenced, Distracter, Measurement error, Grade Equivalents, Percentiles, Normal Curve Equivalent, Scale Score
>
> This is a game of bingo using key vocabulary words from the chapter. Fold a piece of paper into nine equal parts (fold it into thirds, then fold it into thirds again). The instructor will write nine key vocabulary words on the board. Write them in any of the squares (one word per square). After this, students should have different bingo boards. The difference between this bingo and traditional bingo is that the instructor will read the clue and students will have to find the key vocabulary word that matches it. After a match is found, cross out the whole square. Once a student has bingo (three across, down or diagonal), he or she shouts 'bingo!' and the instructor will check the work.

References

AERA, APA, NCME (2014) *Standards for Educational and Psychological Testing*. Washington, DC: American Educational Research Association.

Bracey, G. (2002) *Put to the Test: An Educator's and Consumer's Guide to Standardized Testing*. Bloomington, IN: Phi Delta Kappa Intl Inc.

De Angelis, G. (2021) *Multilingual Testing and Assessment*. Bristol: Multilingual Matters.

FairTest: The National Center for Fair and Open Testing (2004) Torrent of testing errors. https://fairtest.org/article/torrent-testing-errors/ (accessed 22 February 2024).

Poza, L. and Valdés, G. (2017) Assessing English language proficiency in the United States. In E. Shohamy and I. Or (eds) *Encyclopedia of Language and Education. Language Testing and Assessment* (pp. 427–440). New York: Springer International Publishing.

Shohamy, E. (2011) Assessing multilingual competencies: Adopting construct valid assessment policies. *The Modern Language Journal* 95 (3), 418–429.

Zieky, M. (2006) Fairness review in assessment. In S. Downing and T. Haladyna (eds) *Handbook of Test Development* (pp. 359–376). Mahwah, NJ: Lawrence Erlbaum Associates.

Recommended reading

Copeland, G., Finley, S., Ferguson, C. and Alderete, K. (2000) Activity 3: Clapping hands. In G. Copeland, S. Finley, C. Ferguson and K. Alderete (eds) *A Collection of Tools to Promote Instructional Coherence* (pp. 22–28). Austin, TX: Southwest Educational Development Laboratory (SEDL).

This activity deepens understanding of psychometrics through participation in a simulation that physically demonstrates the difference between NRT and CRT and other unintended consequences of assessment. The author highly recommends administering the clapping hands activity on the first night of class. Whole-group activity.

De Angelis, G. (2021) *Multilingual Testing and Assessment*. Bristol: Multilingual Matters.

This is a very thorough book about multilingual testing and assessment. Specific research and an example of 'integrated assessment' are provided in a trilingual community (Italian, Ladin, and English) in Italy.

Kahneman, D., Sibony, O. and Sunstein, C. (2021) *Noise: A Flaw in Human Judgment*. New York: Little, Brown.

The authors set out to focus on the relative weight of bias and noise in total error, but concluded that noise is often a larger component of error than bias is. Examples of noise are given and contemplated in the field of medicine, law and business.

MacSwan, J. and Mahoney, K. (2008) Academic bias in language testing: A construct validity critique of the OPT I Oral Grades K-6 Spanish Second Edition (IPT Spanish). *Journal of Educational Research and Policy Studies (JERPS)* 8 (2), 86–101.

Mahoney, K., Haladyna, T. and MacSwan, J. (2009) The need for multiple measures in reclassification decisions: A validity study of the Stanford English Language Proficiency Test. In T.G. Wiley, J.S. Lee Wiley and R.W. Rumberger (eds) *The Education of Language Minority Immigrants in the United States* (pp. 240–262). Bristol: Multilingual Matters.

7 Accommodations

THEMES FROM CHAPTER 7

(1) We don't need accommodations if we create better assessments for multilingual learners (MLs).
(2) Many accommodations are permitted for MLs, but few of them have research to support that they work.
(3) Linguistic simplification is a promising accommodation.

Key Vocabulary

- Accommodations.
- Direct linguistic support.
- Error.
- Indirect linguistic support.
- Large-scale assessments.
- Reliability.
- Reliability coefficient.
- Standard error of measurement (SEM).

PUMI Connection

This chapter questions the very foundation of PUMI (Purpose, Use, Method and Instrument). The reader is guided to question the concept of accommodations in general and, based on PUMI critical questions, especially in the area of U (Use), whether it is appropriate to even have accommodations. Students first – our students deserve better than to be required to take tests that were not designed for them. There is irony in requiring the wrong test, then doing students 'the favor' of accommodating them with extra time or a glossary for a test that was not designed for them. Further, the fact that standardized tests in the United States are narrowly normed along white, middle-class, monolingual measures of achievement (Rosa & Flores, 2017) makes the success of others nearly impossible. The stakes are high for schools and teachers, and every aspect of PUMI, when it comes to accommodations, should be questioned.

This chapter also comes with a warning. Despite some high-quality research conducted on accommodations for MLs, educators and policymakers should be aware that accommodations alone cannot eliminate the gaps in achievement between MLs and non-MLs or make tests fair. We need to advocate for better assessments of MLs, not try to find ways to fix bad ones. The problem of less reliable test scores for MLs may be addressed if two things are done: (1) state departments of education specify, as part of their contracts with testing companies, that large numbers of MLs be included in every test blueprint; and (2) a large-scale reliability study proving an acceptable level of reliability (similar to that for native English speakers) be presented *before* any test is used to make important education decisions about MLs. Nobody wants to make educational decisions with unreliable data, and accommodations don't 'fix' reliability issues. The *Standards for Educational and Psychological Testing* (AERA, APA, NCME, 2014: 45) include important standards for test design related to reliability and MLs. Standard 2.11 states that 'Test publishers should provide estimates of reliability/precision as soon as feasible for each relevant subgroup for which the test is recommended'.

Translated Tests Aren't Always the Answer

Two states challenged the idea of using unreliable test scores for MLs in state-level courts, but without much success. In Pennsylvania, *Reading School District v. PA Department of Education* (2005) upheld the determination that it is not practical to administer tests in a child's native language (Elliot, 2011). In California (*Coachella Valley v. California*, 2007), a request by nine school districts to not use unreliable tests (Gándara & Baca, 2008) was denied because the state court said it did not have the authority to require the State Education Department to change its testing policy for MLs. Despite testimony from those who constructed the test saying that the test should *not* be used with MLs, the court still chose not to overrule the 'expertise' of the State Department of Education. Translated tests are offered and useful in some situations, but often are not the solution most had hoped for. Also, to address the quality of translated tests, the International Test Commission (ITC, 2018) *Guidelines for Translating and Adapting Tests* offers 18 guidelines organized into six categories when creating translations of tests.

Despite the claim that students will perform better if the test is given in their home or native language, this isn't always the case. The reason for this is that many MLs would not perform well in their home language, if they are not taught in those languages. Even though administering tests in a child's home language is appealing, research results do not support its fairness (Abedi, 2004). A central question when considering translated tests is which language the student has been exposed to academic content in. So, if a child's home language is Spanish but he or she learns math every day in English, the child will likely perform better in math on an English assessment. If the child regularly uses home language support in math, such as a translation of directions, responding in Spanish and English to word problems in both languages, then this is exactly how assessments should be administered to yield more valid results. General rule: Whatever scaffolding is used in instruction must also be used in assessment. Therefore, translated tests are not always the answer. However, some level of using translanguaging in instruction and assessment is always a good thing. The difference is that translated tests are fractional for MLs (monolingual, still only one language) and translanguaging in instruction and assessment is holistic (using a full linguistic repertoire).

However, even if tests are translated into other languages, this still supports a monolingual approach to assessment. A traditional monolingual approach to assessment is the idea that languages are independent of one another. We see this traditional monolingual approach to assessment even in bilingual education programs such as Spanish–English programs in the United States. We also see tests translated into many languages such as the Program for International Student Assessment (PISA) and the New York State Education Department (NYSED) uses alternative-language tests in Chinese, Haitian Creole, Korean, Russian and Spanish. But the tests are still in one language, which supports the traditional monolingual approach to assessment (De Angelis, 2021). Another example of the monolingual view is when in dual-language programs in the United States, MLs are assessed in their home language (Spanish) and new language (English). However, the assessments used treat the languages as separate discrete skills that function independent of one another. The languages are scored and interpreted separately and students may be penalized for using Spanish on the English test and for using English on the Spanish test (Lopez *et al.*, 2017).

There are different ways for a test to be multilingual. When tests are multilingual through translation, they are just translated monolingual versions of an original test. Vast financial and political interests surround monolingual testing and international testing agencies, and, since such powerful forces are not going to disappear overnight, there is a need to look at translation practices more closely and evaluate whether they can be used more sensibly (De Angelis, 2021).

What Are Accommodations and Why Do We Have Them?

In the United States, the latest reauthorization of the Elementary and Secondary Education Act, known as the Every Students Succeeds Act (ESSA, 2015), requires states to assess MLs in a valid manner and provide 'appropriate accommodations' to yield accurate data on what MLs can do in academic content areas. This is a case where federal policy mandates something that researchers haven't been able to clearly identify: accommodations that yield accurate data (see Chapter 2 for more history on assessment policy). This conundrum leaves many teachers frustrated.

Accommodations are changes in the test process, in the test itself or in the test–response format. The goal of accommodations for MLs is to provide a fair opportunity for them to demonstrate what they know and what they can do and to make tests as fair for them as they are for native English-speaking students, but without giving MLs an advantage over students who do not receive accommodations. Accommodations are sometimes referred to as adaptations or modifications. Accommodations for MLs exist because large-scale assessments[1] were designed for English-speaking students and most often do not yield valid results for MLs. It is important not to lose sight of this as we move through this chapter, because thus far, accommodations may not be able to 'fix', 'patch' or 'make up' for this fact.

Let's use the analogy of applying a small bandage (band aid) to fix a very large wound. The bandage might appear to address the wound and the bandage most definitely makes those at stake feel better – at least temporarily – but it will do very little to heal the wound or prevent future wounds from occurring.

If MLs were invited to participate in larger numbers and during the initial stages of test design, there would be less need for accommodations. Or students would need no or few accommodations if tests were designed for bilingual or multilingual students. The usual approach in test development is to develop and field-test items for the intended audience. In the United States, tests are mostly piloted with English-speaking students for whom language is less of a problem or no problem at all. Because the field tests of these items are usually done with small numbers of MLs, the items that become part of the blueprint are naturally above their language level, making it more difficult for them to access the content of the achievement test.

Pressure has escalated over the past two decades to make tests fairer and pilot studies have begun to include more culturally and linguistically diverse students; however, they still do not have enough ML representation, especially across proficiency levels. This matters because test items are designed and modified by the test makers based on the responses given during the pilot study. If the pilot study is conducted with all MLs, they will not respond well to items that do not meet their linguistic and cultural needs and those items will likely be thrown away, resulting in more appropriate instrumentation for MLs.

Furthermore, test-item writers typically do not take into account what is known about second language acquisition, especially language differentiation. To yield more valid results, assessments should include test items with language complexity appropriate to the student's level of second language acquisition. If you (a monolingual English speaker) take a mathematics test administered in Mandarin but do not speak or write Mandarin fluently, you likely will not be able to show what you know in mathematics; in fact, it will appear that you know very little. Accommodations such as having the questions read to you (in Mandarin), giving you extra time or taking the test in a separate location will not make up for your lack of knowledge of Mandarin. Many accommodations are administered – like a bandage – to give the perception of 'fixing the problem' or 'test fairness'. The commonly used accommodations just mentioned are not specifically designed for MLs with language needs; instead, many are borrowed from the field of special education.

The reality for many teachers is that they want to use multilingual accommodations; however, they themselves are monolingual and not fluent in the multiple languages presented in their classrooms. This is when monolingual teachers are teaching in multilingual classrooms with multilingual children. In this situation, the types of adjustments and modifications that can be used are, for example, using bilingual or multilingual scoring rubrics, or using more than one language for test instructions, or allowing for answers to be presented in multiple languages. All of these accommodations to assessments can be made by a monolingual teacher. The next section focuses on a promising modification called linguistic modification.

Linguistic Modifications

A very promising accommodation thus far has been the *linguistic modification* of test items – simplifying or modifying the language of a test without changing the intended construct of the item. By reducing the language barriers to content area tests, such as mathematics, both reliability and validity can increase. According to Abedi (2006), some linguistic features that may interfere with comprehension include word frequency and familiarity, word length, sentence length, voice of the verb phrase, length of the nominal and complex question phrases. These linguistic features may slow down the reader, make misinterpretation more likely and add to his or her cognitive load, unnecessarily. Other linguistic features that may affect comprehension include comparative structures, prepositional phrases, sentence and discourse structure, subordinate clauses, conditional clauses, relative clauses, concrete versus abstract or impersonal presentations and negation (Table 7.1).

Table 7.1 Linguistic features that may affect comprehension of test items

Linguistic feature	Short explanation[a]
Word frequency and familiarity	Words that are encountered more often are interpreted quickly and correctly
Word length	Longer words are more likely to be morphologically complex
Sentence length	Sentence length serves as an index for syntactic complexity
Voice of verb phrase	People find passive voice constructions more difficult to process than active
Length of nominals	Noun phrases with several modifiers are difficult
Complex question phrases	Potential source of difficulty
Comparative structures	Potential source of difficulty
Prepositional phrases	Interpretation of prepositions is difficult
Sentence and discourse structure	Some sentence structures are more syntactically complex
Subordinate, conditional and relative clauses	Contributes to complexity
Concrete vs. abstract or impersonal presentations	Better performance when problem statements are concrete
Negation	Terms like *no, not, none, never* are difficult to comprehend

[a]See Abedi (2006) for a more in-depth explanation.

Table 7.1 shows linguistic features that may cause confusion on tests, unnecessarily. To begin with, it is important to have a clear understanding of what part of the test item is content and what part is language (an in-depth example of this is provided in Chapter 5). The accommodation should not make the content of the item any less challenging; a content area teacher should review the item to assess whether the content has been changed. The list in Table 7.2 is from a 1997 study conducted by Abedi and colleagues, which evaluated the linguistic complexity of 69 national assessment of educational progress (NAEP) math items for eighth-grade students. This study was the first of its kind. Of the 69, some items were flagged as being potentially difficult for students to understand, and their linguistic features were analyzed (Abedi *et al.*, 1997).

Table 7.2 Original and revised test items based on linguistic complexity

	Original	Revised
Familiarity/frequency of non-math vocabulary	A certain reference file contains approximately 6 billion facts.	Mack's company sold 6 billion hamburgers.
	Census	Video game
Voice of verb phrase	A sample of 25 was selected.	He selected a sample of 25.
	The weight of three objects was compared.	Sandra compared the weights of three rabbits.
Length of nominals	Last year's class vice president.	Vice president.
	The pattern of puppy's weight gain.	The pattern above.
Clauses	A report that contains 64 sheets of paper for each report.	He needs 64 sheets of paper for each report.
	If two batteries in the sample were found to be dead.	He found three broken pencils in the sample.
Complex question phrases	At which of the following times?	When?
	Which is the best approximation of the number?	Approximately how many?
Concrete vs. abstract or impersonal presentations	The weights of three objects were compared using a pan balance. Two comparisons were made.	Sandra compared the weights of three objects using a pan balance. She made two comparisons.

Source: Abedi *et al.* (1997) and Abedi (2006).

Solano-Flores (2010) investigated using a sociolinguistic approach to the linguistic modification of tests and reported positive findings. Solano-Flores approaches the topic of assessment through a culturally relevant lens, much like culturally relevant instruction. Culturally relevant assessment is viewed by some as a promising assessment accommodation. Strategies include incorporating the characteristics of how languages are used at school sites and also adopting local dialects for use in tests. This approach takes into account the variation in language use across groups of MLs.

Multilingual Test Instructions and Responses

Lack of comprehension of test instructions is a major problem. As you can imagine, if one cannot understand the instructions of a test, the chances of demonstrating what you know becomes impossible. A common-sense accommodation is to provide test instructions and allow test responses in two languages including translanguaging. There are some research results to support the effectiveness of this approach. For example, Lopez *et al.* (2019) designed flexible mathematics bilingual assessments using a technology-enhanced assessment platform where students can see or listen to the item in English or Spanish and they can say or write their responses in any language or a mix of languages, without being penalized for mixing languages. Researchers in the Congo (Gándara & Randall, 2019) found translanguaging on math assessments to be more appropriate than traditional administration where one experimental group administered the test in French, one in Lingala and one with a mix of the two languages.

Translanguaging on assessments can be done using computer-based testing or paper-based testing. In New York State, schools may allow students to receive test instructions and responses in the following three ways: (1) simultaneous use of English and alternative-language editions which allows students to use both tests (home language and English, print test options only) at the same time and therefore can read directions in both languages; however, the responses have to be given in one language or the other; (2) New York has a limited number of translated tests (Arabic, Bengali, Chinese, Haitian-Creole, Korean, Russian and Spanish); therefore, if a translated test is not available because a student speaks a language other than these, oral direct translation is allowed; and (3) New York State allows students to write responses in the home language, but it is the responsibility of the school district to score. All three of these accommodations in New York support the idea of allowing to some degree multilingual test instructions and responses. The drawback in practice is that each school has the choice to use these accommodations or not, which leads to inconsistent use of these accommodations and adds an uncertain variability to the reliability of these test scores. This New York example demonstrates the idea of accommodations giving the perception that tests are fair for MLs but in reality the end results are still less valid and reliable scores. If states mandated that large testing companies provide instructions and responses in multiple languages or just simplified English, we would begin to see more valid results. The need to develop tests for students with varying language profiles is not a new topic (see Chapter 2), yet the research in accommodations has a long way to go, because it usually focuses on bilingual students, often in homogeneous contexts and in the United States (De Angelis, 2021) According to De Angelis, a test can be monolingual, multilingual by translation, or multilingual by design. (Table 7.3).

An example of a multilingual-by-translation test can be seen in a study exploring ML assessments in Israeli schools, conducted by Shohamy *et al.* (2022). Two types of students participated in this study: immigrants from the former Soviet Union who learn all their school subjects in Hebrew and Arab students who participate in school where the language of instruction is Arabic and some subjects are in Hebrew. An experimental group had a bilingual version of the test and the control group had a Hebrew version only. The experimental test was arranged so that each page included items in two languages, mirroring one another. Figure 7.1 shows the Hebrew–Russian version and Figure 7.2 shows the Hebrew–Arabic version. The results

Table 7.3 According De Angelis (2021) a test can take three formats: monolingual, multilingual-by-translation and multilingual-by-design

Monolingual tests	The instructions and content provided orally or in writing in one language. Students must answer all questions in the language of the test. The use of monolingual tests with multilingual remains controversial due to validity concerns.
Multilingual-by-translation	These are monolingual tests fully translated into multiple languages. For example, PISA is translated into many languages and the New York State Regents is translated into six languages. It is recommended that students have access to two tests (two languages) but it's important that the test layout does not change and has a one-to-one correspondence. These translated tests are expensive to make and may not meet the needs of many students.
Multilingual-by-design	Designed and written in more than one language. For example, instructions can be in one language and content in another, and answers can be accepted in more than one language. In a trilingual school for example, if reading comprehension has been taught using translanguaging pedagogy, students would feel very comfortable completing a test that presents instructions in Language A, content in Language B and responding in Language C. It's important that students are very familiar with this pedagogy. One difficult aspect to Multilingual-by-design is the need for scorers who are multilingual scorers or many scorers who represent all the community languages.

showed that having the first language available on the test contributed greatly to a more relaxed and positive assessment experience (Shohamy et al., 2022).

Computer-Based Supports

In the last five years, many states in the United States have moved to computer-based assessments for their state accountability assessments, mostly due to the previous adoption of Partnership for Assessment of Readiness for College and Careers (PARC) and Smarter Balance (see Chapter 2 for a brief history of these consortia). Although many states no longer participate in these consortia, the trend for technology-based assessments has remained (Wolf et al., 2021). Lopez et al. (2019) designed a flexible bilingual mathematics assessment where supports were delivered via a computer-based test platform which allowed students to select language supports when necessary. Computer-based testing can allow for many language-related accommodations such as a pop up glossary, a read-aloud via prerecorded audio or the text-to-speech function in multiple languages (Wolf et al., 2021). At the time of this publication, Artificial Intelligence (AI) is providing quick ways for teachers to simplify the language of assessments and translate assessments. This author experimented with the integrated AI feature of Quizziz (Quizziz.com) to linguistically simplify and translate classroom-based assessments. AI may hold promise in modifications to assessments, such as linguistic simplification. Continue PUMI to assure alignment.

State Assessment Policies Addressing Accommodations

Around the time No Child Left Behind (NCLB) was passed, Rivera and Collum (2004) launched a research study to investigate policies related to testing accommodations across the United States. They found that in most cases, policies focused on two student groups, MLs and students with disabilities (SWD), with some states treating the two groups together. Of the 75 accommodations listed in state policies,

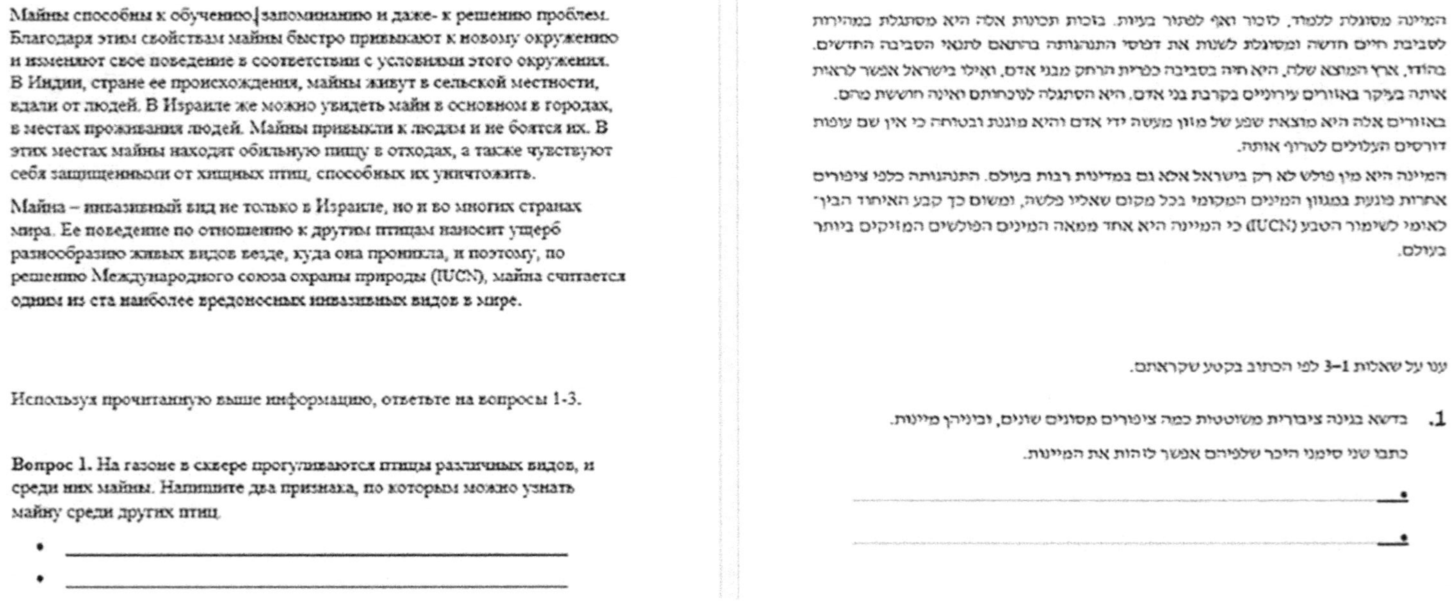

Майны способны к обучению|запоминанию и даже- к решению проблем. Благодаря этим свойствам майны быстро привыкают к новому окружению и изменяют свое поведение в соответствии с условиями этого окружения. В Индии, стране ее происхождения, майны живут в сельской местности, вдали от людей. В Израиле же можно увидеть майн в основном в городах, в местах проживания людей. Майны привыкли к людям и не боятся их. В этих местах майны находят обильную пищу в отходах, а также чувствуют себя защищенными от хищных птиц, способных их уничтожить.

Майна – инвазивный вид не только в Израиле, но и во многих странах мира. Ее поведение по отношению к другим птицам наносит ущерб разнообразию живых видов везде, куда она проникла, и поэтому, по решению Международного союза охраны природы (IUCN), майна считается одним из ста наиболее вредоносных инвазивных видов в мире.

Используя прочитанную выше информацию, ответьте на вопросы 1-3.

Вопрос 1. На газоне в сквере прогуливаются птицы различных видов, и среди них майны. Напишите два признака, по которым можно узнать майну среди других птиц.

- ______________________________
- ______________________________

המיינה מסוגלת ללמוד, לזכור ואף לפתור בעיות. בזכות תכונות אלה היא מסתגלת במהירות לסביבת חיים חדשה ומסוגלת לשנות את דפוסי התנהגותה בהתאם לתנאי הסביבה החדשים. בהודו, ארץ המוצא שלה, היא חיה בסביבה כפרית הרחק מבני אדם, ואילו בישראל אפשר לראות אותה בעיקר באזורים עירוניים בקרבת בני אדם. היא הסתגלה לנוכחותם ואינה חוששת מהם. באזורים אלה היא מוצאת שפע של מזון מעשה ידי אדם והיא מוגנת ובטוחה כי אין שם עופות דורסים העלולים לטרוף אותה.

המיינה היא מין פולש לא רק בישראל אלא גם במדינות רבות בעולם. התנהגותה כלפי ציפורים אחרות פוגעת במגוון המינים המקומי בכל מקום שאליו פלשה, ומשום כך קבע האיגוד הבין־לאומי לשימור הטבע (IUCN) כי המיינה היא אחד ממאה המינים הפולשים המזיקים ביותר בעולם.

ענו על שאלות 1–3 לפי הכתוב בקטע שקראתם.

1. בדשא בגינה ציבורית משוטטות כמה ציפורים מסוגים שונים, וביניהן מיינות.
כתבו שני סימני היכר שלפיהם אפשר לזהות את המיינות.

- ______________________________
- ______________________________

Figure 7.1 An example of multilingual-by-translation Hebrew–Russian Assessment (Shohamy *et al.*, 2022)

Figure 7.2 An example of multilingual-by-translation Hebrew–Arabic (Shohamy et al., 2022)

44 were relevant to MLs and 31 relevant only to SWDs. After analyzing 51^2 state policies, Rivera and Collum (2004) identified the ways in which states determined whether a student was eligible for accommodations: level of language proficiency (language related), length of time in English-medium academic environment (time related), achievement and prior schooling level (academic related) and judgment of school personnel and/or family (opinion related). This flexibility, of course, was changed upon the implementation of NCLB.

The borrowing of accommodations from the field of special education led Rivera and Collum to suggest linking accommodations more closely with the actual linguistic needs of MLs and the available research on second language acquisition. To articulate the accommodations further, they also suggested placing the 75 accommodations in two categories: *direct linguistic support* and *indirect linguistic support*. Direct linguistic support included accommodations such as translation of the test into the native language, simplification of the English language or test language and repetition of the test language; indirect linguistic support includes accommodations such as adjustments to time, schedules or environment.

In 2008, Shafer Willner et al. published a descriptive report identifying the 10 most commonly used test accommodations for MLs as recommended by state policies (Table 7.4). Shortly afterward, these authors published a guide for states to provide general guidance on state accommodation policies and how to make them more responsive to MLs. For example, they distinguished between accommodations for MLs and those for SWDs (Rivera et al., 2008).

Table 7.4 Ten most commonly used test accommodations for MLs as recommended by state policy

Use of dual-language dictionary
Extended time
Reading items aloud
Translating direction orally into native language
Clarifying/explaining directions in English
Repeating directions
Reading direction aloud
Allowing student to respond orally in English and describing responses
Clarifying/explaining directions in the native language
Simplifying directions

Source: Shafer Willner et al. (2008).

What Does the Research Say?

As mentioned above, states' policies list 75 accommodations to be used with MLs. What we don't know is whether these accommodations actually work, with which students and under what conditions. The larger question is: Do accommodations adequately satisfy the legal demands of ESSA to provide valid and reliable assessments for MLs?

The most credible results dealing with accommodations for MLs come from research studies that examine the effects of accommodations one at a time, set up the study as an intentional experiment (as opposed to studying existing data from mandatory testing and looking for trends) and experiment with both MLs and non-MLs to help pinpoint the accommodations that will actually level the playing field between the two groups instead of increasing scores for everyone.[3] Although 75 accommodations are represented in policy, only a few are often studied: (1) testing in the native language or in English with translation (Abedi et al., 1998; Miller et al., 1999); (2) testing in modified English (Abedi & Lord, 2001; Abedi et al., 1998, 2000a; Miller et al., 1999); (3) providing published dictionaries (Miller et al., 1999); and (4) providing a glossary and/or custom dictionary (Abedi et al., 2000a, 2000b).

Jamal Abedi, a US leader in accommodation research, has dedicated much of his career to designing empirical studies with large samples of students to investigate the validity, effectiveness and feasibility of the growing number of accommodations, many of which are already written into state policies. His research studies usually offer the accommodation to both ML and non-ML subgroups in a randomized sample (Abedi et al., 2004). Abedi's research differs from many accommodation studies due to the experimental nature of his research designs. Other studies have investigated the effectiveness of accommodations using large-scale databases, but their research design does not randomly assign MLs to different forms of accommodation and the non-ML group does not receive an accommodation. If the non-ML group does not receive an accommodation as treatment in an experimental research design, we will never know how the accommodation may have affected them. The experimental nature of Abedi's research designs gives his studies an edge over other studies in drawing significant conclusions about the effectiveness of accommodations.

For an accommodation to 'work' for MLs, some would say that it should increase the validity of the test scores for MLs while not affecting the scores for non-MLs. It should not be forgotten, though, that language can be an issue for non-MLs as well. Since Abedi's studies are largely experimental research designs, they usually include a non-ML comparison group. For some non-MLs – for example, native English speakers who struggle with literacy – reducing the linguistic complexity or using other language-based accommodations may work equally well. Technically, if an accommodation increases scores for non-ML and ML groups alike, it is not an effective accommodation for MLs but it is an effective accommodation for all students. Most educators, and members of the general public for that matter, would not argue with increasing the validity of test scores for all students.

Around the time NCLB was proposed, Abedi and his colleagues were conducting research at the National Center for Research on Evaluation, Standards and Student Testing (NCCREST) to investigate the validity and reliability of test scores for MLs and the hypothesis that the linguistic complexity of test items may introduce error to test scores, thus decreasing their validity. These studies (Abedi, 2002; Abedi & Lord, 2001; Abedi *et al.*, 2000a) concluded that test scores for MLs are substantially lower than the scores for native English-speaking students in all subject areas; the linguistic complexity of test items may threaten the validity of test scores; and as the language demands of individual test items decrease, the performance gap between MLs and native English-speaking students diminishes. In test items where the language demands were minimal, the gap between native English-speaking students and MLs essentially disappeared.

Several large evaluative studies have been conducted on the topic of accommodations. Rivera and Collum (2004) reviewed 15 high-quality research studies and concluded that two accommodations hold promise for MLs: native-language versions of assessments and linguistic simplificationor linguistic clarification, of English versions,[4] along with combining some indirect and direct linguistic support accommodations such as bilingual glossaries and extra time. Francis *et al.* (2006) outlined best practice, and Pennock-Roman and Rivera (2011) conducted a meta-analysis of 14 studies showing large effect sizes for extra time and computer-administered glossaries, smaller effects for plain English and very sizable effects (1.45) for Spanish test versions. A Smarter Balanced Assessment Consortium report led by Abedi and Ewers (2013) recommended several accommodations for MLs based on its research results[5] (Table 7.5). All the accommodations listed met five conditions (effective, valid, differential impact, relevance and feasible).

Table 7.5 Recommended accommodations based on meeting five conditions (effective, valid, differential impact, relevance and feasible)

Read-aloud of test directions in student's native language
Picture dictionary (alone, combined with oral reading of test items in English and combined with bilingual glossary)
Test in a familiar environment with other MLs
Traditional glossary with Spanish translations and extra time (content-related terms removed)
Bilingual dictionary

Source: Abedi and Ewers (2013).

Additional accommodations that work for both MLs and non-MLs are not shown in Table 7.5. For example, computer testing shows evidence of validity and effectiveness but may not be feasible for most schools due to the need for one computer per student during large-scale testing time. Abedi (2009) conducted a study that tested the computerized administration of a math test with a pop-up glossary. This feature provided a simple gloss of a word with the touch of a mouse, thereby providing access to non-math words with which MLs typically struggle. Abedi was able to document that MLs spent more time glossing. Therefore, an appropriate accommodation – should your school have computer-testing capabilities for MLs – is to provide a computer-based pop-up glossary combined with extra time.

A report from the Center on Instruction (Kieffer *et al.*, 2012) is a refreshing alternative to the laundry list of accommodations that work with MLs. It provides recommendations for accommodations practice based on the results of research; these are shown, in order of importance, in Table 7.6.

Table 7.6 Recommendations for using accommodations for MLs

(1) Use simplified English in test design, eliminating irrelevant language demands on all students.
(2) Provide English dictionaries/glossaries to MLs.
(3) Match the language of tests and accommodations to the language of instruction.
(4) Provide extended time to MLs or use untimed tests for all students.

Source: Kieffer *et al.* (2012).

The research to demonstrate whether certain accommodations are effective is still unclear. Recently, after conducting a large, randomized, controlled trial design research study investigating linguistic modification and glossary, Wolf *et al.* (2021) did not detect statistically significant accommodations effects. Unfortunately, after more than 20 years of research on accommodations for MLs, the search for a clearly 'effective' accommodation is still outstanding. As a reminder, an effective accommodation is one that will increase the performance of MLs (but not others) and not alter the construct that is being measured (e.g. mathematics). Similarly, in a random control group research design with large samples, Abedi *et al.* (2020) studied four accommodations that show promise: linguistic modification, English read-aloud, English glossary and bilingual glossary; however, in the end many of these accommodations did not produce significant gains for students. Linguistic modification led to ML improvement on a computerized mathematics assessment; however, the results were not significant.

Sometimes, accommodation research focuses on the student perspective of accommodations, which can be thought of as external validity, as opposed to the research studies that focus on the internal part of a test or score (called internal validity studies). De Backer *et al.* (2019) studied multilingual students taking a science test under three conditions: (1) the written science test was in the language of instruction (Dutch); (2) the students received a bilingual test in Dutch plus their home language; and (3) the students received added audio support in both languages. The results showed that students chose the bilingual test and the audio support more often, and the choice depends on personal preference and language proficiency (De Backer *et al.*, 2019).

Due to the lack of clear results showing effective accommodations, this is a good time to refer back to the introduction to this chapter where the existence of accommodations is questioned. The following questions are raised: Why do we have so many accommodations for MLs when we don't know if they work? What purpose do they serve if not an effective accommodation to level the playing fields between MLs and non-MLs? Are there other reasons for giving accommodations, other than effectiveness? Are accommodations a distraction from more important topics, like why are tests so unfair for MLs and why can't we demand better designed tests for MLs?

Formative Assessments can have Accommodations (one example)

Some teachers say they are not comfortable modifying tests based on principle. Some teachers express that they are being 'faithful' to the assessment when they feel obliged to conduct the assessment monolingually, without any accommodations. A more truthful statement when it comes to accommodations is the opposite – the assessment needs to be 'faithful' to the student, more so than to the test. This section focuses on one example of using accommodations with formative assessment. The topic of accommodations is almost always associated with large-scale standardized testing. But the reality is that accommodations are much easier to use with formative classroom-based assessments. This allows educators to adapt the assessment to our students.

Ascenzi-Moreno (2018) points out that we often hear teachers talk about formative assessments as 'tests' and then take a very formal, non-interactive stance when administering an assessment. As a consequence, when teachers choose to limit MLs reading performance to one language, they are not able to detect and respond to the full span of their students' reading abilities, leading to a partial and inaccurate assessment of students (Ascenzi-Moreno, 2018). Through a case study, Ascenzi-Moreno demonstrated that formative assessments can be interactive and student centered by applying a translanguaging lens to a typical monolingual administration of formative reading assessment.

This section describes one of the three students that Ascenzi-Moreno (2018) focused on in her study (see Figure 7.3, Santiago's miscue data form). This miscue analysis is a formative reading assessment administered by Ella (teacher) to Santiago (student). The basic idea with miscue analysis is that a student reads a text and the teacher marks a miscue form to document the miscues (miscues are when students deviate from the text). From Chapter 4, this would be categorized as performance with checklist, because the miscue form is a type of checklist (see Figure 7.3, Santiago's miscue data form). Santiago arrived from Guatemala one year before the study was conducted and the certified English as a new language (ENL) teacher, Ella, has some knowledge of Spanish.

The exact adaptation made to this miscue analysis form was to add two additional components to the usual three. The components L for language and P for pronunciation were added to the form to add opportunity for the assessor (Ella) to have space to document miscues due to language in addition to literacy, a more holistic assessment for students. In Figure 7.3, Santiago read the word 'beard' for 'bird'. When Ella asked Santiago about the word he pronounced as 'beard', Santiago pointed to the picture in the text and said 'pájaro' which means bird in Spanish. By

Differentiated Miscue Analysis Form

Name: Santiago						
Grade: 5						
Text: A Giant in the Forest Text Level:						
Text/Teacher Documentation of Student Reading:	S/C	M	V	S	L	P
Page 4 Every week the little boy's mother gave 　　　　　　　　　　　S/C him a big bar of soap. Then she sent 　　　bear him to the lake to take a bath. 　You "You'll be safe in the lake because the giant can't swim," she always said. "But don't forget to be home before dark. **Page 5** One day when the little boy was going to 　　　　　　　　　beard take his bath, he saw a baby bird on the 　　　failen ground. It had fallen out of its nest. 　　　　　　　　　　the The boy put the bird back in its nest.	1		1 1		1	1 1 1
Types of Miscues S/C=Self Correction M=Meaning V=Visual S=Syntactical L=Language P=Pronunciation						

Figure 7.3 An adapted formative reading assessment (Ascenzi-Moreno, 2018)

interacting with Santiago and opening the reading assessment to his home language, the miscue was marked as a pronunciation miscue (P), not a visual miscue (V: a visual miscue attends to the visual information in a word).

Why does this matter? First. Applying a translanguaging lens to a formative reading assessment allows us to view Santiago through a lens of promise not deficit. Second, the results of the adapted miscue analysis are more accurate (and therefore more valid); the monolingual administration would have overlooked the real reason behind the miscue. Third, Santiago learned that his teacher is interested in him as a reader and not acting solely as an assessor (Ascenzi-Moreno, 2018). This one example demonstrates the importance of using accommodations with formative assessments.

A State Example (New York)

Each state in the United States has its own list of acceptable accommodations. For example, the New York State Policy on Accommodations suggests 'schools may provide testing accommodations to ELLs, as needed…'. Note that this appears to be a suggestion and not a directive because of the phrase 'may be provided'. This allows individual school principals and teachers to decide which acceptable accommodations, if any, should be used; the result is a wide variety of accommodations being employed across districts and schools. Acceptable accommodations in New York State include time extension, separate location, third reading of listening selection, bilingual dictionaries and glossaries (definitions or explanations not permitted), simultaneous use of English and alternative-language editions, oral translation for lower-incidence languages and writing responses in the ML's native language (Table 7.7). An additional accommodation introduced in 2023 is the Next Day Completion, where MLs who are scheduled to take two tests in one day may take the second test the following day. The idea is that once the student reaches proficiency in English or the language of the test, the student no longer needs accommodations (in NY, MLs can have access to accommodation for two years after being reclassified). However, Shohamy (2022) rightly points out that accommodations should not stop after reaching proficiency as ML test takers continue to rely on their whole linguistic repertoire for a long time, perhaps for their whole life.

Nearly all of the research on accommodations focuses exclusively on what works (generalized broadly), but other important questions are ignored. Should we spend time and money researching what accommodations work best instead of using the money to improve the design of tests for MLs? Are all these accommodations equally comparable? How do we control for or even determine whether popular accommodations have parallel effects and are interchangeable in test use?

Despite what looks like a lot of research, even simple questions about accommodations remain unanswered. Should states even use accommodated test scores before we know more answers? Is it legal/ethical to use accommodated test scores to satisfy the accountability policies and laws? Should accommodated test scores be used to evaluate teachers? Decades ago, Shepard *et al.* (1998) raised a number of similar important questions: Can accommodated test results be combined with non-accommodated test results, or should the test score be flagged as 'accommodated'? Will accommodated test scores be used differently from non-accommodated scores? Does the use of accommodations imply a breakdown of the concept of standardization? How does the use of accommodations affect the construct being measured? With a higher-stakes environment currently in place for the assessment of MLs, these questions have become even more important. A concern among educators is whether the test scores for MLs are less reliable than those for non-MLs. The next section discusses the topic of reliability in detail, and the chapter ends with a discussion of reliability. Reliability is usually embedded in the validity section of a textbook; however, the concern for reliable test scores should occur before validity discussions. If scores aren't reliable, they shouldn't be used. Reliability is often the outcome measure for accommodations research studies and it is closely related to the topic of accommodations. The goal of many research studies is to secure more reliable test scores.

Table 7.7 New York state policy on accommodations

Accommodation	NYS policy	Considerations for implementation
Time extension	Schools may extend the test time for MLs taking state examinations. Principals may use any reasonable extensions, such as 'time and a half' (the required testing time plus half that amount), in accordance with their best judgment about the needs of the MLs. Principals should consult with the student's classroom teacher in making these determinations.	Inexpensive. No changes to test necessary. Doesn't close gap because all students do better with extra time.
Separate location	Schools are required to provide optimal testing environments and facilities for all students. They may administer examinations to MLs individually or in small groups in a separate location.	
Third reading of listening selection	Proctors may read the listening passage of the Grades 3–8 English language arts tests or the Regents Comprehensive Examination in English a third time to MLs. This accommodation is not permitted in state examinations in foreign languages such as the Regents Comprehensive Examination in Spanish.	
Bilingual dictionaries and glossaries	MLs may use bilingual dictionaries and glossaries when taking all state examinations with the exception of the Second Language Proficiency Examinations, Regents Comprehensive Examinations in foreign languages and the Regents Competency Tests (RCTs) in Reading and Writing. The bilingual dictionaries and glossaries may provide only direct translations of words; definitions or explanations are *not* permitted. No student may use an English-language dictionary when taking any state examination.	If this includes definitions or simple paraphrases of potentially unfamiliar or difficult words, it is effective for MLs. If it does not, then it is not effective.
Simultaneous use of English and alternative-language editions	When taking state examinations for which the department provides written translations, MLs may use both English and an alternative-language edition of the test simultaneously. However, they must be instructed to record all of their responses in only one of the two editions. The alternative-language edition used by the student should be so indicated on the student's answer sheet. Because the alternative-language editions of the RCTs are not direct translations of the English-language editions, students *may not* be given both.	Difficulty maintaining construct equivalence. Often misaligned with language of instruction. Expensive.
Oral translation for lower-incidence languages	Schools may provide MLs with an oral translation of a state examination when no translated edition is provided by the department. This accommodation is permitted for state examinations in all subjects except English and foreign languages. All translations must be oral, direct translations of the English editions; written translations are *not* allowed. No clarifications or explanations may be provided. Translators may be provided with copies of the English edition of the tests no earlier than one hour prior to administration to become familiar with the material. Translators who also serve as proctors must be familiar with the procedures for administering state examinations. Principals must take the necessary precautions to ensure that the examinations are properly administered and that the students receiving translation services are not given an unfair advantage.	
Writing responses in the native language	MLs making use of alternative-language editions or oral translations of state examinations may write their responses to the open-ended questions in their native language. Scoring the tests is the responsibility of the school.	

Note: These accommodations are acceptable to the New York State Department of Education and may be provided to MLs.

What is Reliability?

Reliability is measured as a coefficient (a number between 0 and 1), which informs us empirically of how much contamination (or error) is part of the overall test score. No test is 100% reliable, but technically sound tests have a reliability coefficient of 0.85 or higher, indicating that at least 85% of the test score is due to actual achievement (for example); the other 15% is due to measurement errors, which for MLs usually take the form of language factors. For example, in one large study (sample size approximately 200,000) conducted by Abedi, reliability coefficients were consistently higher for fluent English proficient (FEP) students than for limited English proficient (LEP) students. In reading, the coefficient was 0.86 for FEPs and 0.75 for LEPs; in math, 0.90 for FEPs and 0.80 for LEPs; in language, 0.80 for FEPs and 0.68 for LEPs; and in science, 0.78 for FEPs and 0.53 for LEPs (Abedi et al., 2004). This means, for example, that 22% of the science test score for FEPS is due to error and 47% of the test score for MLs is due to error! These coefficients are very revealing about how (un)reliable the data really are.

SNAPSHOT: HOW FAR CAN CLARISSA THROW?

The track and field team has an event called the softball throw in which competitors throw a softball as far as they can. Clarissa feels she may be strong in this event; she doesn't really know how far she can throw, so she practices throwing 100 times. Since she consistently throws the softball between 80 and 90 feet, she knows that her true ability lies somewhere between these two distances. During one throw, her hands become sweaty, and the softball slips as she throws it. This causes her distance to be only 50 feet, clearly not her true ability. If Clarissa throws the ball 100 times and takes the average distance, then we can find out a very close estimate to her 'true' distance. If the softball slips, this is not a good measure of the 'true' distance she can throw. If she only throws once, it may not be a reliable (or consistent measure). The same applies to test scores. We would never ask a child to take a test 100 times, but if we did, we could take the average and find out a very good estimate of his or her 'true' score. Test scores are never 100% reliable, and the test scores for MLs are much less reliable than those for non-MLs.

Discussion questions
- How does throwing a softball relate to taking a test?
- Why are ML test scores less reliable than those for non-MLs?

One type of scorer-related reliability that attracts a lot of attention is rater reliability. Inter-rater reliability is when, for example, multiple teachers score a writing response on a language proficiency test – it becomes unlikely they will all have the same score. A similar type of rater reliability is when the same person scores, for example, a writing response, on different days; the extent of this variation is a matter of intra-rater reliability (Green, 2014). Contamination or error in test scores can be caused by guessing, subjective scoring of essays, unnecessarily complex language, fatigue, nervousness and other factors. Figure 7.4 shows drawings by two ML elementary students illustrating how they felt about the Arizona Instrument to Measure Standards (AIMS), a high-stakes test. The first drawing shows how nervous the student was; the second shows other negative factors known to not only affect

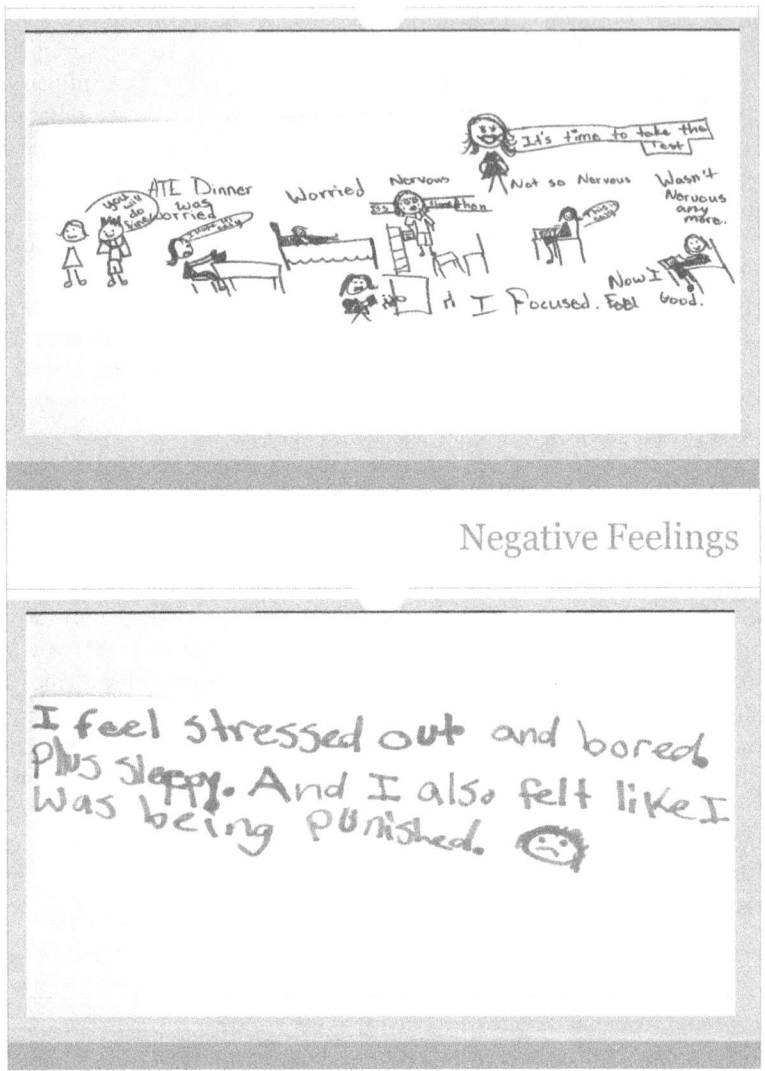

Figure 7.4 Two drawings by ML elementary students in response to a high-stakes test. These drawings are part of an unpublished study to explore the feelings of MLs, through drawing, taking achievement tests in English in a restricted language policy state (Arizona). Mahoney, K., Mahoney, A. and Rossi, R. (unpublished).

the test score but also the student's attitude toward school in general (stressed out, bored, sleepy, being punished). These negative experiences are typically associated with deficit-oriented assessments and not with assessments that lead to promise (see Chapter 1 for this discussion).

A topic almost never mentioned by researchers but well known by educators is the fact that MLs omit items and 'give up' toward the end of the test more than non-MLs. Those omissions are counted as incorrect answers; however, in reality, they are signs of difficulty in understanding the language of a test, lack of time to take a test or fatigue from cognitive and linguistic overload combined with pressure. Empirical evidence showing a higher non-response rate for MLs was reported by Haladyna *et al.* (2003).

The reliability of a test score refers to how *consistent* the score is. For example, suppose a student student takes a 100-item test at 1pm on Monday, then takes the same test at the same time for the next four days. (This would never happen, of course, because he or she would remember items from the test or grow tired of the test, which would affect performance.) Hypothetically, no learning or forgetting has occurred during the one-day intervals. If the ML student has the exact same score each day, this score is very consistent or very reliable and, as such, will have a very high reliability coefficient – close to 1. However, this rarely happens with MLs because things other than the construct (e.g. math) are contributing to the score (Table 7.8).

Table 7.8 Unnecessary linguistic complexity in a mathematics item

A certain reference file contains approximately 6 billion facts. About how many millions is that?

A. 6,000,000
B. 600,000
C. 60,000
D. 6,000
E. 600

The test makers chose this item to see if the student knows how many millions are in 6 billion. However, the language of the item is very complex and may cause MLs who know the math to answer incorrectly. Terms like *certain*, *reference*, *approximately* and *facts* are not needed to measure whether students know the math. Abedi *et al.* (2004) reword the math item to reduce language demands and increase validity.

Mack's company sold 6 billion pencils. About how many million is that?

A. 6,000,000
B. 600,000
C. 60,000
D. 6,000
E. 600

SNAPSHOT: HOW MUCH DO YOU REALLY WEIGH?

Rose is watching her weight, and she decides to weigh herself often to see if she loses or gains any weight. On Friday, she weighs herself on her home scale, and she weighs 143 pounds. While visiting her mother later that day, she weighs herself on her mother's scale and she weighs 139 pounds. Before swimming laps at the school pool the next morning, she weighs herself on the locker room scale and she weighs 140 pounds. Although Rose prefers the results of her mother's scale, she wonders how much she really weighs. The scales in this analogy is like an achievement test, or instrument. The instrument intends to measure the construct – in this case 'weight' or with a test in school, 'achievement'. Like tests used in schools, no scale is perfectly reliable; if Rose averages all three weights, she may have a closer idea of her 'true' weight.

Discussion questions

- How does weighing yourself relate to taking a test?
- Why would different tests (measuring the same thing) produce different results?

Standard Error of Measurement

SEM represents the range of a test's accuracy. A standard procedure for testing companies is to include empirical evidence about the reliability coefficient and the SEM in the technical manual. However, technical manuals are difficult to obtain and difficult to read; therefore, the reliability coefficient for MLs remains largely unknown among educators.

> **END-OF-CHAPTER ACTIVITIES** (Instructors: see advice at the end of the book)
>
> After completing Activities 1–3, the reader will be able to:
>
> (1) Identify nine commonly used accommodations for MLs.
> (2) Answer essential questions about reliability.
> (3) Apply the concept of linguistic simplification (an effective accommodation) to an item.
>
> **Activity 1**
>
> Identify nine commonly used accommodations for MLs.
>
> This is a game of bingo using 9 of the 10 most commonly used accommodations in state policies learned in this chapter. Fold a piece of paper into nine equal parts (fold it into thirds, then fold it into thirds again). The instructor writes nine commonly used accommodations on the board. Write them in any of the squares – one word per square. After this, each student should have a different bingo board. The instructor 'performs' the accommodations so the class can guess what each one is. After a match is found, cross out the whole square. Once a student has bingo (three across, down or diagonal), he or she shouts 'bingo!' and the instructor checks the work, and asks for a student explanation.
>
> **Activity 2**
>
> Answer essential questions about reliability.
>
> Do Inside/Outside Circle. Half of the students are given an index card with one of the questions below written on it and the answer written on the back. Students with the questions form a small circle facing outward, and those without index cards form a circle facing the inner circle. Each student must face another student to state the definition of the term *or* the term when the definition is given. The outside circle rotates clockwise until each student has had a chance. After every student in the outside circle has had a chance, the outside circle switches with the inside circle (which always has the card) and the activity is repeated.
>
> (1) What is reliability?
> (2) How is reliability connected to accommodations?
> (3) If a reliability coefficient is 0.70, what does that mean?
> (4) Can accommodations close the achievement gap?
> (5) What does it mean if a test has an SEM of 3 points?
> (6) What is linguistic simplification?
> (7) Give two other names for test score error.
> (8) Name three common causes of error for MLs.

> **Activity 3**
> Take a math test item and simplify it linguistically.
>
> In small groups (four or fewer), students rewrite the following math item using simplified English. They should focus on how they can simplify the language without affecting the math. Each group names three linguistic features of the changes that they made. After 20 minutes, the groups post their new items in front of the room and prepare to make a short presentation to the class. (This activity is adapted from Abedi et al., 2004.)
>
> If __ represents the number of newspapers that Lee delivers each day, which of the following represents the total number of newspapers that Lee delivers in 5 days?
>
> (a) 5 + __
>
> (b) 5 × __
>
> (c) __ + 5
>
> (d) (__ + __) × 5

Notes

(1) In general, this chapter discusses accommodations for achievement tests given to MLs, not including English language arts (ELA) or other language-related tests which typically do not allow for these types of accommodations. Most state policies prohibit the use of accommodations on ELA tests because they would jeopardize the construct.

(2) Washington, DC was treated as a state for the purposes of this analysis.

(3) Most educators do not oppose making tests fairer for everyone and welcome suggestions on how to do so. However, the quest to find a valid, effective and feasible accommodation for MLs dictates that the performance of non-MLs should be relatively unaffected by the accommodation while improving the performance (and reliability) of the scores of MLs.

(4) After reviewing the idea of linguistic simplification at a teacher workshop in Buffalo, my colleague Dr Erin Kearney introduced a term to describe what is happening in this process which this author likes better: linguistic clarification. Linguistic clarification does not indicate simplifying anything but rather clarifying a rather uncommon register, otherwise known as the language of testing.

(5) 'Recommended based on research results' refers to the results of several studies, plus a thorough review from experts in this field which has deemed the accommodation promising with little or no risk of altering the construct.

References

Abedi, J. (2002) Standardized achievement tests and English language learners: Psychometric issues. *Educational Assessment* 8 (3), 231–257.

Abedi, J. (2006) Language issues in item development. In T. Haladyna and S. Downing (eds) *Handbook of Test Development* (pp. 377–398). New York: Routledge.

Abedi, J. (2009) Computer testing as a form of accommodation for English language learners. *Educational Assessment* 14 (3–4), 195–211.

Abedi, J. and Lord, C. (2001) The language factor in mathematics tests. *Applied Measurement in Education* 14 (3), 219–234.

Abedi, J. and Ewers, N. (2013) *Accommodations for English Language Learners and Students with Disabilities: A Research-Based Decision Algorithm*. Davis, CA: University of California, Smarter Balanced Assessment Consortium.

Abedi, J., Lord, C. and Plummer, J. (1997) Language Background as a Variable in NAEP Mathematics Performance (CSE Tech. Rep. No. 429). Los Angeles, CA: University of California, Center for the Study of Evaluation/National Center for Research on Evaluation, Standards, and Student Testing.

Abedi, J., Lord, C. and Hofstetter, C. (1998) Impact of Selected Background Variables on Students' NAEP Math Performance (CSE Tech. Rep. No. 478). Los Angeles, CA: University of California, Center for the Study of Evaluation/National Center for Research on Evaluation, Standards, and Student Testing.

Abedi, J., Lord, C., Hofstetter, C. and Baker, E. (2000a) Impact of accommodations strategies on English language learners' test performance. *Educational Measurement: Issues and Practice* 19 (3), 16–26.

Abedi, J., Lord, C., Kim, C. and Miyoshi, J. (2000b) The Effects of Accommodations on the Assessment of LEP Student in NAEP (CSE Tech. Rep. No. 537). Los Angeles, CA: University of California, Center for the Study of Evaluation/National Center for Research on Evaluation, Standards, and Student Testing.

Abedi, J., Hofstetter, C. and Lord, C. (2004) Assessment accommodations for English language learners: Implications for policy based empirical research. *Review of Educational Research* 74 (1), 1–28.

Abedi, J., Zhang, Y. and Rowe, S. (2020) Examining effectiveness and validity of accommodations for English language learners in mathematics: An evidence-based computer accommodation decision system. *Educational Measurement: Issues and Practice* 39 (4), 41–52.

Ascenzi-Moreno, L. (2018) Translanguaging and responsive assessment adaptations: Emergent bilingual readers through the lens of possibility. *Language Arts* 95 (6), 355–369.

American Educational Research Association (AERA), American Psychological Association (APA) and the National Council on Measurement in Education (2014) *Standards for Educational and Psychological Testing*. Washington, DC: AERA.

De Angelis, G. (2021) *Multilingual Testing and Assessment*. Bristol: Multilingual Matters.

De Backer, F., Baele, J., van Avermaet, P. and Slembrouck, S. (2019) Pupils' perceptions of accommodations in multilingual assessment of science. *Language Assessment Quarterly* 16 (4–5), 426–446.

Elliot, S. (2011) US legal issues in educational testing of special populations. In S.N. Elliott, R.J. Kettler, P.A. Beddow and A. Kurz (eds) *Handbook of Accessible Achievement Tests for All Students: Bridging the Gaps between Research, Practice, and Policy* (pp. 33–68). New York: Springer.

Francis, D.J., Rivera, M., Lesaux, N., Kieffer, M.J. and Rivera, H. (2006) *Practical Guidelines for the Education of English Language Learners: Research-Based Recommendations for the Use of Accommodations in Large-Scale Assessments*. Portsmouth, NH: RMC Research Corporation. Center on Instruction. See https://eric.ed.gov/?id=ED517790 (accessed 13 October 2016).

Every Student Succeeds Act (ESSA) (2015) Public Law No. 114-354.

Gándara, P. and Baca, G. (2008) NCLB and California's English language learners: The perfect storm. *Language Policy* 7, 201–216.

Gándara, F. and Randall, J. (2019) Assessing mathematics proficiency of multilingual students: The case for translanguaging in the Democratic Republic of the Congo. *Comparative Education Review* 63 (1), 58–78.

Green, A. (2014) *Exploring Language Assessment and Testing: Language in Action*. New York: Routledge.

Haladyna, T.M., Osborn Popp, S. and Weiss, M. (2003) Non-Response in Large-Scale Assessment. Paper presented at the Annual Meeting of the American Educational Research Association, Montreal, Canada.

International Test Commission (2018) *ITC Guidelines for Translating and Adapting Tests* (2nd edn). *International Journal of Testing* 18, 101–134.

Kieffer, M., Rivera, M. and Francis, D. (2012) *Practical Guidelines for the Education of English Language Learners: Research-Based Recommendations for the Use of Accommodations in Large-Scale Assessments*. Portsmouth, NH: RMC Research Corporation. Center on Instruction. See https://files.eric.ed.gov/fulltext/ED537635.pdf (accessed 13 October 2016).

Lopez, A., Turkan, S. and Guzman-Orth, D. (2017) Assessing multilingual competence. In E. Shohamy, I.G. Or and S. May (eds) *Language Testing and Assessment, Encyclopedia of Language and Education* (pp. 91–102). Cham: Springer International Publishing.

Lopez, A., Guzman-Orth, D. and Turkan, S. (2019) Exploring the use of translanguaging to measure the mathematics knowledge of emergent bilingual students. *Translation and Translanguaging in Multilingual Contexts* 52, 143–164.

Miller, E.R., Okum, I., Sinai, R. and Miller, K.S. (1999, April) A Study of the English Language Readiness of Limited English Proficient Students to Participate in New Jersey's Statewide Assessment system. Paper presented at the annual meeting of the National Council on Measurement in Education, Montreal, Canada.

Pennock-Roman, M. and Rivera, C. (2011) Mean effects of test accommodations for ELLs and non-ELLs: A meta-analysis of experimental studies. *Educational Measurement: Issues and Practice* 30 (3), 10–28.

Rivera, C. and Collum, E. (2004) An analysis of state assessment policies addressing the accommodation of English language learners. Commissioned paper synopsis for the NAGB Conference on Increasing the Participation of SD and LEP Students in NAEP. The George Washington University Center for Equity and Excellence in Education, Washington, DC.

Rivera, C., Acosta, B. and Willner, L. (2008) *Guide for Refining State Assessment Policies for Accommodating EBs*. Washington, DC: The George Washington University Center for Equity and Excellence in Education.

Rosa, J. and Flores, N. (2017) Do you hear what I hear? Raciolinguistic ideologies and culturally sustaining pedagogies. In D. Paris and S. Alim (eds) *Culturally Sustaining Pedagogies: Teaching and Learning for Justice in a Changing World*. New York: Teachers College Press.

Shafer Willner, L.S., Rivera, C. and Acosta, B.D. (2008) *Descriptive Study of State Assessment Policies for Accommodating English Language Learners*. Arlington, VA: The George Washington University Center for Equity and Excellence in Education. See http://files.eric.ed.gov/fulltext/ED539753.pdf (accessed 13 October 2016).

Shepard, L., Grace, T. and Betebenner, B. (1998) Inclusion of Limited-English-Proficient Students in Rhode Island's Grade 4 Mathematics Performance Assessment (CSE Tech. Rep. No. 486). Los Angeles, CA: University of California, Center for the Study of Evaluation/National Center for Research on Evaluation, Standards, and Student Testing.

Shohamy, E. (2022) Critical language testing, multilingualism, and social justice. *TESOL Quarterly* 56 (4), 1445–1457.

Shohamy, E., Tannenbaum, M. and Gani, A. (2022) Bi-multilingual testing for bi-multilingual students: Policy, equality, justice, and future challenges. *International Journal of Bilingual Education and Bilingualism* 25 (9), 3448–3462.

Solano-Flores, G. (2010) Introduction and assessing the cultural validity of assessment practices. In M. Baserra, E. Trumbull and G. Solano-Flores (eds) *Cultural Validity in Assessment: Addressing Linguistic and Cultural Diversity* (pp. 3–21) (Language, Culture and Teaching Series). New York: Routledge.

Wolf, M., Yoo, H., Guzman-Orth, D. and Abedi, J. (2021) Investigating the effects of test accommodations with process data for English learners in a mathematics assessment. *Educational Assessment* 27 (1), 27–45.

Recommended reading

Zhao, Y. (2009) *Catching Up or Leading the Way: American Education in the Age of Globalization*. Alexandria, VA: ASCD.

Yong Zhao argues that more standardization, increased outcome-based accountability and testing only a few subjects will not prepare American youth for success in an age of globalization. The author does, however, recognize the strengths of American education, and thus puts forth a vision for American schools to promote creativity, talent and diversity, plus global and digital competencies. American schools should continue to lead the way, Zhao says, not play catch-up with other countries.

Solano-Flores, G. (2016) *Assessing English Language Learners: Theory and Practice*. New York: Routledge.

This book focuses on the relationship among language, culture, and testing.

8 Special Education

(co-authored with Laura M. Geraci)

THEMES FROM CHAPTER 8

(1) There is significant federal and state policy governing the assessment of students who may have special learning needs.
(2) Many challenges regarding the education of multilingual learners (MLs) with special needs hinge on assessment.
(3) It's difficult to disentangle speech or language impairment from new language learning.

Key Vocabulary

- Culturally and linguistically diverse (CLD).
- High-incidence disabilities.
- Curriculum-based measure (CBM).
- Disproportional representation.
- Least restrictive environment.
- Pre-referral.

- Response to intervention (RtI).
- Multitiered system of supports (MTSS).
- Special education (SPED).
- Speech or language impairment (SLI).
- Learning disability (LD).

This chapter is included for teacher candidates who want to improve their knowledge of policies and practice in the field of SPED. This chapter is included to serve as an introduction to assessment and policy related to SPED. A large number of students are classified both as a ML learner and as a student with a disability (SWD). One of the biggest concerns in this field is whether some MLs are classified but shouldn't be (overrepresentation), or whether some MLs should be classified but are not (underrepresentation). Students who are both MLs and SWDs are entitled to the services mandated by law from both the ML classification and the SPED classification. Some of the challenges professionals in this field face include (1) ensuring an appropriate label, (2) determining eligibility for SPED services, (3) encouraging unbiased assessment procedures and (4) making appropriate educational placements.

A large amount of literature is available to document the overrepresentation of CLD students in SPED programs. CLD students are those students different from the dominant culture and language (in the United States, non-white or not English dominant). The authors of this chapter use the term CLD for information pertinent to the larger group of CLD students (more general group) and ML when targeting students learning English as an additional language (more narrow group). ML students and CLD students are different in the sense that you can think of MLs as a subgroup of CLD students, but CLD students are not necessarily multilingual. Unlike MLs, many CLD students are already proficient in English and may have English as their home language as well as being culturally different from the dominant culture (e.g., African American, Native American or Latinx).

The first half of this chapter presents introductory ideas about process, identification and legislation governing services and assessments for students receiving SPED services in US public schools. The second half of the chapter focuses on SLI,[1] a category of SPED that is oftentimes confused with regular second language acquisition (SLA; which does not require SPED services). The chapter ends with an overview of research on SLI among bilingual children and suggestions for determining SPED needs for MLs.

The reason for the inclusion of this chapter in an assessment textbook focusing on MLs is because assessment methods and the policies that govern assessment practice play a central role in determining appropriate services and advocating for needed services. Of special importance is the need to appropriately identify and discern between those MLs who have special learning needs and those who do not. For instance, some behaviors associated with SLI are also associated with LD. Therefore, trained professionals should use assessment methods to discern whether the behaviors are due to SLI or SLA. And, in addition to discerning behaviors, it is important to evaluate holistically whether the student's school and classroom environment are culturally and linguistically available to the student, among other quality schooling factors (quality of instruction, quality of school resources, opportunities to learn, etc.). What we know about assessing language in general, is the importance to assess language in a natural context (like classrooms) and over time – and, at multiple points across time. Assessing language this way may yield more valid results than standardized language test results.

Students who are found eligible for disability categories are sometimes diagnosed through methods requiring judgment or non-standardized evaluations. Assessment methods, when used without rubrics or criteria such as observations and/or interviews, may introduce judgment and de-emphasize objectivity in the process of identification. These types of methods (of diagnosis) are typically found in high-incidence disabilities – those disabilities that are most likely to appear in school for initial evaluation, for example, Learning Disabilities (LDs) and emotional disturbance (ED) (Klingner et al., 2005).

To begin this chapter, we report on some current data published by the US Department of Education (USDOE, 2023) in the Office of Special Education Programs (OSEP). The following three fast facts, about students dually classified as ML and a student with Special needs, demonstrate the need for more research, better assessments and paradigm shifts to better serve MLs. It's important to keep these data to the forefront while reading the remainder of this chapter.

(1) In the United States, the number of MLs with disabilities grew by close to 30% between 2012 and 2020. Fifty-one states saw an increase in the number of MLs with disabilities (USDOE, 2023).
(2) MLs were more likely to be identified with specific LDs and SLI and less likely to be identified with other health impairments, autism and ED as compared to all school-age students (USDOE, 2023).
(3) MLs were more likely to drop out of school, less likely to graduate with a regular high school diploma and more likely to receive a certificate as compared to all school-age children served under the Individuals with Disabilities Education Act (IDEA).

The next discussion focuses on the broader picture of CLD students with special needs. The merging of SPED with CLD individuals requires a unique collaboration – one that includes educational planning that is focused on language proficiency as well as individualized learning plans (Gargiulo & Bouck, 2021). The following sections give an overview of the legislation that governs this collaboration in the United States.

Federal Policy on Special Education in the United States

Individuals with Disabilities Education Act

In the United States, the most notable piece of legislation for individuals, families and educators involved in SPED is IDEA, passed in 1975. IDEA is viewed as a 'Bill of Rights' for those involved in SPED (Gargiulo & Bouck, 2021). At its inception in 1975, IDEA was named the Education of All Handicapped Children Act (EHA) or Public Law 94-142 and quickly became the most important piece of legislation in the field of SPED. Before the passage of this act, children with disabilities were often denied an education or placed in inappropriate settings such as institutions or segregated facilities, and parents were often forced to pay high tuition rates for private schooling. In addition, many states passed laws barring children with certain types of disabilities from attending school (e.g., children who were blind or labeled mentally retarded). Therefore, the main premise of Public Law 94-142 was to ensure that students with disabilities received an appropriate and free public education. The law laid out the entire foundation upon which SPED focuses today and continues to drive current practice (Pierangelo & Giuliani, 2021). The six major tenets of IDEA are listed in Table 8.1, along with the purpose and focus on IDEA (Tables 8.2 and 8.3). The tenet most closely related to the direction of this chapter is 'non-discriminatory assessment' practices.

Table 8.1 Six components of IDEA (1975)

Component	Description
Free and appropriate education (FAPE)	This is the 'zero reject' philosophy. Any student, regardless of the severity of his or her disability, must be provided with an education at no cost to the parent. This also includes other services that a student may require (e.g., speech therapy).
Least restrictive environment (LRE)	Students with disabilities are to be educated to the maximum extent possible with students without disabilities.
Individual education program (IEP)	This document works like a contract and is individually developed to articulate the specific needs of the student. The IEP includes a description of the educational plan's specific services to meet individual needs.
Procedural due process	This is a safeguard measure for parents. It includes confidentiality, native language requirements, evaluation rights and written notice procedures.
Non-discriminatory assessment	Evaluation conducted by a multidisciplinary team that covers all areas in which the student is suspected of having a disability. Assessment measures cannot be racially or culturally biased.
Parental participation	Parents participate fully in all aspects of the decision-making process

Table 8.2 The purpose and focus of IDEA (2004)

(1A) To ensure that all children with disabilities are provided a free and appropriate public education that specifically provides special education services and related services that are designed to meet their unique needs and prepare them for life after graduation (employment, college and/or independent living).
(1B) To ensure that the rights of children identified with a disability (and their parents) are protected.
(2) To assist all those involved in the education of students with disabilities (government and local school systems).
(3) To ensure that educators and parents have what they need to improve educational results for children with disabilities (e.g., research, technical assistance, technology).
(4) To assess the effectiveness of the education of students with disabilities.

Table 8.3 Main tenets of IDEA (2004)

Parental informed consent	Informed consent is defined as: The parent has been fully informed of all information to which consent is being sought.
	Consent must be provided in the parent's native language and/or current mode of communication.
	Parents need to agree in writing.
	The consent form describes the specific activity for which the school is requesting consent.
	The consent form lists any records that will be forwarded and to whom.
	The parent understands that his or her permission is voluntary and can be revoked at his or her request at any time.
Least restrictive environment (LRE)	Students must be placed in the setting (classroom) that will best meet their educational needs.
	Students with disabilities are placed with students without disabilities whenever deemed appropriate.
	Placement decisions begin with full general education consideration and then move through a continuum as deemed appropriate by the academic and behavioral achievement of the student.
	A guiding matrix is applied for how successful the student is learning in his or her current setting.
	Decisions are made following a least restrictive to most restrictive continuum.
Individualized education plan (IEP)	The IEP is the cornerstone of special education.
	This document is often referred to as the legal document that drives the education and planning of students with disabilities. The IEP includes all vital information to ensure success (e.g., goals, assessment and progress monitoring).
Evaluation must be non-discriminatory	In order for an evaluation to be non-discriminatory, the following requirements must be adhered to: • Bias-free instruments. • Multidisciplinary team. A multidisciplinary team is defined as a team composed of professionals from different disciplines. • Assessment materials and assessment procedures selected and administered without racial or cultural discrimination. • Validation of all assessment materials. • Administered by trained professionals. • Must use more than one assessment measure to determine eligibility and/or placement decisions.
Assessed in all areas related to disability	This includes the following (as needed): • Health. • Vision. • Hearing. • Social condition. • Emotional condition. • Intelligence. • Academic achievement. • Communication. • Motor abilities.
All tests and reports must be in the child's native language	Employing a variety of sound evaluation materials and procedures selected and administered so as not to be racially or culturally discriminatory.
Parents and due process	If a parent disagrees on any part of the process, no change can be made until the issue has been resolved through due-process procedures.
Zero reject	Simply put, all children with a disability have a right to free public school education and cannot be denied this education because of a disability.

Source: Adapted from Pierangelo and Giuliani (2012).

IDEA has been revised and sometimes reauthorized approximately every five years since its inception. The most recent amended version is titled the Individuals with Disabilities Education Improvement Act of 2004 (IDEA, 2004). Unlike previous amendments, the 2004 amendment strongly focuses on assessment and accountability and, although initially closely aligned with No Child Left Behind (NCLB), the newest amendment is aligned with the Every Student Succeeds Act (ESSA). The ESSA was signed into law by President Barack Obama on December 10, 2015. The purpose of this updated version of IDEA was to replace and update the NCLB Act which was signed into law in 2002 (ESSA, Table 8.4).

Table 8.4 Every Student Succeeds Act (ESSA) replaces No Child Left Behind (NCLB)

No Child Left Behind (NCLB)	Every Student Succeeds Act (ESSA)
One-size-fits-all plan developed by the US Department of Education for all states	Individualized plans developed by each state
Mandated labels for the lowest performing schools (priority and focus)	No labels for lowest performing schools
School performance primarily measured by math and English language arts test scores	School performance measured by test scores, achievement, growth, English learner progress, graduation rate and school quality and student success
State provided support directly to schools	State provides support to districts, which provide support to schools
Stakeholder engagement not required	Requires meaningful stakeholder engagement
Four-year graduation rate used to determine school success	Four-year graduation rate *and* five-year graduation rate used to determine school success
Focused on achieving proficiency	Focuses on achievement and growth for all students

Source: From https://dese.ade.arkansas.gov/Files/20201126143555_NCLB_vs_ESSA_Flier.pdf.

The ESSA's main purpose is to make sure public schools provide a quality education for all children. The ESSA gives states more of a say on accountability – including the accountability and achievement of 'disadvantaged' students. The ESSA's focus is on greater autonomy for individual states – giving states more control over education standards and policy than NCLB did. Key components include more control over the funding that schools receive, test scores are set by individual states, responding to underperforming schools become the states' responsibility and, lastly, schools now have the power to determine how much weight is given to a school's participation in assessment testing (https://www.linkedin.com/pulse/key-differences-between-new-essa-act-child-left-behind-mcgarrity).

Focus on CLD students

When evaluating for a disability, IDEA 2004 is clear on the need to ensure an unbiased process. Specifically, IDEA 2004 states that all assessments and evaluation instruments are selected and administered so as not to be discriminatory on a racial or cultural basis. This means that the assessments and instruments are to be provided and administered in the child's home language and/or other mode of communication to provide information on what the student knows and can do academically, developmentally and functionally. When IDEA was reauthorized in 2004, evaluating students in their native language was an effort to reduce the erroneous classification of students on the basis of poor English proficiency rather than a true disability (Cioè-Peña, 2017). Despite the focus on CLD, Phuong (2017) researched US federal policy (IDEA and ESSA) through a language policy lens and concluded that these major federal policies tend to support white, normal, abled students who speak English. The following sections provide more detail about the IDEA policies over the years.

Disproportionate Representation of CLD Students in Special Education

In regard to initial evaluations and subsequent assessment measures for MLs, it is imperative that all protocols be closely followed. Disproportionate representation – defined by de Valenzuela *et al.* (2006) as either a higher or lower percentage of students from a particular ethnic group in SPED than is found in the overall student population of a particular school district – is a growing concern for educators. An often-cited metric to quantify this disproportion is called the relative risk ratio. The relative risk ratio compares the risk (of overrepresentation) for different racial and ethnic groups. Basically, if the relative risk ratio is 1.0, then this indicates equal representation between two racial/ethnic groups (e.g., comparing Mexican American to white rates of classification). Any value greater than 1 indicates overrepresentation. For example, if 20% of all Mexican American students are in SPED and only 10% of white students are in SPED, then the relative risk ratio is 20/10 or 2.0, indicating that Mexican American students are two times as likely as white students to be in SPED. In the United States, when disproportionate representation is documented (using the relative risk ratio or some other metric), this is viewed as potential discriminatory practice and monitored by the Office of Civil Rights (OCR). Often, the OCR requires states or regions to develop a correction plan – a plan to correct the perceived discriminatory problem and equalize representation in SPED.

Bicard and Heward (2010) fittingly summarize this critical issue:

> the fact that culturally (and linguistically) diverse students are identified as having disabilities is not in itself a problem… Disproportionate representation is problematic, however, if students have been wrongly placed in special education, if they are segregated and stigmatized or are denied access to special education because their disabilities are overlooked as a result of their membership in a racial or ethnic minority group. (Bicard & Heward, 2010: 333–334)

Other Federal Legislation that may Impact Students with Disabilities in the United States

Section 504 of the Rehabilitation Act of 1973

Section 504 differs from IDEA in the following ways: (1) Section 504 reaches beyond the school setting, (2) schools do not receive funding for students covered under Section 504 and (3) students are found eligible for Section 504 through professional judgment as opposed to test scores. In short, Section 504 is a civil rights law that prevents discrimination against individuals with disabilities by any agency or institution that receives federal monies. It is possible that a student may not qualify for services under IDEA but could be considered for services under Section 504. For example, a student who has severe asthma may qualify for modifications under 504 but not IDEA. A student who needs an individual education program (IEP) and qualifies for SPED in essence needs specially designed instruction in order to achieve success; a student with a 504 plan only needs accommodations and/or modifications. They do not require specially designed instruction or the services of a SPED teacher.

Americans with Disabilities Act (ADA)

The ADA became law in 1990. It is a civil rights law that prohibits discrimination against individuals with disabilities in all areas of public life. It guarantees equal opportunity for individuals with disabilities in public accommodations, employment, transportation, state and local government services, and telecommunications (https://adata.org/learn-about-ada). The ADA is important because it provides for the protection of students with disabilities attending college. It is often viewed as an extension of IDEA because it provides for reasonable accommodations and non-discriminatory treatment beyond the school years (Mastropieri & Scruggs, 2014).

In 2008, the Americans with Disabilities Act Amendments Act (ADAAA) was signed into law. This amendment allowed for a broader legal definition of 'disability'. The focus of this law continues to be on the prevention of workplace and hiring discrimination against employees with disabilities (https://www.investopedia.com/terms/a/americans-with-disabilities-act-amendments-act-of-2008-adaaa.asp).

The Special Education Process in the United States

The SPED process is also regulated at the federal level, where all states are mandated to align state policy with federal regulation. What is SPED? In its simplest form, SPED is specially designed instruction, at no cost to the parent, to meet the unique needs of a child with a disability. IDEA 2004 defines SPED:

(1) Special education means specially designed instruction, at no cost to the parents, to meet the unique needs of a child with a disability, including –
    (i) Instruction conducted in the classroom, in the home, in hospitals and institutions, and in other settings; and (ii) Instruction in physical education.
(2) Special education includes each of the following, if the services otherwise meet the requirements of paragraph (a)(1) of this section of IDEA – (i) Speech-language pathology services, or any other related service, if the service is considered special education rather than a related service under State standards; (ii) Travel training; and (iii) Vocational education. (IDEA, 2004)

Federal legislation in the United States requires six steps that schools in all states must follow to identify and provide services to students with a disability. The following section articulates each of the six steps.

Step 1: Pre-referral

This section begins with a discussion on pre-referral, including Response to Intervention (RtI), and then walks through the remaining steps of the process. RtI is going to be a part of pre-referral strategies and intervention for many students (obviously not for students with visual, hearing or orthopedic impairments or traumatic brain injury, for example). RtI is only specific to Learning Disabilities (LDs) and does not pertain to other categories. All other categories require different processes for identification. In other words, RtI is used for all students, but will only lead to referral for students with an LD. Pre-referral interventions are designed to assist a student who is struggling academically or behaviorally in order to improve learning before a referral for a SPED evaluation. These interventions are designed to provide support to students and to be delivered inside the student's regular classroom. This is usually the first step toward improving the student's school performance (NCLD, 2013).

School districts will typically have a school-based team. These teams go by various names, such as child study team (CST), student assistant team (SAT) or pupil personnel team (PPT). The team may include the following members: the child's classroom teacher, principal, school psychologist, SPED teacher, school nurse, social worker, speech/language therapist and guidance counselor (Pierangelo & Giuliani, 2012). The team's main objective is to use a data-based decision-making model that will review the student's progress and suggest interventions and supports; they then make decisions based on progress monitoring of the interventions and supports. The data-based decision-making model will be used to determine whether to continue with current interventions (that is, interventions outside of SPED) or to move forward to a SPED referral.

In an attempt to deter unnecessary referrals, IDEA promotes the idea of detecting and solving learning issues early, in what is called a pre-referral stage. In 2004, IDEA thus added a new provision titled Early Intervening Services. This provision is designed for a school to use its SPED funds (up to 15%) to design and implement pre-referral interventions for students who are not currently identified with a disability. There is also a strong focus on the need for school personnel to use scientifically based academic and behavioral interventions as well as scientifically based literacy instruction. For example, school districts may send teachers for professional development or provide a direct service to a student such as remedial reading instruction. The goal is to assist students as early as possible in order to reduce the number of unnecessary referrals to SPED.

Owing to the high number of CLD students in SPED, pre-referral strategies are an important way to focus on CLD students who may not have a need for SPED. Pre-referral strategies and teams aim to reduce the number of students from CLD backgrounds who are inappropriately referred to SPED. Examples of pre-referral strategies include (1) team meeting with teachers and parents, (2) parent interviews, (3) medical exam, (4) hearing test, (5) vision test, (6) classroom management techniques, (7) counseling and (8) progress reports sent to parents.

Pre-referral interventions have been found to exhibit several advantages. First, data used during the initial stages of pre-referral can be used to recommend alternative programs or instructional strategies. Second, the nature of a pre-referral allows for an increased amount of collaboration with other professionals as well as with the student's family. This collaboration can strengthen the family relationship and trust with the school and student's teachers. In addition, the initial data and collaboration serve as a gateway to ensure that additional support will occur within the general education setting. Finally, and perhaps most importantly, if a referral to SPED is deemed appropriate, the student is more than likely to have a 'true' disability (Pierangelo & Giuliani, 2021).

RtI

Every time IDEA is reauthorized, there are changes in the newer policy that try to correct for practices we know are not best. Many educators were relieved when RtI replaced the discrepancy model to determine the existence of an LD. The discrepancy model is described below. RtI can function as an alternative for LD evaluations. In practice, IDEA 2004 eliminated the requirement for schools to show a severe discrepancy between intellectual ability and academic achievement in order for a student to be found eligible for an LD (NCLD, 2013). Before IDEA 2004, discrepancies were 'proven' by comparing two test scores: intelligence test and achievement test scores. IDEA 2004's main premise was that by using RtI, school districts can identify students early and reduce referral bias (Pierangelo & Giuliani, 2021).

RtI is an assessment and intervention process for systematically monitoring student progress and making decisions about the need for instructional modifications or increasingly intensified services using progress monitoring data (National Research Center on Learning Disabilities [NRCLD], 2007). Federal policy encouraged school districts to implement a system to support students who were struggling within the general education setting. In addition, the NRCLD (2007) identified the following components of RtI:

- Progress monitoring in the general education setting using appropriate assessment materials.
- Choosing and implementing scientifically proven interventions (interventions that are research based and have proven to be effective for most students).
- Following a problem-solving model – use of formal guidelines – to make decisions on a student's progress or the student's RtI.
- Monitoring the student weekly or at least once every two weeks.
- Ensuring the intervention is provided accurately and consistently.
- Determining the level of support a student needs to be successful.
- Giving parents notice of the need for a formal referral to SPED if a disability is suspected.

RtI is most often carried out within a three-tiered model:

- Tier 1: Screening and group intervention.
- Tier 2: Targeted interventions.
- Tier 3: Intensive interventions and comprehensive evaluation.

Figure 8.1 provides further tier details. It is important to note that at any time during the RtI process, parents may request a formal evaluation to determine if their child is eligible for SPED services. Also, school districts cannot use the RtI process to deny or delay a formal referral to SPED. RtI is also unique in its use of a CBM and progress monitoring to make decisions on a student's progress. A CBM is used to track and record a student's progress in specific learning areas (NCLD, 2013). Pierangelo and Giuliani (2021) describe RtI in the following way:

> RtI is an integrated approach to service delivery that encompasses general, remedial and special education through a multitier service-delivery model. It utilizes a problem-solving framework to identify and assess academic and behavioral difficulties for all students using scientific, research-based instruction. (Pierangelo & Giuliani, 2012: 78)

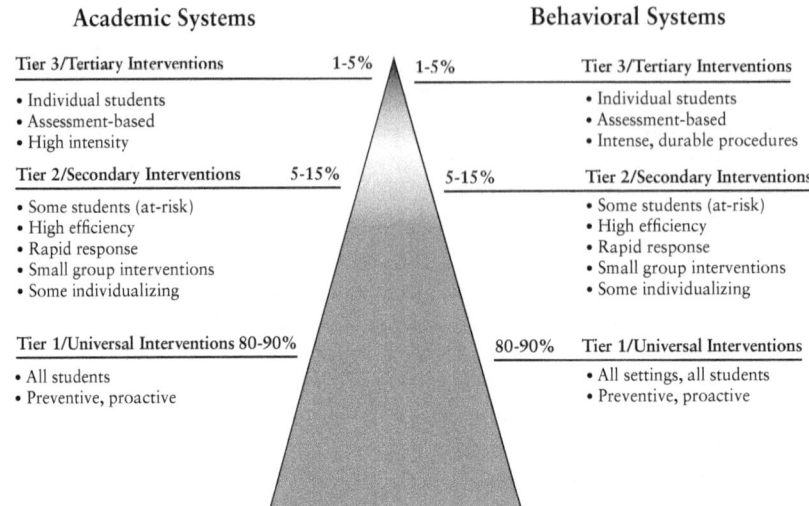

Figure 8.1 An RtI model (https://rtinetwork.org/)

RtI is a three-tiered approach that is used to provide academic and behavioral interventions to students while collecting data to make data-based decisions on the effectiveness of the interventions. In Figure 8.1, the left side of the pyramid focuses on academic tiered interventions. For example, typically all students in a classroom begin in Tier 1; universal or whole-class interventions are provided with a strategic approach on prevention and proactive strategies. As students move up the tiers, interventions become more individualized and target specific learning needs. The same occurs on the right side of the pyramid; interventions and instruction are behavioral in nature and increase in individualization as a student moves up the tiers. In Figure 8.1, the percentages indicate the percentage of students typically in each tiered level in an average classroom. Keep in mind that RtI is not used to make final recommendations about SLI. RtI is primarily used to collect data around potential LDs. This is only 1 of the 13 official categories of SPED.

RtI is not without its challenges and criticism. Initially meant to provide early intervention, at times RtI can prolong the evaluation process. As described above, one of the intentions of RtI was to reduce the number of unnecessary referrals to SPED. Although there are concerns about the overrepresentation of CLD students in SPED, RtI has become a promising strategy to reduce the number of referrals to SPED and to provide culturally appropriate instruction (Mastropieri & Scruggs, 2014).

RtI has the potential to screen learning and behavior problems early to prevent academic difficulties and/or failure of all students, including CLD students with disabilities. RtI also has the potential to bring together professionals from different fields (such as general education, SPED, English as a new language [ENL], speech) even though these fields are typically bound by isolated practices. If RtI is used with culturally relevant practices and prevention, with early intervention and support that views culture and language in a promising way, then it has great potential. Klingner and Edwards (2006) recommend the culturally responsive interventions shown in Table 8.5 to support students from diverse backgrounds. RtI can work for CLD

Table 8.5 Cultural response interventions for CLD students

Tier 1	Interventions should be implemented by teachers who are familiar with culturally relevant teaching.
Tier 2	Progress monitoring should be carefully tracked and culturally relevant.
	Tier 2 teams should also be composed of individuals with expertise in working with diverse students.
Tier 3	Focus is on ensuring that assessment and evaluation measures have been conducted with cultural fairness and use of unbiased measures prior to special education referral.

students if the appropriate responsive protocol is used, including assessment methods and instruments. The bottom line about RtI: the RtI process is only as strong as its strongest assessment method.

MTSS

In addition to RtI, school districts also engage in a framework referred to as an MTSS. Although very similar to RtI, there are distinct differences. Many schools use the terms response to intervention and multitier system of supports interchangeably. However, there is a difference. RtI usually refers to a school's academic support system only. MTSS is more expansive, describing the systems set up in a school to provide coordinated support for both academic and behavioral/social-emotional needs. The Michigan Department of Education defines MTSS as an integrated, multitiered system of instruction, assessment and intervention designed to meet the achievement needs and behavioral health needs of all learners (Quick Guide for Multi-Tiered System of Supports: The Building Level). However, RtI and MTSS are similar in that each offers several levels of intervention support, uses data to identify students requiring services and employs research-based strategies to help at-risk learners (Table 8.6).

Table 8.6 A walk through RtI and MTSS

	RtI	MTSS
Interventions	Academic	Academic behavioral, social, emotional
Target audience	Student becoming eligible for special education service	All students
Resource and support	Target audience	All students, teachers and paraprofessionals
Collaboration	General education and special education teachers work together on Tiers 2 and 3	Stronger focus on collaboration between disciplines
Focus	Intervention and remediation	Intervention, remediation *and* strong prevention focus
Problems addressed	Student level	Included student level as well as system level
Intervention	Centered within the school	School, community and home

Source: Adapted from What is the Difference between RTI and MTSS?

Step 2: Referral or request for evaluation

The second major step in the SPED process is a formal referral to SPED. This occurs after both pre-referral strategies and RtI have proved to be ineffective for the student. At this stage, either the parent or the school district will request a formal evaluation that must be in writing and requires informed consent from the parent (Pierangelo & Giuliani, 2021). This request will set in motion the remaining steps of the SPED process.

Note that although informed consent is required, such a requirement does not give permission for the school district to begin SPED; the informed consent step is solely for evaluation to determine if the student needs SPED. What's more, when the parent or the school district makes the request, the evaluation is conducted at no cost to the parent. This initial referral will be processed by a multidisciplinary team (MDT). This team is responsible for beginning the formal assessment process and working through the remaining steps with parents and students (Pierangelo & Giuliani, 2021).

The evaluation process begins with a review of the pre-referral data. The direction of the assessment process will be aligned with pre-referral information as well as any specific concerns expressed by the referring party. IDEA (2004) defines the evaluation process as follows:

> (1) Uses a variety of assessment tools and strategies to gather relevant functional, developmental and academic information about the child, including information provided by the parent, that may assist in determining (i) whether the child is a child with a disability under Sec. 300.8; and ... (2) Does not use any single measure or assessment as the sole criterion for determining whether a child is a child with a disability and for determining an appropriate educational program for the child; and (3) Uses technically sound instruments that may assess the relative contribution of cognitive and behavioral factors, in addition to physical or developmental factors. (Sec. 300.304: Evaluation procedures). (IDEA, 2004)

Step 3: Eligibility determination

Once the student has been formally evaluated for SPED services, the next step is to determine, based on all of the completed evaluations, whether the student is eligible for services as required by IDEA. At this time, the school district will convene a team, often called the eligibility committee (IEP team), the committee on SPED or the IEP committee. The main focus of the IEP team is to review the assessment results, determine eligibility and make recommendations for classification and placement.

During the eligibility meeting, after the evaluation results have been discussed and the team has determined eligibility, the student will be classified under 1 of 13 disability categories defined by IDEA.

Instead of reviewing all 13 categories, the authors of this chapter decided to define the 3 categories that are known to have an overrepresentation of ML students (ED, LD and SLI).

(1) Emotional disturbance: A condition exhibiting one or more of the following characteristics over a long period of time and to a marked degree that adversely affects a child's educational performance:
   (a) An inability to learn that cannot be explained by intellectual, sensory or health factors.

(b) An inability to build or maintain satisfactory interpersonal relationships with peers and teachers.
(c) Inappropriate types of behavior or feelings under normal circumstances.
(d) A general pervasive mood of unhappiness or depression.
(e) A tendency to develop physical symptoms or fears associated with personal or school problems.
(f) The term includes schizophrenia.
ED does not apply to children who are socially maladjusted, unless it is determined that they have an ED.
(2) Learning disability: A disorder in one or more of the basic psychological processes involved in understanding or in using language, spoken or written, that may manifest itself in the imperfect ability to listen, think, speak, read, write, spell or do mathematical calculations. The term includes such conditions as perceptual disabilities, brain injury, minimal brain dysfunction, dyslexia and developmental aphasia. The term does not include learning problems that are primarily the result of visual, hearing or motor disabilities; of intellectual disability; of ED; or of environmental, cultural or economic disadvantage.
(3) Speech or language impairment: A communication disorder such as stuttering, impaired articulation, a language impairment or a voice impairment that adversely affects a child's educational performance.

A final note on eligibility: IDEA established a two-pronged process to determine SPED services. Prong one states that the student must have 1 (or more) of the 13 categories listed in IDEA. Prong two states that the student must need SPED services in order to be successful in school and to make progress in the general education setting (NCLD, 2013).

IDEA 2004 includes special rules for eligibility to prevent the inappropriate identification of a student as having a disability under any category. The team must therefore ensure that the following factors are not a primary reason for the student's lack of progress in the general education setting:

- Lack of appropriate instruction in reading.
- Lack of instruction in math.
- *Limited English proficiency*.

The main idea in regard to math or reading is to demonstrate that the student did not make sufficient progress to meet age- or state-approved or grade-level standards in math or reading while provided instruction in reading and math from a qualified teacher in the general education setting. For CLD students, documentation must support that the lack of success in the general education setting, given appropriate support and instruction, *is not a result of* the student having limited English proficiency.

Step 4: The individual education program

At this point, the Individual Education Program (IEP) team has reviewed all relevant information provided in the evaluation process, determined eligibility and determined a student's classification category; it will now develop the student's IEP. Simply stated, it is the student's education plan that explains the goals and objectives, related services and where the student will receive his or her SPED series (placement). The IEP is otherwise thought of as the critical link between the student in SPED and the special teaching that the student requires (Pierangelo & Giuliani, 2021).

Step 5: Special education placement

With the IEP developed and actionable, students with disabilities are then placed in the least restrictive environment (see Table 8.3). The *placement* is where the student will receive his or her SPED services. This is the next step in the SPED process – determining the environment into which the student will be placed. Again, this decision is based on the initial evaluation and assessment results. Students are to be placed where they can gain the most without interfering with the learning of others and where they can progress and meet the goals of their IEP. As noted earlier in this chapter and according to IDEA, placements follow a continuum of least restrictive to most restrictive.

Step 6: Annual review

The IEP will be reviewed annually and follow the same process as the initial evaluation process, which makes this process cyclical. The annual review meeting will make recommendations to continue, revise, change or end the student's SPED services. It is important to note that each component of the IEP is determined through assessment measures and will be amended and reviewed using assessment and data-based decision-making processes. The student will also have a triennial review, which is an evaluation conducted every three years to provide current assessment information. In general, federal law informs the policy and the policy informs the regulation and each policy and regulation needs to be aligned with the law (IDEA). State laws provide the framework for educational policy; regulations lay out how the law will be implemented (Pierangelo & Giuliani, 2021). A good grasp of the laws and regulations will assist teachers in being strong and knowledgeable advocates for their students and students' parents.

Obstacles and Challenges with Addressing Special Needs of CLD Students

Sometimes, myths and past practice can be difficult to overcome when it comes to schooling issues. Hamayan *et al.* (2013) identified the following three *myths* or misconceptions that prevail in schools about MLs and SPED. For more detail, or for a continuum of services framework, see Hamayan *et al.* (2013).

(1) **If we label a ML student as having SPED needs, at least he or she gets some help.** Response in short: Not true. The stigma related to the label combined with interventions targeting the wrong needs will lead to more harm than benefit.
(2) **We have to wait three to seven years for MLs to develop their English language skills before we can rule out language as a cause of the student's difficulty.** Response in short: Not true. If a student truly has an intrinsic difficulty, then it exists in the student's entire language repertoire and in most contexts. The

sooner these exceptionalities are identified and supported, the better (Hamayan *et al.*, 2013).

(3) **When a ML student is identified as having SPED needs, instruction should only be in English, so as not to confuse the student.** Response in short: Not true. Students with speech, language or learning impairments can become bilingual and bilingual instruction provides a more culturally relevant environment. Bilingualism and multilingualism have been found to be beneficial for MLs with disabilities, yet they continue to mostly receive services in English only. The reason for this is a persistent and widespread belief that children with disabilities cannot and should not be enrolled in bilingual programs, in part because they would be over-taxed by learning two linguistic systems. Not true. Evidence supports the benefits of bilingualism for this group of students (Cioè-Peña, 2017).

Current schools experience a long list of challenges in the area of educating CLD students. There is a pervasive and historical achievement gap between CLD and non-CLD students. There is an overrepresentation of certain CLD students in SPED, especially in high-incidence disabilities (more commonly found among students). Compared to low-incidence disabilities, high-incidence disabilities represents more CLD students. The assessments associated with high-incidence disabilities tend to be subjective and ambiguous in nature, leaving room for bias. This subjectivity, in combination with a historical devaluation of CLD students in US schools, has opened the door to much of the overrepresentation seen today (Zhang & Cho, 2010). There is also an underrepresentation of CLD students in gifted education. Even though schools that receive federal or state funding must provide unbiased and non-discriminatory assessments, including administering assessments in the home language, this goal has been difficult to achieve. Teacher bias may also result in the misidentification or over-identification of CLD with special needs. African American students in particular have been disproportionately diagnosed with intellectual disabilities, as have Native Americans (Zhang & Cho, 2010).

Although it is unclear exactly what shapes the overrepresentation of certain racial groups in categories of SPED, it is likely that many systemic and historical factors contribute, but most people believe that assessment practices are one of the main sources for the overrepresentation. In particular, the use of culturally and linguistically biased assessments is majorly contributing to the collection of invalid data for CLD students. Despite federal policies mandating fair assessments (IDEA and ESSA) as well as court decisions mandating fair assessments (e.g. *Diana v. State Board of Education [1970]*), the use of biased assessments still occurs regularly. See also *Arreola v. Santa Ana Board of Education (1968)* and *Covarrubias v. San Diego Unified School District (1971)*.

In addition to the problem of using biased assessments, the next prominent obstacle is the shortage of speech and educational professionals who share the same cultural and linguistic background as their students being assessed. Since the early 1980s in the United States, training programs have been funded to try to eradicate the shortage of professionals trained in bilingual education and SPED.

Despite this, four decades later, the United States still has a shortage of bilingual special educators and bilingual speech pathologists. This shortage is one of the major challenges facing the service delivery model to MLs with disabilities. Because of a shortage of bilingual teachers in general, many MLs are often served in English-only settings with relatively few modifications to the instruction/assessment. The shortage of bilingual educators and speech pathologists also causes the problem of not having qualified personnel to administer the assessments (for example in the child's home language).

Some of these challenges are superficial, while others are more deeply rooted, such as general diversity issues. To add to this list of challenges, Martin (2009) writes about the many discourses that construct diversity as a problem. These discourses present diversity and difference as interfering with the smooth running aspects of mainstream society and services. Disruptions caused to mainstream life are seen as the fault of individuals who are diverse or different. Martin (2009) calls this blaming diversity and disabling diversity.

Supporting these discourses is a prevailing amount of research about speech and language difficulties constructed around monolingual children, but very little about bilingual children. Therefore, most of our theories, empirical evidence, assessment methods and interventions are drawn from research on monolinguals. The three categories of language difficulties that have been researched cross-linguistically and in bilingual children are language delay, grammar difficulties and speech difficulties (Martin, 2009). Martin reminds us that having typical overall development except in regard to language learning is what identifies children with SLI. Both monolingual and bilingual children have problems, varying in severity, with speech and/or grammar – both understanding and producing language. They have smaller vocabularies and often atypical patterns in understanding and expressing speech and grammar in comparison with their typically developing peers. These patterns may appear similar to patterns of SLA (Martin, 2009). Martin (2009) also reminds us that bilingualism does not cause speech and language difficulties.

A Review of *Assessing Multilingual Children: Disentangling Bilingualism from Language Impairment*[2] (Armon-Lotem et al., 2015)

This summary section takes the reader out of the US context and examines a non-US context with an emphasis on the assessment methods of bilingual children who potentially have SLI. The problem of overrepresentation of bilingual children with SLI across the Western world led to the funding of the European Cooperation in Science and Technology (COST) and in particular Language Impairment in a Multilingual Society: Linguistic Patterns and the Road to Assessment. Researchers in the Armon-Lotem *et al.* (2015) book come from Israel, the Netherlands, Lithuania, Sweden, the UK, Iceland, Malta, Poland, Denmark, South Africa, Finland, Ireland, France, Germany and Greece. The researchers (Armon-Lotem *et al.*, 2015) provided the following four guidelines that still hold promise for future research and practice in SLI for bilingual children:

(1) Bilingualism and SLI are not the same and can be disentangled.
(2) Bilingual children with SLI show error patterns similar to monolingual children with SLI.

(3) Bilingualism and SLI seem not to show a cumulative effect. Therefore, one factor does not increase the other factor; because of this, we should *not* see more cases of SLI in bilingual children than monolingual children.
(4) Bilingualism might sometimes offer a partial compensatory mechanism for language and cognitive development in children with SLI.

SLI v. SLA

There is a problem across the Western world among bilingual children with disentangling Speech Language Impairment (SLI) from Second Language Acquisition (SLA) for a variety of reasons. It is believed that the number one reason contributing to this problem of overrepresentation (of bilingual children having SLI) is the types of assessments being used.

In general, the assessments used are designed for monolingual children and have not been normed for bilingual children, who in general do not conform to monolingual norms. For example, many assessments count vocabulary size (lexicon) in one language which lends itself to a fractional view of bilingual children. It only makes sense that if vocabulary is measured in one language only (fractional view), then the bilingual child will appear to have a smaller vocabulary than he or she does if vocabulary is measured in both languages in tandem (holistic view). Even though the holistic assessment makes more sense for a bilingual child, the fractional practice is dominant in schools across the Western world. De Angelis (2021) reports promise using multilingual narratives (oral accounts of real or imaginary events) in educational and clinical settings to assess children's language and cognitive development and to identify children with SLI. Multilingual narratives can be valuable tools for assessment as they reflect how children conceptualize, plan and organize content, using languages and cognitive skills (De Angelis, 2021). Further:

> bilingual children are exposed to narratives from an early age, depending on the type of bilingualism they are developing and the language choices their parents have made for them. ... Children typically continue to develop their narrative skills up to school age and by that time have already developed the ability to establish causal and temporal links between characters and events and are able to tell stories using complete episode ... Narratives grow in depth and complexity as children grow older and are progressively able to understand, process, and produce more elaborate input and more complex language. Narratives therefore offer a clear window into children's language development, providing valuable information to teachers who may adopt remedial strategies in the classroom whenever needed. (De Angelis, 2021: 85)

Assessments like multilingual narratives are not common in schools. One of the difficulties of disentangling bilingualism from SLI stems from the many similarities in the linguistic manifestations of SLA and of SLI. This in combination with the fact that there are a limited number of diagnostic instruments to appropriately distinguish between SLI and SLA, more ML children are diagnosed with SLI than should be. If there were no misdiagnoses, then the percentage of bilingual children with SLI should be similar or equal to that of monolingual children (for example, the relative risk ratio of bilingual children to monolingual children with SLI should be 1.0), but it's not. It is believed that inappropriate assessment methods are one reason for the overrepresentation of MLs with SLI.

The impact that monolingual assessments have on referring healthy bilinguals to unnecessary special needs services is great. It can be confusing for teachers to understand the boundaries between behaviors that might be classified as language developmental delays (needs SPED services) or delays typical of second language development (does not need SPED services). As already mentioned, the big question is often characterized as 'SLI or SLA?', otherwise known as 'speech language impairment or second language acquisition?'. Teachers are the first in line to identify concerns about potential delays, so they should be adequately trained to identify and analyze behaviors, and also to advocate against the use of monolingual assessments to make these important decisions about MLs.

This has been a source of frustration for many educators for a long time. Are we asking the right questions? Should we be asking more questions? Kangas (2021) argues that the question 'SLI or SLA?' or more broadly 'disability or language?' has evolved into a pervasive and troubling filter through which educators attempt to make sense of the academic performance and linguistic development of MLs. This question was originally intended to promote equity, but this question may evolve a deficit mindset rooted in ableism (discrimination in favor of able-bodied people) and monolingualism (the condition of being able to speak only a single language) (Kangas, 2021).

Should we be asking bigger questions? Cioè-Peña (2022) views these issues through a decolonization perspective. Decolonizing refers to examining the ways in which colonialism continues to shape modern political, economic, cultural, social and knowledge systems, including education policy and practice. She argues that over and underrepresentation of racialized minorities in segregated learning settings (SPED and ENL, for example) is by design a part of the native speakerism (an ideology that upholds the idea that 'native speakers' are the best model) and gatekeeping in general for racial minorities. These ideas uphold a larger settler colonial logic (Cioè-Peña, 2022a). She suggests that students racialized as Black, Indigenous and Latinx are overrepresented with SLI because underlying these mostly monolingual assessment measures of language is a colonial framework that drives language ideologies and practices worldwide (Cioè-Peña, 2022a).

Next, the big ideas of this chapter are translated into 11 suggestions for teachers and future teachers.

Assessment Suggestions

This chapter ends with Table 8.7, which gives 11 suggestions surrounding the assessment of bilingual students who are under consideration as having special learning needs.

Table 8.7 Suggestions for assessment practice surrounding ML students potentially having special needs

(1)	Answer this critical question: Are the difficulties present in both the child's home language and the new language? Is his or her communication impaired with family members or others who speak the same language? Remember: A child's developmental delay or disability will be observable in both languages and across multiple settings.
(2)	Make all comparisons to 'peer cohorts' or 'true peers' to avoid invalid conclusions. Peer cohorts are groups of children who are bilingual, share the same home language and have similar life experiences.
(3)	Educators who value and reinforce the student's home language in assessment will experience more success with CLD students (and vice versa).
(4)	Use culturally relevant pedagogy (CRP) in all three tiers of RtI. See Gloria Ladson-Billings' (1994, 2021) work on a theory of CRP. Combine with Funds of Knowledge (Gonzalez et al., 2005 work) to capitalize on family/home 'funds' in school. This will create a culturally relevant environment.
(5)	Use translanguaging as pedagogy in all three tiers of RtI to promote a holistic view of a child's language and academic ability (as opposed to a fractional view). See Ofelia Garcia's work on translanguaging pedagogy (2009). This will create a culturally relevant multilingual environment. Cioè-Peña (2022) offers an integrated pedagogical stance called translanguaging and universal design (TRUDL).
(6)	Ask PUMI (Purpose, Use, Method, Instrument) questions whenever an assessment is used with MLs. Only use instruments normed on bilingual children. Do not use instruments normed on monolingual children. You can read the blueprint of the test to find out how the instrument was normed or piloted.
(7)	When selecting assessment methods for language, choose methods *in context* (natural setting, real authentic language use) and *over time*. Avoid pre-made stories, sentences and other pre-made language tasks. These may be culturally incongruent or make no sense to the child. Choose holistic and open-ended language assessments to allow the child to construct language that makes sense to him or her.
(8)	Choose assessment methods that include a holistic perspective (both languages – translanguaging) not a fractional one (one language or the other).
(9)	Ask a cultural expert (preferably someone who shares the home language and culture with the bilingual child being assessed) to analyze pictures and pre-made sentences for cultural relevance and appropriateness.
(10)	Seek information from families about language practice at home. Use questionnaires or interviews; preferably administer in the home.
(11)	Interviews and observations are assessment methods that lend themselves to culturally relevant assessment: they take more time and more trained professionals.

END-OF-CHAPTER ACTIVITIES (Instructors: see advice at the end of the book)

By doing Activities 1–3, the reader will be able to:

Orally or in writing, define each tenet of IDEA and provide evidence to support tenet choice.
Discuss the SPED process.
Organize and map the three disability categories (ED, LD and SLI).

Activity 1
Orally or in writing, define each tenet of IDEA and provide evidence to support tenet choice.

Activity 2
Participate in a gallery walk and discussion of the SPED process.

Activity 3
Develop a mind map of the three disability categories relevant to MLs (ED, LD and SLI).

Activity 4
Think about some of the issues that SPED teachers must face as the number of students from cultural and linguistic backgrounds increases in our schools across the nation. Be prepared to discuss your responses to the following questions.

Questions/Discussion Topics

(1) How might you ensure that, as a teacher, you evaluate a student who has a disability in ways that do not discriminate against his or her cultural or linguistic background?
(2) How can SPED teachers who are monolingual meet the educational needs of linguistically diverse students? Discuss the availability of services in your community that may be supportive to this teacher.
(3) What can administrators representing a school do to create a comfortable learning environment for all students (SPED and general education)?

Notes

(1) The IDEA federal policy uses this acronym for speech or language impairments (SLI). Many terms are used to describe language and communication difficulties. Most terms are deficit focused and specific to one language level (Martin, 2009). For example, specific language impairment (SLI), specific speech impairment, language impairment (LI), specific speech and language difficulties, semantic and pragmatic impairment and pragmatic impairment (Martin, 2009).
(2) In the book *Assessing Multilingual Children: Disentangling Bilingualism from Language Impairment*, the authors refer to SLI as specific language impairment. This is also used in the current chapter.

References

Armon-Lotem, S., de Jong, J. and Meir, N. (2015) *Assessing Multilingual Children: Disentangling Bilingualism from Language Impairment*. Bristol: Multilingual Matters.
Bicard, S. and Heward, W. (2010) Educational equity for students with disabilities. In J. Banks and C. Banks (eds) *Multicultural Education: Issues and Perspectives* (7th edn, pp. 315–341). Hoboken, NJ: Wiley.
Cioè-Peña, M. (2017) Bilingualism, disability, and what it means to be normal. *Journal of Bilingual Education Research & Instruction* 19 (1), 138–160.
Cioè-Peña, M. (2022a) The master's tools will never dismantle the master's school: Interrogating settler colonial logic in language education. *Annual Review of Applied Linguistics* 42, 25–33.
Cioè-Peña, M. (2022b) TrUDL, A path to full inclusion: The intersectional possibilities of translanguaging and universal design for learning. *TESOL Quarterly* 56 (2), 799–812.
De Angelis, G. (2021) *Multilingual Testing and Assessment*. Bristol: Multilingual Matters.
de Jong, J. (2015) Elicitation task for subject–verb agreement. In S. Armon-Lotem, J. de Jong and N. Meir (eds) *Assessing Multilingual Children: Disentangling Bilingualism from Language Impairment* (pp. 25–37). Bristol: Multilingual Matters.

De Valenzuela, J.S., Copeland, S.R., Huaqing Qi, C. and Park, M. (2006) Examining educational equity: Revisiting the disproportionate representation of minority students in special education. *Council for Exceptional Children* 73 (4), 425–441.

Garcia, O. (2009) *Bilingual Education in the 21st Century: A Global Perspective*. New York: John Wiley.

Gargiulo, R. and Bouck, E.C. (2021) *Special Education in Contemporary Society* (7th edn). Thousand Oaks, CA: Sage Publications.

Gonzalez, N., Moll, L.C. and Amanti, C. (eds) (2005) *Funds of Knowledge*. Abingdon: Routledge.

Hamayan, E., Marler, B., Sánchez-López, C. and Damico, J. (2013) *Special Education Considerations for English Language Learners: Delivering a Continuum of Services*. Philadelphia, PA: Caslon Publishing.

IDEA 2004 Regulations: Subpart E – Procedural Safeguards. See http://www.wrightslaw.com/idea/law/idea.regs.subparte.pdf (accessed February 2013).

Kangas, S. (2021) 'Is it language or disability?': An ableist and monolingual filter for English learners with disabilities. *TESOL Quarterly* 55 (3), 673-683.

Klingner, J.K. and Edwards, P.A. (2006) Cultural considerations with response to intervention models. *Reading Research Quarterly* 41, 108–117.

Klingner, J.K., Artiles, A.J., Kozleski, E., Harry, B., Zion, S., Tate, W., Duran, G.Z. and Riley, D. (2005) Addressing the disproportionate representation of culturally and linguistically diverse students in special education through culturally responsive educational systems. *Education Policy Analysis Archives* 13 (38). See http://dx.doi.org/10.14507/epaa.v13n38.2005 (accessed 19 October 2016).

Ladson-Billings, G. (1994) *Dreamkeepers: Successful Teachers of African American Children*. San Francisco, CA: Jossey-Bass.

Ladson-Billings, G. (2021) *Culturally Relevant Pedagogy: Asking a Different Question* (Culturally Sustaining Pedagogies Series). New York, NY: Teachers College Press.

Martin, D. (2009) *Language Disabilities in Cultural and Linguistic Diversity*. Bristol: Multilingual Matters.

Mastropieri, M.A. and Scruggs, T.E. (2014) *The Inclusive Classroom: Strategies for Effective Differentiated Instruction*. Boston, MA: Pearson.

NCLD (2013) IDEA parent guide. See www.ncld.org (accessed February 2013).

NRCLD (2007) *Responsiveness to Intervention in Conjunction with Learning Disability Determination*. Lawrence, KS: NRCLD.

Phuong, J. (2017) Disability and language ideology. *Working Papers in Educational Linguistics (WPEL)* 32 (1), 47–66.

Pierangelo, R. and Giuliani, G. (2012) *Assessment in Special Education: A Practical Approach* (4th edn). New York: Pearson.

United States Department of Education (USDOE) (2023) OSEP fast facts: Students with disabilities who are English learners (EL) served under IDEA Part B. See https://sites.ed.gov/idea/osep-fast-facts-students-with-disabilities-english-learners#:~:text=The%20number%20of%20students%20with,while%20eight%20saw%20a%20decrease (accessed 2 November 2023).

Zhang, C. and Cho, S.J. (2010) The development of the bilingual special education field: Major issues, accomplishments, future directions, and recommendations. *Journal of Multilingual Education Research* 1 (1), 45–61.

Recommended reading

Abedi, J. (2009) English language learners with disabilities: Classification, assessment, and accommodation issues. *Journal of Applied Testing Technology* 10 (3).

In this paper, Abedi discusses issues concerning the accessibility of assessment classification and accommodations for English language learners with disabilities (ELLWD). Abedi presents recommendations for more accessible assessments.

Abedi, J. and Faltis, C. (2015) Review of research in education: Teacher assessment and the assessment of students with diverse learning needs. AERA 39. https://doi.org/10.3102/0091732X14558995

The purpose of this volume is to bring awareness to specific considerations necessary in the use of high-stakes tests with teachers, ELLs and students with special needs.

Artiles, A., Rueda, R., Salazar, J. and Higareda, I. (2005) Within-group diversity in minority disproportionate representation: English language learners in urban school districts. *Exceptional Children* 71 (3), 283–300.

The authors examine EB placement patterns in California urban districts. Disproportionate representation patterns were found to relate to grade level, language proficiency level, disability category, type of special education program and type of language program.

Burr, E., Haas E. and Ferriere, K. (July 2015) Identifying and Supporting English Learner Students with Learning Disabilities: Key Issues in the Literature and State Practice. Report from Regional Educational Laboratory (REL) at WestEd.

This report reviews research and policy in the 20 US states with the largest populations of EBs. It is deemed helpful for education leaders who are setting up processes to determine which EB students may need placement in special education.

Harry, B. and Klingner, J. (2005) *Why Are So Many Minority Students in Special Education? Understanding Race and Disability in Schools*. New York: Teachers College Press.

Harry and Klingner examine the disproportionate placement of black and Hispanic students in special education. The authors examine the experience of children, family interactions with school personnel, the school's estimate of child and family and the school climate that leads to decisions about referrals.

The Iris Center (funded by the US Department of Education's Office of Special Education Programs – OSEP) Dual language learners with disabilities: Supporting young children in the classroom. See http://iris.peabody.vanderbilt.edu/module/dll (accessed 19 October 2016).

These modules provide resources about evidence-based practices for use in pre-service preparation and professional development programs. In addition to this 1 module, there are 15 modules to better understand RtI.

Kormos, J. and Smith, M. (2024) *Teaching Languages to Students with Specific Learning Differences* (2nd edn). Bristol: Multilingual Matters.

The purpose of this book is to help language teachers work effectively with students who have specific learning differences (SpLDs).

MacSwan, J. and Rolstad, K. (2006) How language proficiency tests mislead us about ability: Implications for English language learner placement in special education. *Teachers College Record* 108 (11), 2304–2328.

The authors argue that EB language assessment policy and poor language tests partly account for EBs' disproportionate representation in special education. They present empirical evidence to support this claim.

Paradis, J., Genessee, F. and Crago, M. (2011) *Dual Language Development & Disorders: A Handbook on Bilingualism and Second Language Learning*. Baltimore, MD: Brookes Publishing.

This textbook is designed to prepare speech-language pathologists to work with bilingual children.

Resource links

ESSA: https://www.coordinatingcenter.org/files/2018/09/Every-Student-Succeeds-Act-ESSA-What-You-Need-to-Know.pdf

MTSS: https://resources.finalsite.net/images/v1568836530/resanet/v3v3youp8fkgrbzuivve/BuildingMTSSQuickGuide.pdf

9 Accountability

Source: Gary Huck and Mike Konopacki Labor Cartoons Collection; WAG 264; Box 23; Folder 5; Tamiment Library/Robert F. Wagner Labor Archives, New York University. Reproduced with permission.

> **THEMES FROM CHAPTER 9**
>
> (1) Accountability related to assessment has come to the forefront of education in the last 10 years.
> (2) Accountability based on student assessment results has never been more intense and directly tied to assessment.
> (3) Accountability without validity isn't meaningful (see Chapter 2).

Key Vocabulary

- Assessment literacy.
- Growth model v. status model v. value-added model (VAM).
- Multiple measures.
- Status model.
- Value-added assessment.
- Data-driven instruction (DDI).

PUMI (Purpose, Use, Method, Instrument) Connection: Use

This chapter focuses on the U (Use) in PUMI. Test score results are being used like never before for accountability purposes. After reading this chapter, new teachers will have a clearer understanding of what's behind the accountability terms used in schools today. The chapter begins by introducing the term assessment literacy. Teachers are not the only ones accountable when it comes to the assessment of students. Chapter 9 begins with Table 9.1, which shows the different groups of stakeholders (in addition to teachers) who are accountable to have assessment literacy.

What is Assessment Literacy?

Assessment literacy is not just for teachers. Assessment literacy refers to the knowledge, skills and processes associated with designing, implementing and interpreting assessments to improve student learning. According to Rick Stiggins (2017), everyone involved in the assessment of students has responsibilities to have a high level of assessment literacy. Green (2014) argued that language assessment is inseparable from the teaching and learning of languages and most teacher education programs treat assessment as if it is a distinct activity, one that is marginal to the main job of teaching and learning. Green (2014) also argued that teachers need assessment literacy: they need some knowledge of how assessments are made, scored and interpreted, and to be able to score and interpret useful assessments themselves. Table 9.1 explores who needs 'assessment literacy', according to Rick Stiggins (2017).

Table 9.1 Rank order of the educational community most in need of assessment literacy (adapted from Stiggins, 2017)

(1) Professional test developers	They must create and defend and follow-up on high-quality assessments, including demonstrating evidence about whether or not assessments should be used with MLs.
(2) State and local district assessment directors	This group must be able to translate complex measurement concepts into everyday language to be useful in classrooms. This group should also serve to protect MLs/ their families and teachers of MLs from assessments containing validity concerns, such as construct irrelevant variance (CIV) as well as too many assessments. Local district leaders should be first in line to protect and not disrupt the integrity of bilingual programs by requiring too many English-only assessments and glossing over the appropriate assessment and development of home languages.
(3) Teachers and local school leaders	Teachers spend much of their time on assessment. Their and their student's well-being hinge on the results. Teachers and the school leaders that guide them need to protect[a] students (like an umbrella) from too many low-quality assessments, and unnecessary testing.
(4) Policymakers	This group includes federal, state and local policymakers (anyone who influences policy). This group needs to apply assessment literacy to make sure policy guides assessment practice in appropriate ways. Assessment policies must also protect best practices in English as a new language (ENL) and bilingual programs. For example, policies mandating English-only assessments should not impact the integrity of, for example, a 50-50 language allocation in a bilingual program.
(5) Parents and school community in general	Families have assessment rights (see ML Bill of Assessment Rights in the Introduction of this book). Parents and communities of all language backgrounds need to have access to knowledge of assessment literacy to understand what assessment results mean.

Source: Adapted from Rick Stiggins (2017).
[a]This author (Kate Mahoney) proposes an add-one delete-one policy. To avoid assessing too much and collecting data that will not be used in meaningful ways, if a school district chooses to add a required assessment, they must also remove at least one.

In Europe, the need for assessment literacy also exists. Some European countries use Content and Language Integrated Teaching (CLIL) to deliver instruction. When content knowledge is assessed through a second or other language, several issues of validity and fairness arise. Lo and Leung (2022) propose a conceptual framework for CLIL teachers for assessment literacy (see Table 9.2).

Table 9.2 Assessment literacy conceptual framework for CLIL teachers

(1)	Teacher conceptions (views of teaching and learning, assessment values and principles)
(2)	Knowledge of assessment and purposes
(3)	Knowledge of what to assess
(4)	Knowledge of assessment strategies
(5)	Knowledge of assessment interpretation and action-taking
(6)	Teacher practices and mediation of contextual factors

Source: Lo and Leung (2022).

What is a 'Growth Model' for Accountability?

Accountability is usually emphasized at the district, state and federal level and usually in that direction. These are ways for districts to prove to states and states to prove to the federal government that their schools are working well. Growth models grew out of a general frustration from working with what are called status models. Status models take a snapshot of a subgroup, such as multilingual learners (MLs), at one point in time and compare it to an established target. In the status model, growth may not be rewarded – a fact that frustrated schools with high numbers of MLs. Status models do not work well with MLs learning English because not all MLs – nor all children, for that matter – start at a similar place and grow at the same rate. Second, language acquisition (SLA) rates of growth rely heavily on many factors that vary from student to student. Stated plainly, you can set high standards for all students, but this does not remove the many obstacles that get in the way for some students. In the cartoon at the beginning of this chapter, on the race track, some children have a clear path toward the goal with very few obstacles in their way while others have to overcome nails, potholes and barbed wire.

In general, growth models for accountability refer to models that evaluate the progress of a group of individual students over time. This is much like a longitudinal research study in which individual students are tracked over time instead of being evaluated on a snapshot of their achievement in a single year. Growth models also control for transiency and reclassified students; this means that students are tracked by growth from year to year. If Mrs Smith receives 10 new beginner students from refugee camps in Indonesia in one year, her average won't 'go down'. Therefore, an increase in English proficiency is rewarded, not punished, regardless of the endpoint – or the beginning point, for that matter. Table 9.3 outlines the differences between the status and growth models.

Table 9.3 Growth versus status models of accountability

Growth model	Status model
Recognizes growth in achievement or language proficiency	Recognizes how far a student is from a final goal
Tracks one student or cohort from year to year	Snapshot of students in one year; usually a different group of students is compared from year to year
Controls for individual differences (e.g., socioeconomic [SES], out-of-school factors [OSF])	Does not control for individual differences (e.g., SES, OSF)
Rewards growth	Highlights deficits
Used in many states now as a reaction to the status model	Aligned with original conception of No Child Left Behind

What is Value-Added Assessment?

Most authors consider a value-added assessment model to be a type of growth model, because one of the main assumptions behind the value-added assessment model is to measure change over time in student test scores. In a Value Added Model (VAM), changes are mostly attributed to the teacher. (Note that this ignores out-of-school factors [OSFs].) Value-added assessment models follow individual student achievement over time, and they also intend to show the specific effects of programs and other relevant factors; in practice, however, they mostly target a teacher's instruction. Basically, a student's test score from last year (e.g. third grade) is compared to the current year's (fourth grade); if the fourth-grade test score is higher than that for the third grade, the teacher is 'adding value' to the child's education. If a child's test scores decrease from year to year, the teacher is not contributing value to the child's education.

This model is considered fairer than simply measuring a teacher's value by looking at current fourth-grade test scores (which would be a status model, not a growth model) because the multi-year approach does take into account some background variables. But it also has many identified flaws and the measurement community warns against using it. Plus, we have decades of research results showing how teachers and schools account for only a small portion of the variability in student performance on annual tests. The remainder is explained by other factors, such as class size, curriculum, educational resources, community factors, prior schooling, out-of-school learning opportunities and the internal structure of the test. In November 2015, the American Educational Research Association (AERA) issued a statement on the use of VAM.[1] The statement notes that there are potentially serious negative consequences in the context of evaluation that can result from the use of VAM based on incomplete or flawed data, as well as from the misinterpretation and misuse of the VAM results.

How Do I Identify, Monitor and Reclassify MLs?

In larger, mostly urban school districts, the process of identification may be completed before you meet your students, depending on which grades you teach. However, it is likely that you will be called upon to administer the identification process and/or score the state's language proficiency test on an annual basis. The process is governed by the State Department of Education, including in most cases exactly what instrumentation you will use. Figure 9.1 shows the process of identification for MLs in New York State. This process is governed in New York by Commissioner

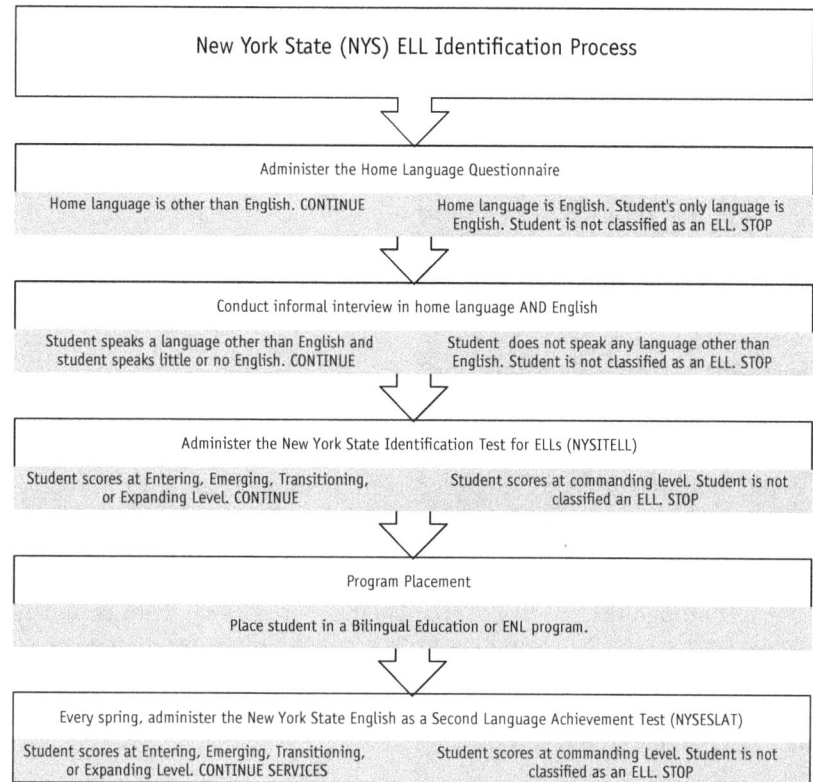

Figure 9.1 The basic process for identifying MLs in New York State. There are details missing from this figure, for example, details related to students with special learning needs and students with interrupted schooling.

Regulation (CR) Part 154, and all schools in New York State are expected to identify MLs in the same way with the same instruments. Each state has a different identification process, but all must meet minimum federal guidelines.

Each state has a law that governs the identification and reclassification process, which also satisfies federal guidelines for identification/reclassification. In New York and most states, the process of identifying, monitoring and reclassifying MLs over-relies on one standardized test that may or may not have evidence of validity for these particular purposes. The data needed to conduct a validity study on the use of the high-stakes test and its cutoff scores for the purpose of identification, monitoring and reclassification are unavailable due to 'test security'.

What is the Appropriate Use of Norm- and Criterion-Referenced Assessments?

When determining the appropriate use of any assessment, one should consider the four-step process called PUMI (see Chapter 1). In general, norm-referenced assessments have fallen out of favor due to their inherent unfairness to groups not represented in the norming sample (such as MLs) and because of the way that the norm referenced are designed to compare test takers to a 'normal group of children', usually not including MLs learning English. Many times when using norm-referenced assessments, test design concepts override content validity considerations. This means that more importance may be placed on test design and the precision of response rates than on whether the items and their responses actually make sense and are used appropriately (validity). Although criterion-referenced tests are more popular now, they too have problems – mostly in regard to the cutoff score. Who is to determine the difference between proficient and not proficient? Upon what evidence will the determination be based? As always, though, neither a norm- nor a criterion-referenced test will be 'valid and reliable' with MLs if they cannot read the test. A thorough discussion of norm and criterion referenced tests is in Chapter 6.

What is Meant by Multiple Measures?

The concept of multiple measures is a long-standing and important one to practice good assessment. It is similar to the concept of triangulation in radio telemetry, wherein multiple directional references are used to confirm location. Multiple measures are also used to increase validity within research studies. For example, a student survey shows that a student perceives himself as a strong reader, he scores high on reading achievement tests and the teacher observes him reading often during his free time. Through the process of triangulation, we can say with confidence that this child is a strong reader. If you measure a construct three different ways and they all point toward the same result, your results are good. Multiple measures, in other words, are different methods of assessment, which allow us to know that a result is near true, and not due to method or format.

SNAPSHOT: ARE THESE TRULY MULTIPLE MEASURES?

A mother is confused when she receives a note from the school indicating that her son Victor will be receiving academic intervention support (AIS) in reading, because she thought he was a good reader. She observes Victor at home reading all the time; his favorite books are fishing encyclopedias and Hardy Boys mysteries. The teacher and the principal assure his parents that Victor indeed has a deficit in reading, and if he doesn't attend intervention classes (where they seldom read but rather focus on phonics and vocabulary), he may fall behind even more. The principal further assures the parents that the school used 'multiple measures' to draw these conclusions.

However, upon closer inspection, this was not true. The school used three views of the *same* method (as opposed to three *different* methods of assessment) – the English language arts (ELA) state test, benchmark to ELA and the district reading assessment. All these measures used standardized, criterion-referenced, highly decontextualized assessments of reading; so similar, they were really one measure, not multiple. They all missed the fact that Victor not only reads but reads a lot, by choice – which to many educators are important indicators of being a good reader. The parents became frustrated and exercised their right to waive AIS, ultimately opting out of standardized testing altogether (an option for parents in New York and other states). The parents are not anti-testing; they feel that the tests are being used inappropriately and the consequences of how the scores are used (multiple hours a day of phonics practice) could potentially deter their child from enjoying reading overall.

What is Data-Driven Instruction?

The focus on test-based accountability has led schools to implement DDI programs and significant amounts of funding/professional development to ensure all decisions regarding curriculum, instruction and assessment are using data. Using data to inform instruction in a cyclical and reflective way is not new and is very similar to many other education initiatives in the past. The decision cycle is one that all teachers have used before, albeit often in different forms.

DDI is generally understood in practice to be the use of quantifiable data (numbers) obtained from measuring articulated goals to determine if a student is improving his or her academic skills or remaining at the same level. The ML educator analyzes the data, which serve as a guide to determine how to modify or design the next steps for instruction. This section draws on the preceding discussion of promising assessment practices and on the PUMI framework to help educators look critically at what DDI for MLs means in their district and schools. This section also introduces the theme of authentic DDI for MLs put forward in this book.

Many new teachers today are given the message that DDI is 'the way' to increase student achievement. Statements such as 'Everything we do is data driven' or 'All instruction is driven by data' are often heard in conversations with school leaders. What do such statements really mean? More and more, data are available in schools each year, but the question about what to do with the data remains primarily unanswered. Not a new idea, DDI can be traced back to 1970s-era debates about *measurement-driven instruction* whereby some states required the use of *outcome data* in school improvement planning and strategic planning. These debates continued through the 1980s and 1990s.

Unlike the previous models of DDI, the current model of school reform, however, narrowly interprets the definition of data and places a greater emphasis and value on the results of standardized achievement and language proficiency tests designed and scored outside a school – usually at the state or commercial level. Schools are drowning in these test data, often at the cost of more valid data. As a result, other forms of data such as the results of portfolios, parent surveys, interviews and oral presentations are used less and less. In fact, most schools spend more time collecting, documenting and organizing data than on processing and reflecting on what the data mean, which data are meaningful and which are appropriate for MLs.

The consequences of drowning in 'one type' of data (standardized test results) include loss of instructional time, diversion away from subjects such as science and social studies (tested less), testing saturation (testing students too much) and rerouting of funding toward data initiatives and away from classroom- and school-level initiatives. Stephen Krashen recommends reducing or eliminating testing to increase instructional time and save money for buying books and hiring more teachers. According to Krashen, we only need a sample of test results, such as the National Assessment of Educational Progress (NAEP)[2] test, a test we've had for many decades. Despite the warnings of excessive testing, all states are full steam ahead in promoting more and more testing and using DDI based on standardized test results.

It is important to recognize that DDI means different things to different people. For some schools, DDI simply means printing out state test scores to determine areas of weakness and then targeting instruction toward those weaknesses. A more complex model of DDI might use multiple measures (use at least three different types of data to draw inferences) and look for patterns to decide what the underlying causes might be. Some schools have hired more administrators or data coaches (at times at the expense of other teaching budget lines) to help manage and coach data uses at the school, grade and classroom levels. Data teams might also include experts such as English as a new/native language (ENL)/bilingual teachers, mathematics teacher-leaders who sift through the data to determine what is worthy of becoming 'actionable knowledge' – in other words, data interpretations worthy of instructional time. After all, not all data and data interpretations should initiate action, especially with MLs. Using the PUMI framework will give educators the questions that they need to ask to determine what data are actionable and what data should be abandoned.

Nobody says that data has to equal the results of standardized tests. Educators should use the results of performance assessments, one-on-one communication and other methods to inform their instruction. Teachers have always used data in the form of the results of essays, multiple-choice quizzes, interviews, portfolios, responses to questioning and parent surveys – using multiple measures – to make instructional decisions. In addition to using the results of assessments, teachers relied on their *experience* with students to help meet the needs of students. Using multiple measures is best practice.

The picture of DDI shown in Figure 9.2 (Institute of Education Sciences [IES], 2009) may lead teachers to believe that DDI involves linear and continuous processes. In real settings, however, educators often skip steps, rely on intuition or hesitate to collect more (or more meaningful) data. Proponents of DDI favor the objective (without judgment) aspect of DDI; however, DDI may involve more judgment (less objective, more subjective) than many realize. The first judgment occurs when the people who make the tests judge whether a test item truly measures the

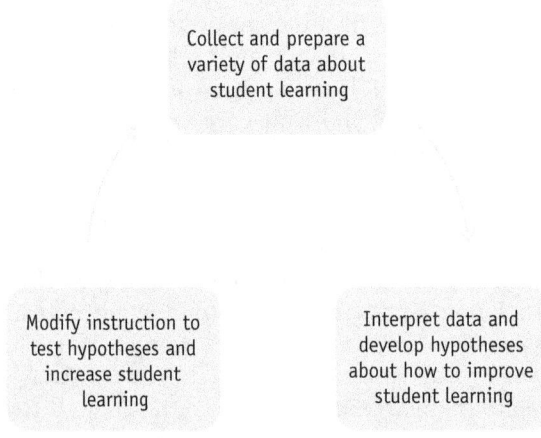

Figure 9.2 Data-use cycle presented by the Institute of Education Sciences (IES)

intended construct. The second judgment takes place when school leadership prioritizes data based on what is meaningful and appropriate (e.g. state, district or school requirements/recommendations). Further judgment is needed to decide what actions to take (increase time on task, change or modify the curriculum, institute more professional development). Even though the process of DDI is empirically based (uses data), it turns out to be less objective than most think.

END-OF-CHAPTER ACTIVITIES (Instructors: see advice at the end of the book)

By completing Activity 1, the reader will be able to:

(1) Answer the following guiding questions about assessment:

- How do I ensure that I'm following national and state requirements? How do I identify, monitor and reclassify MLs?
- What is the appropriate use of norm- and criterion-referenced assessments? What is meant by multiple measures?
- What is meant by DDI?

Activity 1

Answer the following guiding questions about essential assessment:

- What are these buzz words: growth model, value-added?
- How do I ensure I'm following national and state requirements? How do I identify, monitor and reclassify MLs?
- What is the appropriate use of norm- and criterion-referenced assessments? What is meant by multiple measures?

Do Inside/Outside Circle. Half of the students are given an index card with one of the above questions written on it and the answer written on the back (answers written on the back are optional). Students with the questions form a small circle facing outward, and those without index cards form a circle facing the inside circle. Each student must face another student to state the definition of the term *or* the term when the definition is given. The outside circle rotates clockwise until each student has had a go. After every student in the outside circle has had a chance, the outside circle switches with the inside circle (which always has the card) and the activity is repeated.

Notes

(1) See Amrein-Beardsley (2014) for an in-depth and critical view of VAMs.
(2) The National Assessment of Educational Progress (NAEP) started in 1964 and measures student achievement across topics. Using sophisticated sampling techniques, the NAEP takes samples of groups of students to determine 'the Nation's Report Card'; the NAEP does not test all students in all topics.

References

American Educational Research Association (AERA) (2015) AERA issues statement on the use of value-added models in evaluation of educators and educator preparation programs. See http://www.aera.net/Newsroom/NewsReleasesandStatements/AERAIssuesStatementontheUseofValueAddedModelsinEvaluationofEducatorsandEducatorPreparationPrograms/tabid/16120/Default.aspx. Accessed on February 22, 2024.

Amrein-Beardsley, A. (2014) *Rethinking Value-Added Models in Education: Critical Perspectives on Tests and Assessment-Based Accountability*. New York: Routledge.

Green, A. (2014) *Exploring Language Assessment and Testing: Language in Action*. New York: Routledge.

Institute of Education Sciences (IES) (2009) *Using Student Achievement Data to Support Instructional Decision Making: IES Practice Guide*. Washington, DC: US Department of Education.

Lo, Y. and Leung, C. (2022) Conceptualising assessment literacy of teachers in content and language integrated learning programmes. *International Journal of Bilingual Education and Bilingualism* 25 (10), 3816–3834.

Stiggins, R. (2017) *The Perfect Assessment System*. Alecandria, VA: The Association for Supervision and Curriculum Development (ASCD).

Advice for Instructors on Chapter Activities

At the end of each chapter are 'chapter activities' to use in face-to-face teacher preparation courses. This advice chapter provides support for the instructor.

Chapter 1: A Decision-Making Process called PUMI

Instructor guidance for Activity 1

Before class, the instructor prints out all 14 clues from Table 1.1 and tapes them to sticky notes. The 14 clues come directly from the cells of Table 1.1 in Chapter 1 and are associated with either the lens of promise or of deficit.

It's tempting, but it's not as easy as saying one way is good and the other is bad, as Table 1.1 implies. Each approach and point on the continuum has strengths and weaknesses. As the name implies, the lens of promise has more strength for assessing multilingual learners (MLs), including opportunities to provide assessments that are culturally relevant; it sets students up for success, not failure; it focuses on language as asset, not deficit; and it produces more valid results. Weaknesses of the promising practices may be that some of these practices are time-consuming and many times they yield data that are not comparable across districts and states. Weaknesses of the deficit practices include a one-size-fits-all approach that does not account for individual language and culture; decisions on results may not be valid; students have less agency; students may not perform well on test day; and MLs are not usually included in the norm, among others. Strengths of the practices leading to deficit may be that comparison of results can be made across school, district and state. Some might choose deficit approaches (they won't call it that) because large numbers of students can be assessed at the same time and therefore they can be more efficient or there is a need for baseline data. Explore other strengths and weaknesses.

A way to negotiate both views is to make sure that you use many assessment methods, including as many promising assessment practices as possible. Teachers tend to use promising methods when there is a choice and yield to deficit assessment practices when mandated. For example, use observation and checklists (more promising) during class to document academic language proficiency and compare those results to state-mandated tests (more deficit). Include a balance of data to use as a profile of learning in addition to results from state tests. Analyze how checklists, portfolio results, etc., align with state test results. Make collective decisions about MLs using both models; never use the result of one assessment to make a big decision. And use PUMI (Purpose, Use, Method and Instrument) with all assessments so that you can understand them better and raise critical questions when the time is appropriate.

Instructor guidance for Activity 2

Bring to class four index cards labeled P, U, M and I for each pair of students in your class. If you have 20 students, bring 10 sets because students will be working in pairs. After discussing PUMI and giving the students examples, ask them to complete Activity 2. If you are in a WIDA Consortium member state, give students general information about ACCESS for English language learners (ELLs; https://www.wida.us/assessment/access/) and ask students to complete a PUMI table (Table A.1 shows an example) to better understand the English proficiency test used in your area.

Table A.1 PUMI chart for ACCESS[a] for ELLs

P (Purpose)	U (Use)	M (Method)	I (Instrument)
To measure English language proficiency (ELP) (reading, writing, speaking, listening)	To monitor student progress every year. To help determine when MLs have gained full proficiency	Criterion-referenced[b] test (CRT)	Pre-ordered printed tests from WIDA

[a]ACCESS for ELLs (Assessing Comprehension and Communication in English State-to-State for English Language Learners) is a secure large-scale ELP assessment given to kindergarten through twelfth graders who have been identified as ELLs. It is given annually in WIDA Consortium member states to monitor students' progress in acquiring academic English.
[b]Because this is a criterion-referenced test, by design it is not intended to compare student to student or grade level to grade level (that would be more like norm referencing). It is intended to compare student performance on this test to the set of ELP standards published by WIDA.

Table A.2 PUMI chart for the process of identifying Multilingual Learners (MLs) in New York State

Name	P (Purpose)	U (Use)	M (Method)	I (Instrument)
HLQ	To assess language-use in the home	To determine if students continue to 1b for NYS Identification Process	Selected response, written response, Interview	Home Language Questionnaire (HLQ) print out
Individual Interview	To assess oral language fluency in English and Home Language	To determine if students should proceed to Step 2 (NYSITELL) for NYS Identification Process	Interview in English and home language	Prompts developed locally
NYSESLAT	To measure English Language Proficiency	To assign performance levels, to determine minutes of service & staffing, accountability system for district and state, to determine classification (ELL status)	Selected response, written response, conversation with rubric	NYSESLAT booklets
NYSITELL	To measure English Language Proficiency	To assign performance levels, to determine minutes of service & staffing, accountability system for district and state, to determine programming, to determine classification (ELL status)	Selected response, written response, conversation with rubric	NYSITELL booklets
NYS ELA	To assess content (English Language Arts)	To place students in AIS, to reclassify students from ELL status	Selected response, written response	NYS ELA test (paper or computer based)

Chapter 2: History: How Did We Get Here?

Instructor guidance for Activity 1

Purchase a roll of adding machine paper in advance. A roll of adding machine paper (the paper used for older adding machines – great for creating timelines) can be purchased in paper supply stores. Split adding machine paper so that each pair of students can have one strip to fit across their desks or table. Ask students to pair up and give each pair 10 sticky notes; then ask them to copy 10 events from the board and order them on their 'timeline'. Ask students to post their timeline in front of the class on completion. Use Table 2.2 to verify the order of events after students have finished their timelines.

To open and close Activity 1 as a whole group and to integrate movement into the activity, the instructor might model the timeline by asking 10 students to stand in front of the class, facing the class. For this whole-group activity, the instructor might have 10 sticky notes prepared with a historical event (not date) written on the sticky note; then, the instructor 'sticks' one on each student out of order. The instructor then calls on two students at a time to come up and reorder the students until the order is correct. The instructor should ask students to explain why they reordered and what the event means. The instructor clarifies and adds details.

Instructor guidance for Activity 2

The instructor prepares a blank word web (a diagram with the question *Why do some students succeed and others don't?* in the middle, from which branches extend with different arguments) and projects it in front of the class. (See Figure A.1 below, designed in less than one minute using MS Word SmartArt.) The instructor comes to class familiar with arguments for school failure as described in the introduction of Guadalupe Valdés' (1996) book *Con respeto* or another framework for understanding school success/failure.

Ask students why some students succeed and others don't. Categorize the reasons students give on a whiteboard according to arguments presented in this chapter (Valdés, 1996) – genetic, cultural or class analysis or another framework of your choice. Construct the word web in front of students as they each give one reason for school success/failure. Identify the categories *after* the students brainstorm and discuss findings. Ask the students to guess the categories before you name them (cultural, difference and deficit, genetic or class analysis).

The instructor listens to students' comments and decides where they belong in the word web. The instructor leads a whole-group discussion: How does testing and assessment play a role in answering this question? What does testing and assessment have to do with this? This should lead to a thoughtful open discussion.

Instructor guidance for Activity 3

(1) The two main accountability validity scenarios discussed in this chapter are less accountability/more validity and more accountability/less validity. Less accountability/more validity describes the pre-No Child Left Behind (NCLB) climate, wherein MLs were largely exempt from large-scale testing and its consequences, which led to less accountability. More accountability/less validity

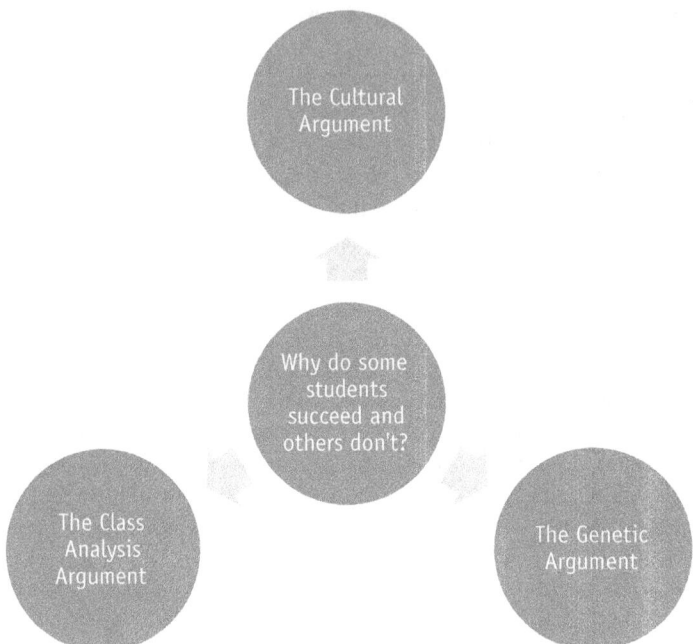

Figure A.1 Example of a word web, designed using MS Word SmartArt

describes the climate after NCLB, wherein all MLs must take tests even though they don't know English yet; a consequence of higher accountability is less valid test results that misrepresent what MLs really know.

(2) Two examples of less accountability/more validity could include a state law that exempts MLs from achievement testing for three years and teachers using portfolios to show how MLs are meeting English and language arts (ELA) standards. Two examples of more accountability/less validity could include NCLB allowing no exemptions from achievement testing in English – even for non-English speakers – and a river project cancelled to spend more time on test preparation for MLs.

Instructor guidance for Activity 4

The instructor comes to the academic discussion prepared with open-ended questions about themes explored in this chapter. To document the results of the academic discussion on one sheet of paper, the instructor prepares a class list with three columns, one for each category in the rubric above and with student names in rows. The following recording sheet is for the instructor only.

Student name	Quality of comments	Resource/document reference	Active listening
Student A			
Student B			
Student C			

Students lead the discussion, not the instructor. As students add comments to the discussion, the instructor marks points according to the rubric. All comments should reference some detail from the book. Students can shift the discussion at any time; if students have already contributed twice, they should yield to those who have not yet contributed to the discussion. One discussion with a class of 20 students takes approximately one hour. Point out to students that you are modeling authentic assessments in this assessment.

Chapter 3: Validity

Instructor guidance for Activity 1

The instructor will pass out blank index cards and ask students to discuss the definition of a unified view of validity as a group. After about 20 minutes of discussion, the instructor will call on one person per group to write on the board and share the group's definition. At the end of the activity, students submit their own definition on an index card with their name to the instructor for review; the instructor returns the cards at the end of class or the next class.

The instructor stresses that each student should have a unique definition that makes sense not only to them, but also to others around the table and in the classroom. They should also feel comfortable saying their definition of unified validity at school faculty meetings and in discussions with administrators and parents in the context of discussions of test scores for MLs. Be sure to do this in a constructive way so that each student's definition is unique and accurate.

Example definitions: (1) *Validity as a unified concept takes into account all aspects of traditional validity, plus new ideas like test interpretation, test use and social consequences.* (2) *Validity is a very complicated topic that includes both science and ethics and should be considered each time schools use test scores for MLs in different ways.* (3) *Validity as a unified concept advocates for validating test use for MLs on a case-by-case basis, not just validating the test.*

Instructor guidance for Activity 2

The instructor comes to class prepared with a marker, sticky notes and a list of key vocabulary words related to the unified view of validity (use the list at the beginning of the chapter) and provides a brief review. It is suggested that the instructor always be the model for this activity. Model for your students how to play vo-backulary so that they can see what you want them to do. Use the following key vocabulary terms and suggested definitions in a sentence related to MLs. Possible hints, answers and use in a sentence with MLs are given below for six key unified validity vocabulary words.

- Example Hint #1: This describes the way we use test scores for MLs. This is different from the purpose and is an important idea in the unified view of validity. *Answer: test score use*. It is important to pay attention to test score use for MLs because many times test scores may be used in questionable ways.

- Example Hint #2: This is a difficult part of validity to study because it involves making judgments to some degree. This is the part of validity that involves ethics, values and ideologies. *Answer: test score interpretation.* Test score interpretation always involves ideologies such as language ideologies that often do not favor MLs.
- Example Hint #3: These include results such as being retained in a grade, when parents feel that their child is not smart or when a teacher doesn't get tenure. *Answer: social consequences of test score use.* One factor that makes unified validity different from most definitions of validity is that it includes social consequences. When a note is sent home saying that a ML student is a limited speaker of Spanish and English, it affects the child and family's social identity and is a social consequence of test score use.

Instructor guidance for Activity 3

The instructor comes to class with five or six printed copies of your state accountability law regarding teacher and principal evaluation and highlighter pens. Together, find the areas that discuss teacher–principal–school accountability and test scores. Split the class into small groups by counting (to mix up students), then review the above assignment.

Possible advocacy statements could include some of the following: *It is important to examine the intended use for a test. The tests used by this state for accountability were not designed (as articulated in the technical manual) to evaluate teachers, but rather were designed to measure achievement among dominant English speakers. Teachers with high numbers of MLs are evaluated unfairly compared to teachers with few or no MLs because many MLs cannot fluently read the items on the test; as a result of this, effective teachers of MLs are being evaluated negatively. If test scores increase or decrease, what does this really mean for MLs when they are given a test in English, a language in which they are not yet proficient? Sometimes this means that the test items were practiced over and over, which may not indicate a true increase in true learning. There are better ways to evaluate teachers, principals and schools and it is time to advocate for better use of test scores. It is not enough to say a test is valid; rather, the actual use of a test should be validated.*

Instructor guidance for Activity 4

Students may need some assistance to interpret this statement and feel confident making a decision about whether they agree or disagree with it. The instructor can project the statement onto a screen in front of the class and use the Microsoft highlight feature to highlight key words in order to help students understand what the statement means. Deconstruct the statement with the students before asking them to agree or disagree with it.

Set up a value line (I usually set mine up in the hallway before class starts) where students need to take a stand about whether they agree or disagree with the statement. Allow students in small groups or pairs to discuss the meaning of the statement, their stance and the reasons why they agree or disagree. Draw the numbers 1 (strongly disagree) through 10 (strongly agree) across the whiteboard or use small posters with the numbers 1 through 10 in the hallway. Place the numbers far enough apart to allow sufficient room for all students to stand near the numbers at the same time. When all students are standing near the number representing their agreement, select three or four to explain why they chose that number and ask the other students whether they disagree or agree and why. As a follow-up question, ask if any students can connect this to the arguments for school success/failure introduced in Chapter 2. This is a whole-group activity.

Chapter 4: Methods

Instructor guidance for Activity 1

Ask students to brainstorm activity and mark on chart paper 10 ways to use multiple languages to create assessment products. To scaffold students, give them the first column and ask them to complete the second column. Think of more.

Final product	Add translanguaging
Write persuasive reviews about local restaurants	Write one in English and one in the home language to target more audiences.
Write about causes/effects of World War II	Create a short audio recording summarizing causes/effects of World War II in the home language.
Research a country of their choice	Take notes in the home language and English. Read research on the internet from home language websites and English websites.
Write a document-based question (DBQ)	Write a DBQ in the home language. Include one sentence in English and English key vocabulary words.
Write a story	Use the home language and English to write a story.
Create campaign advertisement	Create one advertisement in the home language and one in English.
Critique a poem	Choose a poem in the home language and create a PowerPoint in English to explain the poem to peers. Include a comparison of English to the home language. Give an oral presentation in English.

Instructor guidance for Activity 2

See the example checklist and rubrics presented in this chapter. Model how to go through the process of writing language and content objectives to creating a checklist for observation and two rubrics to support the documentation of assessments. In small groups, students should use MS Word, Excel and/or Artificial Intelligence (AI) to create checklists and rubrics. Answers will vary.

Chapter 5: Content and Language

Instructor guidance for Activity 1

Create one set of clue cards per group (six or eight is good, depending on the number of groups you organize) using 3 × 5 index cards. Do not put the answers anywhere on the clue cards. (Clues and answers are shown below.) Be sure to collect clue cards at the end of this activity, using a paper clip for each set so that you can easily reuse them in a future class. Ask each group to sort them by the five categories and discuss for 15 or so minutes. Come to class with five lunch-sized paper bags) labeled with each content target category (knowledge, reasoning, key practices, products and dispositional) and set them in a central location. One by one, a representative from each group will come up and deposit their clue card in the correct bag and explain why. To make it more challenging, the instructor should select the clue card. To make it less challenging, allow the group to select the clue card. Because there are 10 cards, each group will participate twice. The categories of content are not mutually exclusive and therefore may cause confusion or discussion; for example, an act of reasoning could perhaps be classified as reasoning or key practices. Ask the students to go with where they think it fits best. For example, if the learning focuses directly on reasoning, it should be labeled reasoning. If the primary focus of the learning is on practicing (usually through written or oral expression), it should be key practices. An extension of this activity could be to have students make their own clue cards and test one another.

Clue	Answer
A square with side length 1 unit, called 'a unit square', is said to have 'one square unit' of area.	Knowledge
Genes are located in the chromosomes of cells, with each chromosome pair containing two variants of each of many distinct genes.	Knowledge
Analyze how two or more texts address similar themes or topics in order to build knowledge or to compare the approaches the authors take.	Reasoning
Compare the interactions between individuals, events and ideas in a text (e.g., how ideas influence individuals or events and how individuals influence ideas or events).	Reasoning
Use tiling to show in a concrete case that the area of a rectangle with whole number side lengths and b + c is the sum of a × b and a × c.	Key practices
Use an oral and written argument supported by evidence to support or refute the idea that a square is also a rectangle.	Key practices
Assessing attitudes toward learning English is something many educators of MLs do.	Dispositional
Shyness, motivation and attitude are all factors in the affective filter hypothesis. ML educators want to keep the affective filter low for MLs.	Dispositional

Instructor guidance for Activity 2

Answer for Table 5.12; answers will vary.

Objectives	Instruction	Assessment
Content: SW (Student will) be able to compare and contrast the attributes of a square and a rectangle.	Is a square a rectangle? TW (Teacher will) model use of blocks to identify the characteristics of a square and a rectangle. SW use a graphic organizer to collect evidence for or against.	Content. Selected response. TW play Find the Fib* (selected response game where two truths are told about squares/rectangles and one fib).
Language: SW be able to produce a written argument for why a square is a rectangle.	TW model using a graphic organizer to write arguments and how to turn those arguments into a short paragraph.	Language. Written response. SW write a short paragraph using supporting evidence to argue why a square is a rectangle.

Source: Adapted from Echevarria et al. (2008).

Answer for Table 5.13; answers will vary.

Objectives	Instruction	Assessment
Content: SW (Student will) be able to calculate the number of protons, electrons and neutrons in an element, given its atomic number and atomic mass.	TW (Teacher will) use clue cards which have a question side and an answer side. SW rotate cards around small circle and practice reading and answering chemistry Q&A.	Content. Selected response. Survey using selected response (yes/no) is given to students to assess whether they met the objective. Modality is self-assessment.
Language: SW be able to listen to a question and tell a partner the number of protons/electrons/neutrons in an element.	In pairs, each student will listen to their partner read a chemistry clue card and practice answering it.	Language. One-to-one communication. Questioning is used in a peer-to-peer modality.

Instructor guidance for Activity 3

The instructor should model the process of writing language objectives from standards and practicing PUMI at least once before asking students to complete this activity. For the activity listed above, Step 2 might be stated as: Students will follow oral instructions to categorize objects according to their length. A variety of language objectives align with this standard, so perhaps give a few examples. The important thing about language objectives is that they are observable and measurable. Avoid using phrases such as 'students will think' or 'students will know' because these are difficult to observe. If students write objectives using such words, ask them, 'How will they know that?' 'What will the teacher observe the student doing?'. This should help articulate language objectives. Remind students that language objectives are narrower than English language development (ELD) standards and they can think of objectives as the little steps that students and teachers need to take to 'meet' the standard.

Step 3 is the real assessment piece; if students use PUMI, an appropriate standards-based method can be selected. As shown below, after considering all of PUMI, observation is an appropriate standards-based method for assessing this language standard, using a simple checklist (they followed instructions or they didn't).

P	U	M	I
To measure listening skills in the context of a math lesson	To inform instruction	Observation	Checklist

Instructor guidance for Activity 4

Familiarize your students with MS Word SmartArt if possible; however, this activity can be done without SmartArt. SmartArt is a great tool in general for developing quick and easy graphic organizers for instructional purposes. For this assignment, it is suggested that students review the graphic organizers under the 'list' or 'process' category under the insert (SmartArt) tab. Other popular ways to create graphic organizers is through the use of applications such as Canvas (canvas.com) and Padlet (Padlet.com), among others. To warm up for this activity, have students recite the levels of language proficiency used in your state (these will vary) and use movement in some way to physically demonstrate the different levels of language proficiency. The purpose of this warm-up is to use creativity and physical movement for instruction, as well as to become very familiar – by memory – with the language proficiency levels used in your state English language proficiency (ELP) standards document. For the purposes of this book, the six WIDA levels are used.

Chapter 6: Psychometrics

Instructor guidance for Activity 1

Here are answers to the questions posed to students above:

(1) Scale scores are derived from the raw score and they are very useful to show how a student is doing from year to year within one language domain. Do not compare scale scores across domains because they are scaled differently.
(2) Proficiency levels are cut scores designed by the test developers based on a set of standards. Because they are derived from the scale score, they also cannot be compared to other domains; however, if you stay within one language domain, both scale scores and proficiency levels can be compared across years.
(3) The only scores that are *not* composite are listening, speaking, reading and writing. Composite scores in this report add about half of the numbers, which may lead to confusion due to too much unnecessary data; you should cross out composite scores when you are first looking for meaning in the data and stay in the listening, reading and writing domains, the main domains. Composites are a combination of the main domains anyway and you can easily overlook a problem. For example, oral language = listening + speaking; literacy = reading + writing; comprehension = listening + reading; and overall = listening + speaking + reading + writing. Don't worry about composite scores until you have studied the main domains thoroughly; domain scores may give you the information you need without the possibility of losing meaning or hiding something. In fact, you may never need composite scores.
(4) Table 6.4 shows data reported for three high school students across three years. It is important to think about what tier the students have taken and also, who decides what tier they will take. Each form of a test has three tiers (except kindergarten). Within each grade-level cluster, there are three tiers to account for three levels of language proficiency. Tier A is for beginners, Tier B is for intermediate and Tier C is for advanced. The ACCESS interpretive guide states that Tier A is for newcomers, students with limited or interrupted formal schooling, or MLs whose initial literacy development is in their native language. Pay attention to tiers, because Tiers A and B have capped scores. In other words, due to the leveled nature of the tiers, students taking Tier A cannot score above proficiency level 4 and students taking Tier B cannot score above proficiency level 5. Therefore, students taking Tiers A and B cannot demonstrate ELP until they take Tier C. Equipped with this information about tiers, you can notice two peculiarities when scanning the data. The first is that Students A, B and C do not progress through the tiers as we would expect them to. Student A takes Tier B in 2010, Tier A in 2011 and Tier B again in 2012. We would expect to see a progression from A to B to C, not from B to A to B. The same pattern shows for Student B. Student C progresses from Tier C in 2010 to Tier B in 2011, then remains in Tier B for 2012. The other peculiarity involves the performance level of 5.4 that Student C scored in 2012. The WIDA ACCESS interpretation guide states that students taking Tier

B are capped and cannot score above level 5, yet the data show level 5.4. The simple explanation for this is probably that the Tier C students cannot score a 6 or above. The reason for administering the Tier B and then regressing to Tier A is unknown. Perhaps the different tiered test may have affected Student A but not Students B and C. In general, proficiency levels can be used to make comparisons between domains and across tiers. However, whenever a different form of a test is used to determine any score, some precision in comparison is lost.

(5) Year 2 (2011) for Student A is showing some outlier data, but Years 1 and 3 appear to make more sense. For example, it seems strange that second language development in listening would decrease as much as it did in Year 2 (2011) and then go back up in Year 3. Year 2 was also the only year out of three when Student A was given a differently tiered test. Therefore, this analysis will focus on Years 1 (2010) and 3 (2012) and gather other evidence of how the student performed in 2011 instead of ACCESS scores. Student A had very small growth in all areas except speaking, which showed the most growth. Investigate background and school factors more for this student.

(6) Student B showed a large increase in English language development over the three years, especially in listening and speaking. The ELD growth of this student is aligned with the research showing how long it takes to learn academic language (4–9 years).

(7) Student C is showing large growth across the years in all language domains and is on a similarly positive trajectory as Student B.

In short, Student A is not doing so well and needs to be treated as a case study; more evidence is needed, along with interviews with his or her teacher. Students B and C are progressing well and current programming or other school factors appear to be supporting ELD.

Instructor guidance for Activity 2

Make your own bingo board (3 × 3) so that students can see what it looks like. Keep reading the clues until one student shouts 'bingo!'. Keep track of the words you called, review the winner's board word by word and discuss each term. Use clues and terms below.

Clue	Term
A measurement scientist.	Psychometrician
By definition, half of all test takers score at or above the 50th percentile.	Norm referenced
Score performance is in reference to criteria.	Criterion referenced
The wrong answers presented in a multiple choice question.	Distracter
No test is perfectly accurate because of this.	Measurement error
A child in fourth grade brings home a test and because of this score her parents think she should be moved to seventh grade.	Grade equivalents
Line up all students from lowest score to highest score. Don't average this score because of unequal intervals.	Percentiles
Was developed to try and remedy the problems concerning grade equivalents and percentile ranks.	Normal curve equivalent (NCE)
This score can be used to show growth within one domain from year to year.	Scale score

Chapter 7: Accommodations

Instructor guidance for Activity 1

From the 10 accommodations listed in Table 7.4, write 9 where the students can see them. Make your own bingo board (3 × 3) so the students can see what it looks like. Then, 'perform' the accommodations so that the class can guess what each one is. Before class, download test item samples from your state content test to help you perform the accommodations. (This is like a role-play activity.) Continue performing clues until one student shouts 'bingo!'. Keep track of the words you called, review the winner's board word by word and discuss each term. Ask students which accommodations they have observed in schools during field study.

Instructor guidance for Activity 2

Prepare index cards before class with one of the eight questions on one side and a brief answer on the other. Each question is discussed in this chapter. Try to keep answers to paraphrases. Walk around, listen to the answers and help the students to clarify concepts. Rotate the group every two minutes; after all of the students have had a chance to answer the questions, ask them what needs to be clarified. Modification: Do not put the answer on the cards. The instructor clarifies any confusion at the end. There are eight questions, so this will accommodate a class size of 16. If a class is larger, simply ask new questions. Answers to questions may include the following:

(1) What is reliability? *Reliability has to do with the consistency of a score. Is the score due to chance or error or is it due to true achievement? If a score is reliable, it should have little error.*
(2) How is reliability connected to accommodations? *Accommodations are designed to address the barriers to testing, such as language. If accommodations work, the reliability of a score will increase.*
(3) If a reliability coefficient is 0.70, what does this mean? *It means that roughly 70% of the score is due to true achievement and 30% is due to error.*
(4) Can accommodations close the achievement gap? *No. Accommodations can decrease some of the obstacles to testing experienced by MLs, especially language barriers, but they will never close the achievement gap.*
(5) What does it mean if a test has the standard error of measurement (SEM) at 3 points? *SEM is a range in which the true score is located, but we never really know the true score. This means that if a student scores 68 on a test, the true score is somewhere between 65 and 71.*
(6) What is linguistic simplification? *This is a promising accommodation for MLs in which test items are simplified linguistically without changing the construct of the item.*
(7) Give two other names for test score error. *Test pollution, test contamination, garbage or nuisance variables.*
(8) Name three common causes of error for MLs. *Language of the test, fatigue, nervousness or anxiety.*

Instructor guidance for Activity 3

Bring chart paper to class and distribute one blank piece to each small group. Briefly discuss possible linguistic modifications by drawing the students' attention to Table 7.2 and review line by line with brief explanations. With the revised item, students may employ some of the following linguistic changes to make revisions to the language: conditional clause changed to separate sentence; two relative clauses removed and recast; long nominals shortened; questions phrase changed from 'which of the following' to 'how many'; item length changed from 26 to 13 words; number of clauses changed from 4 to 2.

Chapter 8: Special Education

Instructor guidance for Activity 1

After discussing the six major tenets of the Individuals with Disabilities Education Act (IDEA) with students, provide brief scenarios that are linked to each tenet. Ask each student to pick which tenet they believe is being described and provide support for their choice. Students can do this individually or in small groups.

Instructor guidance for Activity 2

Label six pieces of chart paper with the following headings: referral, evaluation, eligibility, individualized education plan (IEP), placement and annual review. Have students put one big idea for each heading on chart paper. Circulate until chart paper and/or headings are conclusive. Generate a group discussion on the muddiest points.

Instructor guidance for Activity 3

Provide the following directions to students to complete a mind map. First, explain the concept of mind mapping as a visual representation, similar to a graphic organizer. Offer the opportunity to work in pairs. Have students design their mind maps with the following characteristics: define the category, define the identification and referral process and provide four recommended educational practices. Students can present their mind maps to the whole class and submit a written document that includes one interesting component, with citation; one thing to learn more about; design rationale; what they learned from the experience; and how the assignment could be used as a resource and in a classroom.

Chapter 9: Accountability

Instructor guidance for Activity 1

Prepare index cards before class with one of the eight questions on one side and a brief answer on the other. Each question is discussed in this chapter. Try to keep answers to paraphrases. Walk around, listen to the answers and help the students to clarify concepts. Rotate the group every two minutes; after all of the students have had a chance to answer the questions, ask them what needs to be clarified. Modification: Do not put the answer on the cards. The instructor clarifies any confusion at the end. There are eight questions, so this will accommodate a class size of 16. If a class is larger, simply ask new questions.

Note

(1) The kindergarten form of ACCESS for ELLs includes proficiency levels to be used for instructional purposes and proficiency levels to be used for accountability levels. All other grades levels have accountability only.

Reference

Valdés, G. (1996) *Con Respeto*. New York: Teachers College, Columbia University.

Glossary

Accommodations: Changes in the test process, in the test itself or in the test response format.
Annual professional performance review (APPR): The annual professional performance review takes the idea of evaluating students through standardized test scores and applies it (in principle) to teachers. It is a way to give teachers and principals a 'grade', or an effectiveness rating.
Assessment: A broad term that can be thought of generally as the use of information from various sources to make decisions about a student's future instruction/schooling.
Assessment lens of deficit: Highlighting what the student doesn't know relative to one measure and does not provide a culturally responsive context.
Assessment lens of promise: Highlighting what the student knows, grounded from ideas of dynamic bilingualism and sociocultural assessment, it is used to guide educators of MLs on how to assess and instruct MLs within a meaningful and culturally responsive context.
Class analysis argument: Ascribes school failure to the role of education in maintaining class differences (that is, maintaining the power of some over others).
Construct: What the learner is being measured on; these ideas are constructed by experts in the field and informed by a theoretical or conceptual framework chosen to guide the test construction, for example 'language proficiency' and 'academic achievement'.
Construct irrelevant variance: The major threat of validity for using ML test scores and the systematic measurement error that reduces the ability to accurately interpret scores or ratings. Otherwise known as bias.
Construct validity: Takes into account how the test will be used, the consequences of using it in those ways and for whom the test was intended.
Content or language target: Knowledge and associated processes such as analyzing, producing, constructing, reasoning, defining, developing and using that help articulate the purpose (in PUMI).
Criterion referenced: Students' performances are compared to a set of behaviors, usually standards.
Cultural argument: Proposes that children who perform poorly in schools are either culturally deprived or culturally different and therefore mismatched with schools

and school personnel; problematic when children and families are identified as having deficits instead of the school.

Culturally and linguistically diverse (CLD): Students who are distinguished from the mainstream culture and language (in the United States, non-white or not English dominant).

Curriculum-based measure (CBM): Assessment derived directly from the curriculum being taught; characterized by frequent, direct measures of school behaviors; formative in nature; allows teachers to make instructional decisions about teaching and curriculum while learning is taking place.

Cut scores: Determine the point between proficient and not proficient; many times problematic.

Data-driven instruction (DDI): Using data to inform instruction in a cyclical and reflective way.

Direct linguistic support: Includes accommodations such as translation of the test into the native language, simplifying English language or test language and repetition of test language.

Dispositional: Dispositional targets help educators understand factors affecting second language acquisition (SLA) such as motivation, attitude, negative and positive experiences with immigration or English or school.

Disproportional representation: A greater number of students from diverse groups placed in special education programs when compared to mainstream students (such as white, middle class).

English language learner (ELL): Students who are in the process of learning English as a new language.

Error: When testing, can be caused by guessing, subjective scoring for essays, unnecessarily complex language, fatigue, nervousness and other factors.

Eugenics: The science of improving a human population by controlled breeding to increase the occurrence of desirable heritable characteristics.

Formative assessment: Formative assessments gather information in order to 'form' or shape student learning. This kind of assessment is ongoing and happens most often in classrooms. Benchmarks, which are mini-goals set to scaffold a student to reach an end goal, guide formative assessments. Most assessments used in classrooms are meant to show how students are progressing toward language and content goals throughout the year. The results of formative assessments also help shape and form the teacher's instruction. Good formative assessments should lead to better summative outcomes.

Four categories of methods: Selected response, written response, performance and one-to-one communication.

Four categories of modalities: One to group, one to one, group to group or to self (e.g., teacher to student, student to student or peer assessment, student to group, student to family or teacher to family).

Genetic argument: The view that some groups are genetically more able than others, and because of these inherent differences, children of different racial and ethnic groups perform differently in schools.

Growth model: In general, growth models for accountability refer to models that evaluate the progress of a group of individual students over time. This is much like a longitudinal research study in which individual students are tracked over time instead of being evaluated on a snapshot of their achievement in a single year.

High incidence disabilities: Those disabilities that are most likely to appear in school for initial evaluation and are usually diagnosed by non-medical personnel after a student starts school (e.g., learning disabilities, emotional disturbance).

Indirect linguistic support: Includes accommodations such as adjustments to time, schedules or environment.

Instrument: The last step in the PUMI process where teachers and administrators decide what instruments will be needed (tests, prompts, realia, rubric, checklist, etc.).

Key practices: Practices or procedures (what we do with content) are sometimes called *key practices*; the idea of key practices within a content area can be thought of as 'things we do with the content' or otherwise thought of as the application of content.

Knowledge: Knowledge can be defined in many ways, but within a school setting it is usually defined as the subject matter content that teachers want MLs to master.

Large-scale assessments: Assessing large numbers of people on their progress at local, state or national level.

Learning disability (LD): A disorder in one or more of the basic psychological processes involved in understanding or using language, spoken or written, which may manifest itself in an imperfect ability to listen, speak, read, write, spell or do mathematical calculations.

Least restrictive environment: Students with disabilities are to be educated, to the maximum extent appropriate, with students without disabilities.

Method: The third step in the PUMI process where teachers and administrators decide what method is most appropriate for the language or content purpose.

Multilingual learner: In the context of New York State, Multilingual Learner (ML) refers to all students who speak or are learning one or more languages other than English. **Multiple measures:** Multiple measures are different methods of assessment, which allow us to know that a result is near true, and not due to method or format.

Multitiered systems of support (MTSS): A coherent continuum of evidence-based, system-wide practices to support a rapid response to academic and behavioral needs, with frequent data-based monitoring for instructional decision-making to empower each student to achieve high standards.

Norm referenced: Students' performances are compared to another group of students' performances to judge how well they learned.

Normal curve equivalent (NCE): This was designed to correct for the lack of equal intervals in grade equivalent and percentile rank by having a normal curve line graph accessible and compare the percentile rank scale to the NCE.

Oral interview: (one-to-one communication) educators can ask questions (input) and evaluate answers from MLs (output).

Percentile rank: Tells where a student stands in regard to other students; should be used with caution.

Portfolio: (may include all or a mix of selected response, written response, performance assessment and one-to-one communication) Contains samples of student work, selected by the student and the teacher systematically and purposefully to show evidence that the student is learning core standards.

Pre-referral : (for consideration in special education) Beginning of the assessment process that gathers data on student academic and behavior progress; reviews strategies and student's response to interventions.

Proficiency level: Scores that are an interpretation of scale scores and are a result of choosing a cut score for each level.

Psychometrics: The science of measuring mental capacities and processes.

Purpose: The first step in the PUMI process where teachers and administrators define the purpose (or target) of a particular assessment.

Raw score: A score that is not ranked or compared to groups of children and that nothing has been done to it yet.

Reasoning: Most people think knowledge gives rise to *reasoning*, and some think knowledge and reasoning grow together. Reasoning means that students will think, understand and form judgments using logic.

Reliability: The extent to which a test yields the same results on repeated trials.

Reliability coefficient: How reliability is measured (a number between 0 and 1), which informs us empirically how much contamination (or error) is part of the overall test score.

Response to intervention (RtI): A three-tiered process that determines if a student is responding to empirically validated, scientifically based interventions. In the United States, RtI is required and used with suspected *learning or emotional disabilities only*.

Role play: Invites students to speak or act through the identity of others; provides an authentic context for students to learn language and content and for teachers to assess it.

Rubric: A tool to keep data collection systematic and focused on the same purpose or target and can be used in different modalities, perhaps by the teacher, the student or even a parent.

Scale score: Derived from the raw score, and links together all test forms within one content area.

Special education: A customized instructional program designed to meet the unique needs of an individual learner.

Speech or language impairment (SLI): Impairments in communication and/or language function, which adversely affect a student's educational performance.

Standard error of measurement (SEM): Represents the range of a test's accuracy.

Standard score: A set of scores that have the same mean and standard deviation so that they can be compared.

Standardized: Everything is the same – the items, the amount of time, the responses, the directions, etc. Typically, standardized tests consist of some combination of selected response and open response, and are usually given to a large group of students at the same time.

Stanine: A method of scaling test scores on a nine-point scale with a mean of 5 and a standard deviation of 2.

Status model: Status models take a snapshot of a subgroup, such as MLs, at one point in time and compare it to an established target. In the status model, growth may not be rewarded – a fact that frustrated schools with high numbers of MLs.

Story retelling: (performance assessment) MLs read or listen to text and then retell the main ideas and some details.

Student learning objective (SLO): SLOs are used to gauge student growth in areas such as art, PE or those areas for which student achievement tests are not given (pre-K–2). They must be aligned to the state standards (for most states these are the Common Core Learning Standards) and be written as measurable and observable objectives.

Summative assessment: Summative assessments are intended to 'summarize' the progress of a program or a child after a long period of time such as a marking period or an academic year. Summative assessments often look like grades, final exam scores, regents tests, a research project or a language proficiency test score.

Teacher observation: (performance assessment) The teacher continues to observe and make instructional decisions based on what he or she sees.

Test fairness: Test norms based on native speakers of English either should not be used with individuals whose first language is not English, or such individuals' test results should be interpreted as reflecting, in part, their current level of English proficiency rather than ability, potential, aptitude or personality characteristics or symptomology.

Test interpretation: How the test developers want the test to be interpreted. A rationale should be presented for each intended interpretation of test scores for a given use, together with a summary of the evidence and the theory of bearing on the intended interpretation.

Test misuse: Using tests as gatekeepers to advance some groups over others. State mandates requiring testing students in a language that they do not know yet are increasing. Achievement test scores will not accurately reflect knowledge of a specific subject area if the student is not yet proficient in the language of the test.

Test score use: The way a test developer uses the test results, for example, giving grades, deciding a program, deciding promotion, ML classification or SPED certification in some cases.

Testing: One measuring instrument that produces information used in assessment.

Title III: Title III awards are granted to states who meet the set requirements; the funds are targeted to help MLs meet English and content standards (Title III replaced the Bilingual Education Act, formerly known as Title VII).

Translanguaging: In assessment, students use their home languages and literacies during instruction and assessment to learn content and language in meaningful ways.

Unified view of validity: An integrated evaluative judgment of the degree to which empirical evidence and theoretical rationales support the adequacy and appropriateness of inferences and actions based on test score (Messick).

Use: The second step in the PUMI process where teachers and administrators decide how the results of a particular assessment will be used.

Value-added assessment: In a value-added model, changes are mostly attributed to the teacher. (Note that this ignores out-of-school factors [OSFs].) Value-added assessment models follow individual student achievement over time, and are supposed to show the specific effects of programs and other relevant factors.

Index

Abedi, J. 38, 43, 58, 59, 115, 152, 154, 155, 160, 161, 162, 167
Aboriginal languages 23
academic intervention support (AIS) 202
academic language skills 109
ACCESS for English language learners 140, 147t
accessibility 137, 138
accommodations 150–73, 181
accountability 197–206
 –and deficit-based assessment 7
 –Every Student Succeeds Act (ESSA) 48
 –and home language assessment 12
 –measurement community 64
 –and No Child Left Behind 37–40, 43
 –and objectivity of standardized tests 143
 –social consequences of test score use 64
 –summative assessment 77
 –and validity 38–9, 60, 199, 201
acculturation 67
achievement and language proficiency links 58–9, 67
achievement gaps 37, 42, 137
active learners, students as 91
adaptations *see* accommodations
adapted miscue analysis 23
Adelman Reyes, S. 67, 92
adequate yearly process (AYP) 40–1
adult learners 94, 96
affective filters 10, 39, 65, 111, 167
AIMS 167
Alim, S. 77
American Educational Research Association (AERA) 10–11, 33, 60, 63, 134, 137, 151, 200

American Psychological Association (APA) 10–11, 33, 60, 63, 134, 137, 151
Americans with Disabilities Act (ADA) 181
Americans with Disabilities Act Amendments Act (ADAAA) 181
Amrein-Beardsley, A. 205n(1)
annual measurable achievement objectives (AMAO) 47t
annual performance review (APR) 61
anxiety 65, 111, 169
Anyon, J. 34–5
approximations 123
Armon-Lotem, S. 190–1
Artificial Intelligence (AI) 96, 157
Ascenzi-Moreno, L. 23, 124, 125, 163
assessment consortia 46t, 157, 161
assessment events, history of 43–7
Assessment for Learning (AfL) 79–80
'assessment inputs' 115
assessment literacy 198
assessment vs. testing 8
assimilationist policies 49
'at-risk' students 48, 185
attitudes to learning 111, 167–8
audio recordings 9t, 89, 90
audio support as accommodation 162
August, D. 33
Australia 23
authentic assessment
 –integrated language assessments 117–18
 –interviews 87
 –lesson plans 107
 –for listening assessment 122
 –and method 22
 –portfolios 91
 –and promise-based assessment 9t

–role play assessment methods 94–6
–for speaking assessment 121
–special education 193t
–story retelling 89
autism 176
autobiographical writing 124
autonomous minorities 35

Baca, G. 151
Bachman, L.F. 117
Baker, C. 48, 49
baseline data 58
Bauer, E. 25
bell-shaped curves 128, 129
benchmarks 76–7, 94
Berliner, D. 42
bias 39, 56, 57, 59, 87, 113, 136–7
 see also construct irrelevant
  variance (CIV)
Bicard, S. 180
bilingual bias 136
Bilingual Education Act 44–5t, 49
bilingual schools 15
Bingo 83t
blueprints 21, 60, 137, 139, 170
Bouck, E.C. 176, 177
Bracey, G. 141–2
Briceño, A. 123
Britton, M. 65, 79, 80
Bush administration 38, 41, 44t

Canada 94
categorical scales 139
Celic, C. 20, 92, 112
Center for Applied Linguistics (CAL) 38
Center on Instruction 162
Chandler, J.T. 32
Chappuis, J. 19, 75–76, 79, 80, 102
checklists 100–3, 121, 121t see also rubrics
China 42
Cho, S.J. 189
Cioè-Peña, M. 36, 180, 192, 193t
City University of New York Initiative
  on Immigration and Education
  (CUNY-IIE) 35
City University of New York-New York
  State Initiative for Emergent Bilinguals
  (CUNY NYSIEB) 19, 86
clarification, linguistic 171n(4) see also
  simplification of language

class analysis argument for success/ failure
  34–5
classifying skills 109
Coachella Valley v. California 151
cognitive effects of failure 39
cognitive load 154
cohort groups 135, 193t
Collum, E. 157, 159, 161
colonialism 35–6, 66, 192
common assessments/interim assessments 76
Common Core Learning Standards (CCLS) 38
Common Core State Standards (CCSS) 46t
communication of results 143–4
communicative activities in language targets 84
comparability of test scores 139
comparing and contrasting skills 109
composite scores 141
computer-based testing
 –accommodations 157
 –student choice of language 15, 156
conceptual/ theoretical frameworks of tests 21,
  128, 139
conditional clauses 115, 154t
consistency in scoring 169
construct
 –confounding constructs 122, 123
 –construct irrelevant variance (CIV) 33,
  56–7, 109t, 137
 –definition of 57
 –rubrics 102
 –underrepresentation 57
 –wrong constructs 9
contaminant variables 57
contamination of test scores 167 see also error
content 106–32
 –checklists 100–1
 –content assessment 13–14, 24
 –content targets 84–5
 –content vs. medium of access to content
  58
 –formative assessment 76
 –key practices 110
 –knowledge (type of content) 108–9
 –and language 112–16
 –linguistic modifications to access 154–5
 –reasoning (type of content) 109
 –role of language 112–16
 –standards 84
 –using interview to measure language use
  88–9

Content and Language Instruction Performance (CLIP) 17
content and language integrated instruction (CLIL) 112, 199
contextualization of assessment 9t *see also* culture
continuum of assessment practices 7–8, 9t
co-regulations 80
COST (European Cooperation in Science and Technology) 190–1
'cost of testing' 16
Council of Europe 92
Courtney, L. 94, 95
Covid-19 49
craniometry 32
creative writing 124
criterion-referenced testing (CRT) 135–6, 138–9, 202
critical language testing (CLT) 68
critical thinking skills 112
CTB/McGraw Hill 144
culturally and linguistically diverse (CLD) students 175, 176, 179–80, 182, 184–5, 187, 188–9
culture
 –acculturation 67
 –checklist for validity checks 59
 –and content 113
 –cultural argument for success/ failure 34
 –cultural assumptions 56
 –cultural ecological theory 35, 36
 –culturally relevant assessment 18, 96, 138, 155
 –culturally relevant pedagogy 193t
 –culturally sustainable pedagogy 67, 77
 –decontextualized tests 122, 128
 –group cultural identity 12
 –inclusion in NCME 'eight factors' 11
 –integrated language assessments 118
 –'local norms' 137
 –sociocultural assessment 7
 –sociolinguistic modification of tests 155
 –story retelling 89
 –tests represent dominant culture 67
 –threats to cultural diversity 23
 –and validity 56, 59, 66–8
 –validity threats 56
 –and writing assessment 125–6
curriculum narrowing 39
curriculum-based rubrics 100

cut scores 138–9

data-based decision-making models 182, 188
data-driven instruction (DDI) 203
De Angelis, G. 134, 136, 138, 152, 156, 157, 191
De Backer, F. 162
de Valenzuela, J.S. 180
decolonial theory 36, 192
decontextualized tests 122, 128
deficit, lens of 7–8, 9t, 17–18, 33, 49, 78, 168, 192
descriptive feedback 77–8
developmental sequences/progression 139
dialects 25
Diana v. State Board of Education 189
Dice Talk 82t
dichotomous data collection 101
dictionaries, use of 160, 162, 166t
difference argument for success/ failure 34
differentiation 96, 153
digital portfolios 90
direct linguistic support 159, 161
discrepancy model 183
discrete point assessments 122
dispositional targets 111
'diversity as a problem' discourses 190
Dorner, L.M. 49
Dos Puentes school, NYC 12
drama (as assessment method) 94–6
dual language bilingual education (DLBE) programs 39, 46t
Dual Language schools 49
'dumbing down,' accusations of 115
dynamic bilingualism 7, 19

Early Intervening Services 182
Echevarria, J. 81, 82t
Educating All Students (EAS) 43
Edwards, P.A. 184
Elementary and Secondary Education Act (ESEA) 38, 44t, 46t, 152
Elliot, S. 151
ELPA21 (English Language Proficiency for the 21st Century) 46t
emotional disturbance (ED) 176, 186
emotional dynamics of assessment 10, 39, 65, 78, 89, 111, 167
English, as language of assessment 16–17
English as a New Language (ENL) 20

English as a Second Language (ESL) 18
English language arts (ELA) 39, 41, 47t, 61, 84t, 89, 145
English language proficiency (ELP) standards 39, 41, 46t, 47t, 48, 84, 109, 139
English learner (EL) designation 18
English-only movement 49, 67, 88
error 59, 114, 123, 143, 166–7
Escamilla, K. 99, 117
Espinosa, C. 124, 125
essays with rubrics 81
ethics 64–6, 165
eugenics 31
European Cooperation in Science and Technology (COST) 190–1
evaluation of teachers 60, 61, 69
Every Student Succeeds Act (ESSA) 30, 42, 44t, 46t, 47t, 48–9, 67, 109, 152–3, 160, 179, 180, 189
evidence-based test design 12
Ewers, N. 161t
experimental research 160, 162
expository writing 124
expressive/ narrative writing 124
extra time accommodations 151, 153, 161, 162, 166t
extraneous variables 57

fairness in testing
 –accommodations 153
 –accountability 201
 –fair measure 9
 –history of assessment 33
 –history of misuse of tests 30
 –and the measurement community 10–11
 –psychometrics 136–8
 –special education 189
FairTest.org 144
family linguistic maps 12–13
fatigue 168–9
feedback, formative 75–7
Find Someone Who 82t
Find the Fib 82t
Fine, C. 23–4, 25
Flores, N. 151
fluency 89, 121
foreign language anxiety (FLA) 65
formative assessment 19, 21, 23, 25, 75–80, 114, 118, 125, 163–4
four guiding assessment principles 18–19
fractional views 190, 191, 193t

Francis, D.J. 161
Fu, D. 124
Funds of Knowledge 193t
Fung, D. 112

Gándara, P. 151, 156
García, O. 7, 19, 193t
Gardner, H. 90
Gargiulo, R. 176, 177
General Home Language Reading Assessment Rubric 22
General Home Language Writing Assessment Rubric 85–6
Genesee, F. 121
genetic argument for success/ failure 34
 see also eugenics
'gifted' children 31, 32
Giuliani, G. 178t, 182, 183, 186, 188
globalization 42
glossaries 161, 162, 166t
Gonzalez, N. 193t
'good education,' definitions of 37
Google Translate 111
Gottlieb, M. 92, 94, 95t
Gould, S. J. 32
Government Accountability Office (GAO) 41
grade level equivalent rankings (GE) 139, 141–2
grade point average (GPA) 143
Green, A. 8, 167, 198
'Growth Model' for accountability 199–200

Hakuta, K. 33
Haladyna, T.M. 169
Hamayan, E. 188
Harcourt Assessment Company 144
hegemony, cultural 68
Henderson, K.I. 39, 49
Heritage, M. 79, 80
Heward, W. 180
high stakes tests
 –cut scores 138–9
 –Every Student Succeeds Act (ESSA) 48
 –and labelling as 'non-nons' 127–8
 –negative consequences of 61, 168–9
 –and No Child Left Behind 38, 39
 –'pineapple has no sleeves' 145
 –single tests, decisions based on 200
 –standardized tests as 96
 –use of test scores 8, 21, 57
higher thinking skills 109, 112
high-quality assessments 19

history of assessment 29–54
holistic models 19, 20, 91, 98, 102, 117, 191, 193t
home languages *see also* translanguaging
    –accommodations 156
    –in assessment methods 97–8
    –assessment of 16–18
    –communication of results 144
    –and core standards 85
    –culturally and linguistically diverse (CLD) students 179–80
    –dispositional targets 111
    –General Home Language Reading Assessment Rubric 22
    –General Home Language Writing Assessment Rubric 85–6
    –and ideology/ culture 66–8
    –inclusivity 14–15
    –for knowledge assessment 108
    –lack of bilingual special educators 189–90
    –native-language versions of assessments 161
    –reading assessment 23
    –and reading assessment 123, 124
    –role play assessment methods 94
    –in SLI assessments 191
    –snapshot example 22
    –story retelling 89
    –teacher observation methods of assessment 94
    –teachers who don't know students' 14, 25
    –translated tests 151–2
    –typically undervalued 12
    –use for assessment of other subjects 13–14, 19 *see also* content; translanguaging
    –using non-teacher resources for assessment 14, 25, 111
Hopis 67

IDEA Proficiency Test (IPT) 64, 127
ideology 66–8
immigrant minorities 35
inadequacy, feelings of 39, 40
inclusivity 14–15, 138
Indigenous languages 24, 25, 67
indirect linguistic support 159, 161
Individual Education Programs (IEPs) 177–8t, 187–8
Individuals with Disabilities Education Act (IDEA) 127, 176–9, 180, 181–4

inequities 66, 124
informed consent 177–8t, 186
input and output 115
instruments 22, 100–3
integrated language assessments 117–18, 134
intelligence testing 30–2
interactive journals 116t
interactive process, assessment as 18
International Test Commission 151
interpretation of tests 139–40
interpreters, using 111
inter-rater reliability 167–8
interviews 87–9, 89t, 116t, 203
involuntary minorities 35

Kangas, S. 39, 192
Kanno, Y. 39
Kearney, E. 171n(4)
key practices 110
Kieffer, M. 162
kindergarten 25
Klein, A. 123
Kleyn, T. 36, 67, 92
Klingner, J.K. 176, 184
knowledge (type of content) 108–9
Krashen, S. 42, 111, 203

Ladson-Billings, G. 18, 69, 193t
Language Assessment Scales-Oral (LAS-O) 64
Language Portfolios 92–4
language proficiency
    –and academic language skills 109
    –assessment vs. testing 8–9
    –and content assessment 112–16
    –cut scores 138–9
    –narrowness of tests 57
    –and No Child Left Behind 38
    –school-related language assessments 112–29
    –statewide standardized testing 62
    –summative assessment 77
    –validity 64
    –validity threats 58–9
language targets 84
languaging 57 *see also* translanguaging
learning disability (LD) 175, 182–4, 187
learning targets 20
least restrictive environment (LRE) 177–8t
Lee, O. 84

lens of deficit 7–8, 9t, 17–18, 33, 78, 168, 192
lens of promise 7–8, 9t, 17–18, 78, 168
Leslie, M. 31
lesson plans 84t, 107, 130–1t
Leung, C. 199
lifelong learning 79
Lindquist, E.F. 10
linguistic modifications 154–5, 161–2
linguistic repertoires
 –accommodations 165
 –and content assessment 78, 114
 –formative assessment 78
 –reading assessment 124
 –translanguaging 19, 25
 –transmodality 23
linguistic simplification 115–16, 154–5, 161, 169
Linquanti, R. 38
listening, assessment of 90t, 116t, 118, 122–3
Literacy Squared project 99
literacy testing 30, 85–6, 99, 123
Lo, Y. 112, 199
local norms 137
Lopez, A. 15, 16, 152, 156, 157
Lord, C. 160, 161
Lorde, A. 36
low-tech and interactive techniques 82–3t

machine scoring 96
MacSwan, J. 64, 127–8
Mahoney, K. 63, 113, 128, 168
mainstreaming of bilingual students 18, 62, 127
mandatory testing 58
manuals/ blueprints 21, 60, 137, 139, 170
maps
 –language assessments akin to 8
 –personal/family linguistic maps 12–13
Martin, D. 190, 194n(1)
mastery 19
Mastropieri, M.A. 181, 184
matching exercises 98t, 108, 116t
math 48–9, 84t, 88t, 91–2, 100–3t, 112–14, 156
McNeil, L. 44t
measurement community 8–10, 33, 60, 63, 64, 134, 137, 151, 198
measurement error 59–60
Menken, K. 15, 39
Messick, S. 19, 62, 63, 67, 68

method 21–2, 74–105
Miller, E.R. 160
minimal pairs 122
minorities
 –cultural ecological theory 35
 –culturally and linguistically diverse (CLD) students 175, 176, 179–80, 182, 184–5, 187, 188–9
 –immigrant minorities 35
 –involuntary minorities 35
miscues 23, 124, 163–4
misuse of assessment, history of 30–3
misuse of test scores 33–4, 61–2, 68, 126
modalities 57, 75, 81, 82–3t, 84, 87, 98, 101
modifications for MLs *see* accommodations
monolingual bias 136, 152, 192
monolingual children, inclusion in multilingual test designs 11
monolingual norms 190–1
monolingual writing assessments 117
motivation 111, 116
multidimensionality 9, 10, 25, 90
multidisciplinary team (MDT) 186
multilingual identities 112
Multilingual Learners' Bill of Assessment Rights 5
multilingual learners, use of term 5
multilingual narratives 191
multilingual-by-design tests 11, 156–7, 159
multiliteracies 123
multimodality 57
multiple choice methods 81, 98t, 108, 116t, 135
multiple intelligences 90
multiple measures 202, 204
multisemioticity 23
Multi-Tiered System of Supports (MTSS) 185
Mystery Word task 82t

narrowness of tests 57
National Assessment of Educational Progress (NAEP) 203
National Board certification 61
National Center for Research on Evaluation, Standards and Student Testing (NCCREST) 46t, 161
National Council on Measurement in Education (NCME) 10–12, 33, 60, 134, 137, 151
National Opt-Out Movement 43

National Research Center on Learning Disabilities (NRCLD) 183
National Research Council (NRC) 33
Native American cultures 35–6, 67
native-speaker norms, tests based on 33, 84, 102, 136, 153, 192
negative emotional effects of testing 65–6, 168
New York City 15–16 *see also* Dos Puentes school, NYC
Next Day Completion 165
Nguyen, D. 92, 94, 95t
No Child Left Behind (NCLB)
　–academic language skills 109
　–accommodations 157–8, 161
　–accountability with(out) validity 37–40
　–criterion-referenced testing (CRT) 139
　–doubts about 42–3
　–effect on testing manufacturers 144
　–fairness in testing 33
　–in history of assessment events 45t
　–and home language development 15, 16
　–and IDEA (Individuals with Disabilities Education Act) 179
　–support for 43
　–and teacher evaluation 69
Noguerón-Liu, S. 124
non-discriminatory assessment 177–8t
non-nons, labelling as 126, 127–8
normal curve equivalents (NCE) 142
norming groups 135–6, 142
norm-referenced testing (NRT)
　–accountability 201–2
　–content assessment 128, 129
　–psychometrics 138, 139, 142
　–in standardized testing 135
　–and validity 67
　–vs. criterion-referenced testing 135–6
nuisance variables 57

Obama, Barack 38, 46t, 48, 179
objectivity of tests 59, 143, 176, 204
observation methods of assessment 94, 95t, 116t, 123
Office of Civil Rights (OCR) 180
Office of Special Education Programs (OSEP) 176
Ogbu, J. 34, 35, 36
one-to-one communication
　–as assessment method 81, 82t, 87–9, 109t
　–for dispositions 111t
　–for key practices 110t

　–for reasoning assessment 110
open response methods 114, 135 *see also* written response
opportunities to role play (ORP) 94–6
opting out of testing 43, 59
oral language development *see* speaking, assessment of
out-of-school factors (OSFs) 42, 200

Palmer, A.S. 117
Palmer, D. 39, 49
parental informed consent 177–8t, 186
Paris, D. 77
Partnership for Assessment of Readiness for College and Careers (PARCC) 46t, 157
passive vs. active voice 115, 154t
pathway to success, seeing 78–9
Pearson 76, 144, 145
peer and self-assessment (PASA) 4, 75, 82t, 83t, 87, 91
peer/cohort groups 135, 193t
Pennock-Roman, M. 161
percentile rankings (PR) 139, 142
performance assessment
　–as assessment method 81, 82t, 89–90, 94–6
　–data-driven instruction (DDI) 204
　–for dispositions 111t
　–for key practices 110t
　–for knowledge assessment 108, 109t
　–for reasoning assessment 110
performance reviews, teacher 60 *see also* teacher evaluation
personal/family linguistic maps 12–13
persuasive writing 124
Phuong, J. 180
Pierangelo, R. 178t, 182, 183, 186, 188
piloting of tests 56, 153
'pineapple has no sleeves' 145
Pinkwater, D. 145
PISA (Program for International Student Assessment) 152
pivotal portfolios 92
Plakos, J. 32
poetry portfolios 92–3
policymakers 10, 64, 198
political ideologies 68
political power 57
pollution, test *see* error
Popov, S. 65
portfolio-based language assessment (PBLA) 94

portfolios 17, 90–4, 118, 203, 204
positive effects of testing 66
poverty 42
power relationships 36, 57
Poza, L. 139
pre-assessments 125–6, 127
pre-referral (in special education process) 181–4
privilege of certain forms of English 57
productive versus receptive language development 11–12
proficiency level scores 140–1
project-based assessments 110t *see also* performance assessment
promise, lens of 7–8, 9t, 17–18, 78, 168
prompts 13–14, 15, 18, 115, 155–6
pronunciation miscues 163–4
psychological constructs 57
psychometricians 10
psychometrics 133–49
Public Law 94-142 177
PUMI (Purpose, Use, Method, Instrument)
 –accommodations 151
 –accountability 197, 201
 –content 107, 114
 –data-driven instruction (DDI) 204–5
 –description of 7
 –framework 21–2
 –in the history of assessment 30
 –and lesson planning 107
 –method 74–105
 –and portfolio assessments 90–1
 –psychometrics 134
 –school-related language assessments 116t
 –for speaking assessment 121
 –and validity 56–7
purpose
 –integrated language assessments 118
 –and method 81–2, 102
 –in the PUMI framework 20–1
 –reading, assessment of 123
 –in role play 96

quantity of tests 16
Quick Writes 91–2
Quizziz 96, 157

Race to the Top (RTTT) funding 38, 46t
racial discrimination 31, 68, 189
racialization 36, 192

Randall, J. 156
Ravitch, D. 43
raw scores 140
read-aloud accommodations 162, 166t
reading, assessment of 23, 116t, 123–4
Reading School District v. PA Department of Education 151
reasoning (type of content) 109
referral processes for special education 185–7
reflective learning 91
Rehabilitation Act (1973) 180–1
relative risk ratios 180
reliability 59–60, 151, 165, 166–9, 202
 see also validity
reliability coefficients 59
report cards 143
response boards 82t
Rhodes, R.W. 67
Rivera, C. 38, 157, 159, 161
role play assessment methods 94–6, 97t, 116t
Rolstad, K. 64
Rosa, J. 151
Rossi, R. 168
RtI (Response to Intervention) 181–4
RubiStar 102–3
rubrics
 –bilingual rubrics 99–100
 –content assessment 107
 –as instruments of assessment 100–3
 –integrated language assessments 118
 –multilingual test instructions and responses 155–6
 –in role play 96
 –school-related language assessments 116t
 –for speaking/ listening assessment 122
Ruiz, R. 12
running record methods 116t, 123

scaffolding 21, 58, 76, 77, 80, 96, 112, 121, 152
scale scores 140
Schissel, J. 25, 30, 66
school-related language assessments 112–29
science 24–5, 59, 84t, 162
Scruggs, T.E. 181, 184
second language acquisition (SLA) 41, 109, 199
Section 504 of the Rehabilitation Act of 1973 180–1
selected response
 –as assessment method 81, 96–8
 –and content assessment 108, 113–14
 –for dispositions 111t

—in standardized testing 135
selected response methods 83t
self-assessment 19, 91
self-confidence 111
self-efficacy, sense of 19
self-esteem 116
Seltzer, K. 20, 92, 112
separate tests for separate languages 16–17
Shafer Willner, L.S. 159–60
Share Bear 82t
Sheltered Instruction Observation Protocol (SIOP) model 80–1, 82–3t
Shepard, L. 165
Shohamy, E. 57, 68, 137, 158–9, 165
side effects of testing 65–6
simplification of language 115–16, 154–5, 161–2, 169
single tests, decisions based on 9, 9t, 200
Smarter Balanced Assessment Consortium 46t, 157, 161
social class differences 34–5, 67
social consequences of test score use 64–6
social inequities 66
social media 145
sociocultural assessment 7
sociocultural/ sociolinguistic ideologies 11, 68
sociolinguistic modification of tests 155
Solano-Flores, G. 155
Solorza, C. 15, 39
solutions-focused assessment 19
sorters, schools as 36, 135–6
speaking, assessment of 88t, 90t, 116t, 118–21
special education 12, 159, 174–96
special educators, shortage of bilingual 189–90
speech or language impairment (SLI) 175, 176, 187, 189, 190–2
standard error of measurement (SEM) 170
standard vs. non-standard English 57
standardized tests
  —and accommodation 165
  —as assessment methods 96–8
  —benefits of 135
  —data-driven instruction (DDI) 203
  —definition of 135
  —interpretation of test scores 139–40
  —misuse of test scores 61–2, 126
  —objectivity of tests 143
  —psychometrics 134
  —selling to untrained legislators 10
  —summative assessment 75–6

—white norms 67, 151
standards, measurement against 20–1
Standards for Educational and Psychological Testing, The (AERA, APA, NCME, 2014) 10, 33, 134, 137, 151
standards for validity 60–1
Stanford English Language Proficiency (SELP) 62
Stanford-Binet Intelligence test 30, 31
state standards 84–5, 157–8
status models 199
Steele, C. 23
Stefanakis, E. 7, 18, 32, 90
Stiggins, R. 4, 5, 10, 19, 36, 39, 43, 65, 75–76, 79, 80, 102, 198
story retelling 89–90, 123, 124
strengths-based frameworks 125
student-centred assessment 18–19, 75
students with disabilities (SWD) 157, 159, 174–96
students with interrupted/inconsistent formal education (SIFE) schooling 22
student-to-family modalities 87
subtractive bilingualism 49
success and failure, theories explaining 34–7
summative assessment 19, 21, 75–7, 79, 80, 126
synthesizing skills 109, 124

teacher evaluation 60, 61, 69
Teacher Improvement Plan (TIPs) 60, 69
teacher observation methods of assessment 82–3t, 94, 95t, 116t, 123
teacher recruitment 68
teacher-controlled assessment versus government control 20
teachers' assessment literacy 198
teacher-to-family modalities 87
technical manuals ('blueprints') for tests 21, 60, 137, 139, 170
term bias *see* construct irrelevant variance (CIV)
Terman, L. 30
terminology 5
test anxiety 65
test policymakers 10, 64, 198
test score use 56, 60–1, 63–4
test validity vs. test score use validity 56
'testing the test' 60
testing vs. assessment 8

theoretical/ conceptual frameworks of tests 21, 127–8, 139
time taken to achieve proficiency 41
Title III 45t
translanguaging *see also* home languages
– accommodations 156
– accountability 166t
– in assessment methods 97–8, 99
– communication of results 144
– computer-based testing 15
– and content assessment 24, 107–8, 112, 114, 115–16
– as design principle 23–6
– formative assessment 78, 163–4
– in formative assessments 23
– as guiding principle 19
– home languages used for assessment 14
– input and output 15
– interviews 88–9
– for knowledge assessment 108
– within language assessments 116–17
– portfolios 91
– and PUMI 13
– and reading assessment 123, 124
– role play assessment methods 94
– Sheltered Instruction Observation Protocol (SIOP) model 80–1
– special education 193t
– in standardized testing 15
– story retelling 89
– translanguaging and universal design (TRUDL) 193t
– using non-teacher resources for assessment 25, 111
– writing skills 126
translated tests 151–2, 156, 159, 161, 166t
translations (of home language), using 111
transmodality 23
triangulation of tests 9t, 202
true/false exercises 81, 98t, 108, 116t, 135
Trump administration 49
Two Truths and a Lie 82t

unified view of validity 56, 63–4
universal design of tests 137
Upshur, J. 121
US Department of Education (USDOE) 176
'us versus them' attitudes 57
use
– accommodations 151

– and accountability 197
– and formative vs. summative assessment 76
– in the history of assessment 30
– psychometrics 134
– in the PUMI framework 21
– and validity 56, 60–1

Valdés, G. 34, 84, 139
Valenzuela, A. 44t
validity 55–73
– accommodations 152, 161, 162
– and accountability 38–9, 60, 199, 201
– confounding constructs 122
– and fairness 136
– history of assessment 33
– integrated language assessments 118
– and No Child Left Behind 37–40
– norm-referenced testing 201–2
– and standardized tests in English 30
– test validity vs. test score use validity 56
– as a unified concept (guiding principle) 19
– unified view of validity 56, 63–4
value-added assessment 200
video recordings 61, 90, 96
VIVA (validity, inclusivity, viability and accessibility) 138
Vogt, M. 81, 82t

weighted (composite) scores 141
white norms 30, 67, 151
whole school responsibility for MLs 43
WIDA 27n(6), 46t, 140–1, 147t
WIDA 'Can do' philosophy, descriptors and rubrics 7, 118, 119–20
Wolf, M. 157, 162
Wright, W. 39, 41, 48, 49
writing, assessment of 85, 86t, 116t, 117, 124–9
written response
– as assessment method 81, 82t, 109t, 116t
– and content 114
– for dispositions 111t
– for key practices 110t
– for reasoning assessment 110
wrong constructs 9
Wylie, C. 79

Zhang, C. 189
Zhao, Y. 42
Zieky, M. 137

For Product Safety Concerns and Information please contact our EU Authorised Representative:

Easy Access System Europe

Mustamäe tee 50

10621 Tallinn

Estonia

gpsr.requests@easproject.com